This book purchased
with donations made to the

Artwork by Julie Paschkis

"Help Us Make $1 Million
for the Library" campaign.

The Seattle Public Library Foundation

More Praise for *The Responsible Business*

"I am eternally grateful to the author of this book, Carol Sanford, for giving me the skills to not only build a number of profitable businesses, but to do so responsibly for all the stakeholders along the way."
—*Bob Raynsford, founder and chairman, Agriwise*

"Carol is a very early thought leader, way beyond the pack. She has an exceedingly high level of intelligence for working on very complex subjects, with workable approaches. Whole enterprises change permanently for the better. I know. I have been engaged with the work in this book for decades in several successful entrepreneurial start-ups and as an executive in Fortune 500 companies."
—*Pravin Jain, serial entrepreneur, CEO and founder, Synergen Energy*

"In *The Responsible Business*, Carol offers a rare exception to all the hype on CSR, providing practical hands-on advice to launch deep systemic change for your entire organization, your external partners, your investors, your community, and the planet that depends on us all. She and this book are gems."
—*Brad Reddersen, President, SIRA Technologies, Inc.*

"In this visionary and hugely exciting book Carol Sanford shares the insights gleaned from a lifetime of working with path breaking businesses. She takes us behind the scenes at companies that have transformed how they think about themselves and the world—and in the process generated not only sustainable prosperity but levels of meaning and commitment that most firms only dream of. This path has the potential to transform our world."
—*Rebecca Henderson, Senator John Heinz Professor of Environmental Management, Harvard Business School*

"Carol Sanford gives us a new paradigm for going beyond CSR and SRI to a marketplace where business creates both positive impact on society and the environment and value for shareholders. Who doesn't want that?"
—*Andrew Kassoy, Bart Houlahan, and Jay Coen Gilbert, founders, B Lab*

"*The Responsible Business* advances a most welcome approach that is more encompassing than most work on responsibility, sustainability, and climate change. Yet it is elegantly simple in its execution. It gives hope and meaning on some of the biggest issues of our time. In many parts of the world natural resources are stretched to their limits. The book argues that ecosystems and communities are not "externalities" but part and parcel of the "whole." This leads to regeneration and revitalization of industries, communities, and ecosystems, building from each unique culture and ecology. It is the *new* corporate responsibility."
—*Mohamed El-Ashry, Senior Fellow, UN Foundation, former CEO and chairman, Global Environment Facility (GEF)*

"An evolution biologist who sees how all sustainable species, in our business world as much as in our greater biological world, must mature from hostile competition to collaborative community, Carol Sanford has written a book brilliantly vital to our future. Any business adopting and practicing her mantra of Agency, Ableness, and Affectiveness will thrive as it contributes to a best possible future for all. Read this book to find out *how*!"
—*Elisabet Sahtouris, Ph.D., evolution biologist; futurist; author,* Earth Dance: Living Systems in Evolution

"This is a bold and inspiring book; one of those game-changing books that come around only once in a decade. It will change how I teach organizational behavior and management. I return to different sections repeatedly and gain something new each time."
—*Pam Hinds, Stanford University, Management Science and Engineering; co-director, Center for Work, Technology & Organization*

"A Responsible Business thinks strategically, comprehensively, and inclusively with all stakeholders. Carol Sanford's book provides executives and investors with the tools and examples to build a better world while seeking positive human impact and profit. She shows how the leaders accomplish this for their firms, shareholders, and society."
—*R. Paul Herman, CEO, HIP Investor Inc., registered investment adviser; author,* The HIP (Human Impact + Profit) Investor: Make Bigger Profits by Building a Better World

"Developing the potential of every stakeholder (customer and investors as well) in the way you do business is good for business. *The Responsible Business* presents companies who have done it successfully and illustrates precisely how you can make it part of your strategy, leadership approach, and build it into your work design. Take the high road and feel grounded and successful in doing it."
—*Chip Conley, CEO, Joie de Vivre Hotels; author,* Peak: How Great Companies Get Their Mojo from Maslow

"*The Responsible Business* is a remarkable book that pushes the overhyped concept of corporate responsibility beyond punitive mandates to innovation solutions deeply grounded in the fundamentals of business. From her broad experience, Ms. Sanford has culled a rich collection of varied, and, quite frankly, enjoyable stories that shed new CSR light on tried and true business directives such as "know and align your stakeholders," and others like "think and act systemically" more recently introduced into the business canon. Through its business-minded practicality, *The Responsible Business* will hopefully push corporate responsibility even further: beyond the Corporate Citizenship department and into the profitability-focused boardroom."
—*Drew Banks, head of marketing at Prezi, co-founder of Pie Digital, and coauthor of* Beyond Spin *and* Customer.Community

"The road to corporate responsibility today demands a new level of courage: to recognize that a fundamental change is in the offing, and to act accordingly. Carol Sanford shows us how to put two simple yet essential truths into practice: that we are all part of a single interconnected world, where each part genuinely matters; and that people will take complete responsibility to transform their situation when challenged to look for and create the unexpected right where they are. *The Responsible Business* shows us how to tap into the hidden potential for practical innovation, and reinforces what every good business leader already knows—that a living spirit of commitment, once activated, renews everything. Read this book to discover its practical secrets."
—*William Isaacs, Senior Lecturer, MIT Sloan School of Management; author,* Dialogue and the Art of Thinking Together

THE RESPONSIBLE BUSINESS LEADER PROJECT . . .

. . . is out to identify as many Responsible Business Leaders on the planet as we can. They often go unrecognized if they are not the CEO. They are everywhere: top to bottom of the business; on every continent; in for-profit and not-for-profit; and in local, provincial, state, and national governments.

They often go against the grain and do what is right by

- Considering customer's well being in creating products and services
- Considering the uniqueness of people involved in the work as equals in thinking
- Considering suppliers as full participants in the creative process and help improve their lives in the process
- Considering how to create a healthier planet by decisions the business makes
- Considering the uniqueness of each community, supporting distinctive expression and increasing vitality—that is, where their suppliers live, where their distribution is significant, where their business facilities are located
- Considering investors worthy of enduring returns based on understanding what makes a Responsible Business, Responsible Industries, and Responsible Capitalism

Join us in "ID-ing" Responsible Business Leaders around the world. Let's honor them for their courage and contribution at

www.theresponsiblebusinessleader.com

While you are there, select a free article to spark a conversation with colleagues.

THE RESPONSIBLE BUSINESS

Reimagining Sustainability and Success

Carol Sanford

Forewords by Chad Holliday and Rebecca Henderson

JOSSEY-BASS
A Wiley Imprint
www.josseybass.com

Published by Jossey-Bass
A Wiley Imprint
989 Market Street, San Francisco, CA 94103-1741—www.josseybass.com

Readers should be aware that Internet Web sites offered as citations and/or sources for further information may have changed or disappeared between the time this was written and when it is read.

Limit of Liability/Disclaimer of Warranty: While the publisher and author have used their best efforts in preparing this book, they make no representations or warranties with respect to the accuracy or completeness of the contents of this book and specifically disclaim any implied warranties of merchantability or fitness for a particular purpose. No warranty may be created or extended by sales representatives or written sales materials. The advice and strategies contained herein may not be suitable for your situation. You should consult with a professional where appropriate. Neither the publisher nor author shall be liable for any loss of profit or any other commercial damages, including but not limited to special, incidental, consequential, or other damages.

Jossey-Bass books and products are available through most bookstores. To contact Jossey-Bass directly call our Customer Care Department within the U.S. at 800-956-7739, outside the U.S. at 317-572-3986, or fax 317-572-4002.

Jossey-Bass also publishes its books in a variety of electronic formats. Some content that appears in print may not be available in electronic books.

Library of Congress Cataloging-in-Publication Data

Sanford, Carol, 1942-
  The responsible business : reimagining sustainability and success / Carol Sanford ; forewords by Chad Holliday and Rebecca Henderson. – 1st ed.
        p. cm.
     Includes bibliographical references and index.
  ISBN 978-0-470-6-4868-1 (hardback)
  ISBN 978-0-470-9-4855-2 (ebk.)
  ISBN 978-0-470-9-4860-6 (ebk.)
  ISBN 978-0-470-9-4861-3 (ebk.)
  1. Social responsibility of business.   2. Corporate culture.   3. Strategic planning.   I. Title.
  HD60.S249 2011
  658.4'08–dc22

                                                                    2010049179

Printed in the United States of America
FIRST EDITION
HB Printing   10 9 8 7 6 5 4 3 2 1

CONTENTS

A Foreword from the Boardroom   xiii
    Chad Holliday

A Foreword from Academia   xvii
    Rebecca Henderson

Acknowledgments   xxiii

Prologue: A New Business Mind   xxv
Procter & Gamble (P&G): Responsibility Prototype   xxvii
P&G's Guiding Principles   xxx
Bringing It Home   xxxiii

Introduction: The Responsible Business   xxxv
New Problem, Old Mind   xxxv
Evolve Corporate Responsibility by Evolving
    Business Responsibility   xxxix
Three Forks in the Road to Responsibility   xl
A Framework for the Responsible Business   xlii
From Add-on Responsibility to Full-on Responsibility   xliv
About This Book   xlv

About the Author   xlvii

PART ONE: THE RESPONSIBLE BUSINESS: REIMAGINING
    BUSINESSES OF THE FUTURE   1

1   Stories from Three Continents   3
Herban Feast: Caring for Customers   3
Kingsford: Creating Collaboratively   7
Colgate, South Africa: Localizing Identity and Destiny   11
Seventh Generation: Regenerating Planetary Systems   15
E. I. DuPont: Engaging Shareholder Value   19
Panning for Gold   23
Conclusions   24

2 Stakeholders as Systemic Collaborators 25

The Meaning of *Stakeholder* 25
Stand in the Stakeholder's Shoes 26
Stakeholders Affect Responsibility 27
Five Key Stakeholders and Their Stakes 29
Conclusions 37

3 Geometry of the Responsible Business 38

Systemic Stakeholder Framework 39
The Logic of the Pentad 41
Integrate Stakeholder Initiatives 44
Conclusions 48

4 Be Value-Adding, Not Value-Added 49

Value-Added Is Not Value-Adding 51
Energize Caring Through Value-Adding Processes 52
Five Stakeholder Imperatives 53
Conclusions 81

5 Making the Responsible Business Pentad Work 82

Revolutionizing Business Models: Red Hat 82
From Commodity to Nondisplaceability: Kingsford 85
Deeply Connect to Your Customer: Herban Feast 108
Mission-Driven Meets Future-Proof:
   Seventh Generation 114
Change the World by Changing the Business:
   Colgate, South Africa 122
Conclusions 129

**PART TWO: MAKING IT WORK: THE MAP
   TO THE TERRITORY 131**

6 Teaching an Organization to Star 133

Retrofit an Existing Business 134
Reverse Phases for a Start-up Responsible Business 150
Conclusions 152

7 Nonhierarchical Decision Making 154

Hierarchical Management Is Irresponsible 154
Self-Organizing Decision Making Is Responsible 156
Four Self-Organizing Capabilities 157
Conclusions 171

PART THREE: IRRESPONSIBILITY HAPPENS:
     REFRAMING HOW CHANGE WORKS   173

8   Responsibility Running Backward   175
     Running Faster in the Wrong Direction   176
     A 360-Degree Business Perspective   179
     Make Something for Someone   180
     From Backward to Forward Spin   182
     Conclusions   185

9   Our Own Worst Enemies: Turning People Around   186
     Brain Works   187
     Three-Brained Decision Making   188
     Triad of Mental Frames   189
     Familiarity Is the Enemy of Creativity   192
     Incentives Narrow the Mind   195
     Narrower Frames of Reference Cause the Pentad
          to Spin Backward   196
     Leading from the Purposeful Mental Frame   196
     Personal Development and Critical Thinking Skills 198
     Conclusions   199

10   Cautionary Tales: Design for Prevention and Cure 200
     Six Common Hazards   201
     An Ounce of Prevention   216
     Conclusions   218

PART FOUR: THE BIG PICTURE OF RESPONSIBILITY   219

11   A Responsible View of Capital   221
     Stakeholder Return on Investment (ROI)   222
     Conclusions   242

12   Assessing Responsibility   243
     Systemic Responsibility Indicators   244
     Conclusions   259

13   The Future of Responsibility   261
     Getting from Here to There   262
     Alternative Business Approaches   263
     Responsible Investing Within the Current
          Legal Framework   275
     Conclusions   277

Epilogue: Developing Capability for Responsibility   279
Three Capabilities Underlying Responsibility   280
A Final Reflection   283

Notes   287
Index   293

To Mark and Tamara, my children by birth, and Oné Alm, my daughter by choice, as well as Max, my grandson—all who taught me how to love and open my heart

To Charlie Krone, who challenged my thinking and developed my mind to see a world that most people miss. I am grateful daily for his wisdom and commitment to my growth.

A Foreword from the Boardroom

The Responsible Business describes a more complete, connected, and systematic way to think and act on decisions and problems. While I was chairman and CEO of the DuPont Corporation, I had firsthand experience with this way of working and thinking for over twenty years. I had many opportunities to apply it to hundreds of practical problems. In fact, rarely a day goes by that I do not call on this way of thinking and looking at the world. It is useful in most walks of life, and in taking on the big business decisions that so many of us face every day.

Our company, and each leader in it, was much better for it. Our path was unique to us, and in this book you will also learn how others in other organizations applied the ways of working presented here, specific to their businesses, industries, and national cultures. *The Responsible Business* offers enlightened approaches for leaders from the board of directors to the front lines sales teams, and for government and not-for profits as well.

Please accept two particular challenges as you read this book as areas for great opportunity to improve all of our thinking. I have taken these two on myself.

The Natural Resource Dilemma

In 1950, if you had the nerve to suggest to a general audience that sixty years later humanity would face a monumental natural resource challenge to its very existence, your ideas would have been quickly dismissed by the mainstream of authorities. Yet as the world's population has expanded from 2.5 billion to nearly 7 billion over the past sixty years, we are pushing the limits of our natural resources. Just consider the approximately 2 billion people who wake up every morning and wonder if they will have enough food and water. That same 2 billion also know they will have no or very limited access to electricity. Just as we have hit the limit of our natural resources, we have hit the limit of thinking in the old way.

Yet at the same time, we are converting science into practical technology at an even faster rate. As the American Energy Innovation Council described, "If today's computer chips were the same size and cost as they were in 1975, Apple's iPod would cost $1 billion and be the size of a building." The question is, how do we focus our scientific might on the really important problems? The foundation of an answer, I believe, lies in the systemic thinking laid out in *The Responsible Business*.

Highest Ethical Standards

Business is under constant attack in most places in the world. Yet letting the free market work is critical to our success. To earn trust, business must operate to the highest ethical standards. At Bank of America, we have a relationship with one out of every two households in the United States. They trust us with a piece of their future. We must earn that trust every day. Bank of America further maintains that trust by adhering not just to high but to the highest ethical standards and best business practices, and by lending, investing, and giving back to the communities we serve through our environmental initiatives, our philanthropic activities, and our support of the arts and culture.

Businesses go off track and lose the public's trust when they stop thinking about issues from their essential core. We need the new business mind described in *The Responsible Business* to redefine what success really means. We cannot "rationalize away" acts that don't consider all stakeholders. You will find the foundation of the systemic thinking required to take on these challenges more comprehensively portrayed in *The Responsible Business* than in any other book I've ever read.

I am not saying this way of working will be easy. It calls for building a capability that is not common; to consider decisions and learning from a systems view. It will make you think. However, if you apply its ideas, it can help you solve some really big problems like the two I just described. The way of thinking about running a business offered in *The Responsible Business* is a critical source of possibilities for a re-imagined future.

February 2011   CHAD HOLLIDAY

Chad Holliday *is chairman of Bank of America Corporation since 2010; chairman, CEO, and president emeritus of E. I. Dupont Corporation; founder and board member of United Nations Global Compact for Sustainability; and founder and member of the American Energy Innovation Council.*

A Foreword from Academia

What role should business play in solving the social and environmental problems that we face? Stubbornly high rates of unemployment, increasing income inequality, and soaring drug and alcohol abuse are straining the social fabric in many communities. At the same time, the evidence that greenhouse gas emissions are heating the planet is continuing to accumulate, we are threatened with worldwide shortages of fresh water, extinction is claiming thousands of species, and toxic chemicals continue to accumulate in our environment—and in our tissues—at alarming rates.

Few suggest that as a society we should not respond to these challenges, but there is little agreement as to how to move forward and less still as to whether business should be at the leading edge of any response. Much of the current debate starts from the premise that the "the business of business is business," suggesting that private firms will naturally take advantage of opportunities that increase the value of the firm—reducing energy use as prices rise, for example, or introducing "green" products if consumers want them—but that beyond this point managers seeking to act "sustainably" are indulging in philanthropy at the expense of the shareholders, and very possibly at the expense of the long-term viability of the business. Within this framework, many people suggest that our best way forward is to rely on taxes and regulatory mandates to change firm behavior—if as a society we believe it should change—and/or to highlight the fact that the challenges we face are already creating great opportunities for private profit.

The book you hold in your hands suggests that this approach is at best radically incomplete and at worst a fatal distraction.

Carol draws on a lifetime of work with a wide variety of companies to argue that when firms focus first on "doing the right thing" and on serving all the stakeholders to whom they are responsible—from customers to employees, to local communities, investors, and the earth itself—they can not only transform their economic performance—dramatically increasing sales, profits, and market share—but also play a central role in healing the social and environmental systems on which we all depend.

At first glance this proposition might seem wildly improbable. If "doing the right thing" and, more broadly, taking advantage of the approaches that Carol describes here has such powerful implications, why isn't every firm using them? For me this is the sixty-four-thousand-dollar question, and it is precisely what makes this book so potentially important.

For Carol is not the first. There is a long, quiet tradition of work suggesting that there is something radically wrong with the way we run most organizations: that it is indeed possible to unlock huge reserves of energy and creativity and to create firms that outperform their competitors so dramatically they reshape industries. Researchers working within the human potential movement, for example, have focused on changing individual behavior, on developing the capacity for self-reflection, and on the dynamics of small groups. Work in system dynamics has highlighted the power of "system thinking." Those studying blue-collar work have documented the transformative impact of treating employees as problem solvers and of creating effective cross-functional teams that can in turn create "learning organizations." Others have focused on the roles that cultures of commitment, purpose, and trust can play in generating and sustaining order of magnitude improvements in performance, and on the importance of focusing on process and qualitative measurement rather than (solely) on short-term quantitative targets. Again and again the stories have surfaced of firms where employees brought their whole selves to work; of environments of trust, respect, and huge creativity; of projects completed in 10 percent of the normal time; of delighted customers; and—often—of very significant economic success.

For years most work in management and economics ignored this work, dismissing it as based on anecdotes or as a function of idiosyncratic circumstances that couldn't be replicated. Conventional "best" management practice continued to stress a view of the world that saw employees as self-interested "agents" who must be tightly managed with short-term quantitative targets, incentivized with cash bonuses (or threats) to work, and in which the central purpose of the firm is the maximization of shareholder return.

More recently, a combination of the financial collapse, recent work in psychology and behavioral economics, and careful empirical research has focused attention on the shortcomings of the conventional approach. An accumulating body of research confirms that some firms outperform their rivals by very significant amounts, that this difference endures, and that it is correlated with exactly those factors the early literature suggests might be important (Gibbons and Henderson, 2010; Bloom and Van Reenan, 2007). Most important, perhaps, it is becoming only too clear that relying on the conventional wisdom as a solution to the crises we face is problematic, and the risks of serious climate change and environmental degradation only continue to increase.

At this moment of challenge, this book is critical. In the first place, it integrates the individual factors that have been associated with high performance into a coherent whole. Carol suggests that it is unlikely that the piecemeal adoption of single "new" organizational practice can have any great affect, and demonstrates how successful firms adopt a "bundle" of approaches that are mutually reinforcing. Second, she helps us to understand why the seemingly radical claim—that firms have responsibilities beyond shareholder return not only to employees but also to communities and natural systems—may not only be morally plausible but also economically critical.

Carol's central argument is that focusing attention beyond shareholder return to the relationship between the firm and its other stakeholders triggers a powerful self-reinforcing dynamic. Not only does it move the organization beyond a dangerous reliance on third party market research and outmoded customer characterizations to a holistic understanding of customers and consumers that can unlock powerful opportunities for new products and services, but in explicitly speaking to/working with "the whole person"—social, economic, moral—it unleashes levels of personal and group creativity and ways of working that are transformational. From Carol's perspective, factors such as "trust," "commitment," "work teams," and "cross-functional processes" are symptoms, not primary causes. Treat your stakeholders as autonomous adults with their own needs and strengths. Trust them, and give them problem-solving responsibility. Let them link their sense of themselves as whole people—embedded both in their community and in the natural world—to their work and you will see incredible outcomes: a failing regional manufacturer claiming 50 percent of the U.S. market; a subsidiary on the verge of bankruptcy not only roaring back to profitability but changing South African history; one of the world's largest chemical companies solving seemingly impossible problems.

In describing just how some firms have been able to achieve these kinds of results, Carol also sheds light on two critically important questions. First, she gives us some clues as to why it is that some firms seem able to behave in such productive ways and to reap such great rewards as a result, while others cannot. Carol is reticent about her own role in the cases she describes, but my guess is that having a coach/advisor of her caliber available who "knows the way" may be very helpful. She is a person of tremendous integrity and great personal passion who is able to make deep personal connections and to ask the "right" questions—a gift that, I suspect, makes a tremendous difference to those groups with whom she works. Her case descriptions also hint at the idea that the determined leadership of key individuals can make an enormous difference. Throughout the book we encounter individuals who signal their commitment to acting in new ways by asking new questions, by behaving quite differently themselves, and by following through on their commitments in very tangible ways.

The second question her book addresses is equally central. Carol asserts strongly and consistently that corporations have much wider responsibilities than we commonly assume. There are at least two ways to think about this idea. The first is fundamentally instrumental. One could assert, and much of the book seems to suggest, that firms that adopt this stance are, in the end, much more successful and profitable than firms that focus only on shareholder returns, and that for an organization to focus only on shareholder returns is a mistake, even if one believes that firms do not, in fact, have any inherent responsibility for the wider health of the social and natural communities in which they are embedded. Taken literally this would imply that we should advise even the most hard-bitten, mercenary managers to adopt Carol's stance—not because they believe it to be true but because it will make them rich. Something about this doesn't feel quite right!

But Carol is making a more subtle point. I don't think she would assert that acting "responsibly," as she defines it, is the only way for a firm to make money. Firms have made money for hundreds of years by actively destroying common resources, or by burning up "natural capital." Nor do I think she believes that acting ethically always guarantees financial success. Rather she is pointing to the importance of imagination, commitment, and innovation in creating great businesses. I think we know that most of the great high technology-based businesses of the last fifty years were founded and grew great not because the employees wanted to be rich but because they were fascinated by a technology and deeply excited by its potential to meet new human needs. They wanted to change the world—and they did.

Carol is suggesting that something similar is possible in the case of the great transition that we face: that those firms who can learn to act on their deepest moral beliefs and sense of connection will blaze a trail that will not only make them exceedingly rich but that will also build entirely new industries and ways of working. But they will succeed not because they cared primarily about money but because they focused on what matters most—on the customers they serve, on the social and natural communities in which they are embedded, and also, and Carol is quite clear about this, on the needs of the investors who provide them with capital.

Can you change your own business and simultaneously change the world? The stakes are huge: for each of us individually and for our children—and given the news each day it is easy to become discouraged. But this book suggests that the answer

to this question is emphatically "yes," and that business can indeed play a leading role in building a more sustainable society.
Let's begin today.

February 2011 REBECCA HENDERSON

Rebecca Henderson *is Senator John Heinz Professor of Environmental Management at Harvard Business School.*

REFERENCES

Bloom, Nicholas, and John Van Reenen (November 2007). "Measuring and explaining management practices across firms and countries," *Quarterly Journal of Economics.*

Gibbons, R., and R. Henderson. (2010). "Relational Contracts and the Origins of Organizational Capabilities." In R. Gibbons and J. Roberts (eds.), *The Handbook of Organizational Economics.* Princeton, NJ: Princeton University Press.

Acknowledgments

"No man is an island," John Donne said. And neither is any author. Until I wrote my own book, I never realized the profoundly large and devoted community it requires. Although the stories and experiences in this book are mine and I made all final decisions on content and how it was said, I am grateful to have the most extraordinary set of colleagues and professionals who have made this a much better book.

Ben Haggard should get an award for patience, creativity, and downright determination to ensure every story was rigorously examined. He also contributed to the sections on Earth from his own experience as a permaculture practitioner and member of the Regenesis Story of Place team. He took down every word I said, exactingly, and then restructured and essentialized it to find its elegant essence. I owe him more than is possible to say or pay. On his team was Shannon Murphy, who ruthlessly and lovingly made sure the logic flowed and the arc of the book could be followed. Kit Brewer was the detail czar and creator of the straightforwardness that resulted. I love you all. I also much appreciate Lynn Geri, who first believed I should write some of my life stories and sat with me for hours to discover how to get them out of me. Thank you, dear friend.

Members of the Regenesis team (Pamela Mang, Shannon Murphy, Joel Glanzberg, Nicholas Mang, and Tim Murphy) rearranged their lives and work, repeatedly, ensuring I got the stories, the editing, and the courage to keep my way clear. There were several people who were generous enough to read drafts and sometimes more than once. Endless thanks to Gregor Barnum, Glenna Gerard, Ariyah Desouza, Kala Fleming, and Tom Sprimont. Bob Mang was repeatedly helpful in untangling the web of complexity in order to look at investors as stakeholders. I mostly took all of their suggestions but did sometimes ignore their advice. They did the best they could with a stubborn author and I greatly appreciate their wisdom and precision.

I have loved working with Jesse Wiley, my dedicated Jossey-Bass editor, and his editorial assistant, Dani Scoville, both of whom made it fun and fulfilling to write a book I believed in. Thanks for having confidence in me and my voice and appreciating my positive contrarian messages. Thanks to Drew Banks who got me connected to Jossey-Bass and its amazing creative team. Barbara Hendricks, Dennis Welch, and Rusty Shelton of Cave Hendricks Communications, my public relations firm, graciously worked with the book design and other decisions long before it went to press and then brought their high energy and creativity to managing me as a spokesperson for my ideas. I grew a lot along the way. All of these fine professionals made the creation of this book and communicating about it pure joy.

I must also thank the leaders in this book who trusted me and gave me chances of a lifetime to make a difference, particularly Stelios Tsezos, Will Lynn, Jeffrey Hollender, Chad Holliday, Pravin Jain, and BJ Duft. Working with Paul McNamara is a joy and I appreciate his harking back to his days at Red Hat for a great story. And to the two dozen executives who reflected on their experiences with Google, Apple, and W. L. Gore as clients and suppliers, I hope I pass on the discovery of unheralded examples of responsibility. I also thank Neel Mehta, senior manager of Adsense Sales, for opening doors that made it possible to interpret the history of Google.

Finally, I also want to acknowledge the countless other people in these companies and countries who opened their hearts and minds to this way of working and changed their own lives and the fortunes of their company and country, along with those of their fellow citizens and colleagues. I hold you all in awe.

Prologue: A New Business Mind

I remember the moment vividly. In June 2006 Al Gore had just stepped to the podium in the Walmart convening hall in Fayetteville, Arkansas. The audience roared to its feet, cheering enthusiastically. Two rows down and visibly moved stood Scott Burns, one of the producers of *An Inconvenient Truth*. The moment was historic and the crowd knew it: one of the world's least sustainable companies was taking on sustainability leadership. H. Lee Scott, Walmart's CEO and one of climate change's most vocal skeptics, had turned on a dime and committed his company to do their part in reversing global warming. Even doubters in the audience were electrified by this monumental shift.

Scott's passion and commitment inspired the room. "Even the most recalcitrant among us," he said with an embarrassed smile, "can change and see what they had not seen before."[1] That day I knew that Walmart was serious. This was no lip-service marketing campaign; the company was making a real commitment to increase responsibility and use the mega-distributor's unprecedented leverage to create global change. It was thrilling—and deeply disappointing.

The intention was so good, yet the ways of thinking proposed to guide the change were so far from adequate. My disappointment wasn't with capitalism or corporatism. I believe that corporate business will be among the critical sources for solutions to the problems we now face as a species on Earth. Nor did I question Scott's sincerity. My disappointment was with the way Walmart framed its vision and the strategies it proposed for realizing it, which I believed were going to limit or even prevent success.

Almost exactly a year later I was a speaker and workshop leader for the annual Ceres conference, an ambitious gathering of the most pioneering companies working in the arena of corporate responsibility. Ceres networks investors, environmental organizations, and public interest groups to work together on sustainability challenges. The conference was a great place to be on a bright spring day. The world, I thought, seemed to be waking up. But here, too, I was disappointed.

Once again I expected to hear about real change. Jim Rogers, the president of Duke Energy, spoke with inspiring passion about his company's commitment to producing alternative energy at a reasonable cost. His speech laid out specific commitments to doing what is necessary and setting an example with regard to sustainability.

He was followed by Paul Keller of Bank of America; Steve Elbert, vice chairman, British Petroleum, America; Jeff Swartz, CEO of Timberland; Gary Hirshberg of Stonybrook Farm; Theodore Roosevelt IV, managing director at Lehman Brothers; and a few dozen other industry titans—a *Who's Who* of important companies. All had had a "come-to" moment, realizing that they were part of the problem and must become not only part of the solution, but also solution leaders.

At so many of the gatherings that I've attended in my capacity as an expert on responsible business development and strategic management, business leaders share their inspiration and their commitment. Organizations describe what they're doing to reverse damages and prevent further harm, and they exchange best practices for becoming sustainable. People take notes on techniques for energy conservation, for shifting behavior, and for changing policy. Yet I am increasingly disturbed and distraught.

I don't like what I see happening in the field of corporate responsibility. I believe all these well-intentioned people and laud their commitment. I'm concerned because the responsibility-sustainability train is finally leaving the station, and it's going the wrong way. Companies are seeking and implementing solutions with exactly the same fragmented mind that created the problems in the first place. There is no shift in how they think, only a shift in what they are thinking about. Failure to work on *how to think* slows the pace of change, and in many cases exacerbates the problems.

PROCTER & GAMBLE (P&G): RESPONSIBILITY PROTOTYPE

Fifty years ago, a small cadre of visionary thinkers in Procter & Gamble's (P&G's) detergent products group launched an era of new design for business systems. The ranking member of the team was Bob Seitz, a manufacturing division manager. Bob had first-hand experience with compelling innovations in work systems that were fostering important changes in the company's spirit and performance. He had been deeply engaged with these innovations, and he wanted to try extending the management designs from manufacturing to an entire business. He decided that the place to start was at a new detergent business unit he was bringing on line in Lima, Ohio. He recruited Charles Krone, an engineer at P&G's Kansas City operation for which Bob had line responsibility, to help him.

To avoid delays on the Lima startup, Bob engaged corporate leadership with the vision and helped them see how it would serve P&G's long-time commitment to innovation. Bob received promises from P&G executives to support expanded boundaries for this organizational design initiative. He committed to meeting extraordinary goals and targets, something for which he already had an established reputation. Howard Morgens, P&G's CEO, was happy to have Bob's help in growing the detergent businesses through the application of innovative practices.

Bob brought over my long-time friend Ken Wessel, who was then one of P&G's key business and manufacturing brand managers. He was asked to manage the new P&G, Lima, venture's business side and Charles Krone would handle the work-design side. In a relatively short time they had teams in place and launched a new operation and cross-functional relationships with colleagues in sales, marketing, R&D, and other departments.

They set out to change thinking, ethos, and values of everyone involved and to challenge every outworn paradigm that held business captive. They connected the entire workforce directly to the market and the business's financial and market context. They innovated with regard to every part of the product development, manufacturing, and marketing process. Bob made a firm rule they were not to associate with the organizational development group in P&G's human resource (HR) department and were not to attend outside seminars or host unapproved visitors. His principle was that Lima was a business strategy and the team needed to avoid confusing it with a social experiment.

Lima's teams were built in an entirely new way. Focus was placed on developing team members' capability for systemic thinking. Prior to this, teams had focused narrowly on their tasks and efficiencies, and the new demands placed on them—responsibility for the totality of the business—required a profound educational process.

Early in their education, the teams were asked to delve into the inner workings of their raw materials in order to understand them thoroughly by themselves and how they interacted with the environment. To accomplish this, the teams had to engage the company's R&D department in a collaborative discovery process. It wasn't long before they discovered that the phosphates used in their detergent formulations were producing disturbing results in their laboratory tests.

Phosphates, they realized, had the potential to negatively affect water and the biological systems of rivers and wetlands. This led them to do a literature search, which uncovered confirming evidence from universities and research labs and notes of alarm from communities around the country.

They pulled in more technicians and went to work looking for alternative materials. They interviewed their raw material suppliers and nearby universities, testing ideas and formulations, searching for a way to make a superior, nonpolluting product.

This mission to reinvent detergent got a boost in momentum when the teams hired a new technician, Louis Risser. Lou was a successful entrepreneurial farmer who wanted to do something new and challenging. He was a keen observer and had noticed the effects of phosphate-based fertilizers on water quality in a variety of waterways.

Lou joined the cross-functional team that was working on phosphate-free formulations to make detergents harmless to rivers without inhibiting their cleaning capabilities. They built a system to switch out old formulations and began working with engineering, product development, sourcing, and sales to make a transition. They were diligent but did not highly accelerate the launch of improved products. They were going slow to do it right.

In response to studies released by the University of Michigan and other university laboratories, the Michigan legislature suddenly began to move to outlaw phosphates. Lou knew that the two biggest sources of phosphate pollution were fertilizers in farmland runoff and poor sewage management. He and other technicians in the brand leadership team approached Michigan legislators to inform them of P&G's support for a ban on phosphates and to reassure them that P&G's own research clearly showed that viable alternatives existed.

What they were not successful in communicating was how important it would be for the legislature to simultaneously address the more significant issues of fertilizer and sewage in the same piece of legislation. Lou decided to take his case to the agencies that could do something about the problem. With the full support of P&G, Lou set out to educate state water agencies, municipalities, and farm bureaus on ways to change their own systems.

Although the bill to ban phosphates was moving rapidly through the legislature, the cross-functional teams at Lima were hastening to speed up their raw materials transition. Because of their commitment to do the right thing, they were well ahead of the competition. Suddenly they had the opportunity to become the only company that could adequately and immediately meet the new regulatory requirements. When it became clear that the bill was coming to a vote, they had less than two weeks to complete the transition.

The biggest challenge was relabeling existing cartons. Lima teams pulled in corporate help from P&G sourcing, marketing, and sales. Ken Wessel found a label-printing company that could respond immediately once the new legal wording was in place. The teams also had to augment packaging machines so that they could "blow" cover-up labels onto existing cartons. This kind of modification had been tried without success on many occasions, but making it work this time was the only way to meet the legislative timeline.

Five days after they began the effort, the Michigan legislature passed the bill. It was noon on Thursday. All of the outlawed detergent products were to be removed from stores throughout the state by Friday midnight. Would a day and a half give the Lima teams enough time to replace their products?

When Ken saw the way the teams responded, he knew that something miraculous was happening. P&G was succeeding in doing the right thing for their customers and for the planet, and they were meeting an impossible deadline.

In stores all over the state, drivers were met by salespeople who helped them clear shelves and stock them with reformulated P&G products packaged in cartons that met the legal ingredient requirements. They filled not only their own shelf space, but also the spaces of all their competitors, every one of which had failed to meet the crucial deadline and would not be able to get products on the shelves for another few months.

P&G's business market share increased irreversibly, by more than twenty points in most parts of Michigan. Their achievement was simultaneously a terrific success for the planet, distributors and consumers, and P&G's employees and investors.

P&G's Guiding Principles

These innovative business practices produced a financial powerhouse, but they did much more. Staff at P&G's Lima plant worked alongside local community and state agencies to clean up water and sewer management, protecting water decades ahead of current mandates. P&G redesigned manufacturing systems to reduce carbon emissions and other pollutants decades ahead of other companies. It redesigned products to remove damaging chemicals and eliminate harmful processes. It changed the way women and minorities were hired, developed, and promoted inside the business and outside in the community. Incredibly, it did these things not because they were legally mandated or demanded by activist groups. It did them simply because *it was the right thing to do*.

The P&G pioneers were among my early mentors. Fifty years ago they birthed a way to create social and planetary health while building a business that was innovative, creating a great place to work and live, and delivering an excellent return on investment. They worked to change practices, formulations, and logistics fast—really fast. They never set sustainability targets, but they were more sustainable in the 1960s than most businesses are today. The P&G story is not offered here to illustrate a set of best practices or a generic development template. It describes a way of doing business that evolved naturally over time, a way of living a principled life. Instead of rules and procedures, the Lima teams were guided by five essential principles.

1. *Do what is right.* In a recent conversation, Ken pointed out to me that the term *stakeholder* did not exist as part of business language in the 1960s, but the concept was understood. "We affect a lot of people and systems when we act. We should take them into account" (personal communication, March 23, 2010). It wasn't complicated, and it worked.

2. *Work together.* The staff at P&G's Lima plant committed to engage and develop all the people and groups who were necessary for success and effectiveness. All were given respect and the opportunity to contribute in a way that mattered to them personally and to the work itself. All working sessions included time for improving team members' thinking capacities.

3. *Get results.* Although the process was important, it wasn't an end in itself. Lima's people changed the way they worked in order to get different outcomes. They gathered daily for work sessions, not meetings. They continually asked themselves how to improve the way they were working and exceed their performance commitments. Progress was shared publicly so that people could get involved. Results were routinely *twenty to thirty times* greater than what they had promised.

4. *Develop continuously.* This was the deepest innovation in the system. The P&G pioneers believed you could not grow a business without growing people. In addition to regular training, they worked to become *systems thinkers,* practicing and reflecting on innovative ways to plan and evaluate work. Regardless of their levels in the organization, everyone worked to become more self-managing with regard to thinking and behavior. They understood that ego and reactivity could undermine their effort. They reasoned that a lack of self-managing capability leads to excuses, politics, and distractions. Rather than make suggestions and hand off responsibility, they made decisions collectively and took responsibility together for the

whole. As a happy consequence, employees' family members also became better thinkers and decision makers and everyone's ability to see the effects on planetary and social systems expanded as they learned to understand systems better.

5. *Do it all—simultaneously.* Lima employees developed a fifth principle, which they articulated in just two words: *same time.* They learned to apply all of the principles simultaneously, as part of their daily work. They understood that the principles were holistic and could not be applied selectively. They learned through doing, working together, seeking to do the right thing, never against one another, always as unique individuals contributing to something bigger than themselves.

The P&G workforce in Lima also discovered that their principles were applicable to a host of social issues. Seeing the world through their lens made injustice and inequity obvious. Embracing *Do what is right* led to a rejection of corporate diversity programs by African American as well as white employees. They discovered that race sensitivity programs had a tendency to encourage classification of people by race within surprisingly narrowly defined boundaries. The new Lima system had been designed to care deeply about individuals, all of them. The Lima employees stated it as an integrated principle: "Everyone is equal with regard to our principles. We work together. We each, and all, get results. We develop everyone to bring more of his or her potential into the work" (personal communication, Ken Wessel, March 23, 2010).

One highly engaged employee, Lily White, served on five boards in the community, including the school board. As an African American, she was highly concerned about the African American youth of her community and worked to make a better future than history predicted they were likely to have. When race riots hit in the late sixties, she worked with students and community leaders to create dialogues that helped defuse the situation and built a new foundation for people to engage deeply with one another. Lily and her husband hosted "Hamfests" in a building they built in their backyard for this purpose. She reasoned that people have to listen if they are eating. Chewing gave everyone time to talk and reflect.

Lily White was known and loved inside and outside of P&G. When she died, people flew to her funeral to remember and honor her contribution. Crowds spilled over into adjacent buildings. It was Lily's nature to care and work tirelessly to grow community. In P&G's innovative Lima program she found a place to work that strengthened this capability and actively supported her efforts—her colleagues were Hamfest regulars.

Almost half of the Lima workforce was involved on local boards and in other social organizations. They were a new kind of activist, living and transferring their principles into the life of the community. They regularly reflected on how well they were living up to their principles and made changes to get it right.

Bringing It Home

The work at Lima was profoundly original, but it wasn't an anomalous success. Instead, many of the people who built the Lima, Ohio, detergent business moved on to P&G Ivorydale, a union plant with a hundred-year-old history, and repeated their success there. Bob Seitz enlisted executives to support change in what was often referred to as P&G's "mother" plant. This time he was backed by a set of performance indexes from Lima that set the standard for the industry in every business and social category.

From Lima and Ivorydale, leaders moved on to other businesses, inside and outside of P&G, and they continued to produce amazing results. Though the P&G experiment has been reported extensively, the real story remains largely undocumented. As Bob is fond of saying, "It was so different that outside people couldn't even see it. They didn't get it." He eventually banned visits from outsiders, saying, "They printed the wrong stuff and led people astray." *Bob is right—most people don't get it.* Most sustainability and social efforts work on symptoms, parts, and pieces. However well-intentioned they may be—and most are founded on fearless and imaginative commitments to social process—almost all approaches to sustainability and fair trade start from false premises. The Responsible Business framework described in this book offers an alternative, building a systemic approach that follows the P&G

principle of a *same time* business transformation—simultaneous, systemic, and ubiquitous.

Leadership Lessons from the P&G Prototype

1. Working on the business as a whole is the only path to simultaneous business and values success. Many popular programs lead to fragmentation and thereby limit creativity and success.
2. Working with a business can affect the corporation it is part of. The Lima venture is often cited by P&G CEOs as the beginning of real innovation in their company.[2]
3. The P&G endeavor was designed uniquely for this business and was based on principles rather than preexisting programs or popular concepts. In fact, it defied most of the popular concepts of its time.
4. Significant shifts at a business level can affect an entire industry. P&G's detergent business was studied for decades because of its distinctiveness and market effectiveness. According to Bob Sykes, over twelve hundred books and case studies were published on the topic between 1970 and 2000.
5. Courageous leadership based on a steadfast connection to principles rather than personal credit and reward is required.

P&G, Lima, used radically new methods to build a business. In 1960, almost no one in any industry was talking about carbon, pollutants, climate change, and social justice. Yet the P&G group naturally generated systemic solutions that addressed these and other challenges because *it was the right thing to do.*

P&G's methods are now fifty years old but they have yet to be adopted by most companies, in spite of validated results. In the following Introduction I will outline some fundamentals of responsible business development, most of which have evolved from the principles and methods that were first developed—in some cases extensively—at P&G.

Introduction: The Responsible Business

According to conventional business practice, responsibility has no inherent or fundamental connection to business, so responsibility needs to be added in. When added, it's usually in the form of a department or program assigned by management to an individual or group. The very concept of "corporate responsibility" puts emphasis in the wrong place, so it's one I've spent my professional career challenging.

New Problem, Old Mind

When I first began my work with businesses and other organizations, I systematically and intentionally violated the majority of business practices held sacred in the corporate world. I even violated some of the conventional beliefs about business ethics. Throughout my entire contrarian career I have swum against the current, always seeking the birthplace of authentic business thinking and practice. I pushed companies to move beyond their dependency on market research, environmental scans, and trends analysis in strategy. I pleaded with people to stop incentives and reward-and-recognition programs across all functional levels. I argued against performance reviews and, later, 360-degree feedback. I suggested that lists of leadership competencies reduced the quality of leadership. I opposed setting environmental goals and creating officer posts for promoting environmental ethics on the grounds that this would actually reduce ethical practices and environmental improvements. In other words, I spent a lot of energy in opposition to a lot of "best practices."

No, this is not a true confession about how I have repented my youthful indiscretion and come back into the mainstream fold with regard to the way to conduct business and improve global social and planetary concerns. In fact, the companies with the courage and vision to adopt the approaches described in this book became highly viable and nondisplaceable in their markets, growing at accelerating rates over decades. Their workforce and supplier relationships became more agile and innovative while their costs to deliver plummeted. Without even one sustainability or social responsibility officer or program in place, their work and operations practices developed increasing social activism and eco-logical leadership. It took over twenty years but the research has finally caught up with this way of doing business. When such ideas are embedded in business design itself, the result is the *Responsible Business.*

Responsibility isn't a set of metrics to be tracked or behaviors to be modified. It is central to both the purpose and the prosper-ity of a business and must be pervasive in its practices. The question of how to be Responsible Business is therefore relevant to all organizations—including nonprofits, governments, and schools—that usually don't see themselves as businesses as well as those corporations that don't imagine themselves to be interested in responsibility.

The word *corporation* derives from the Latin root *corpus,* or "body of the whole," and describes an integrated entity that is recognized by law as an independent being with full standing in society. In other words, a corporation is an invented person, char-tered to provide community benefits that individuals would not readily be able to create for themselves. A business is also a corpus that may or may not be part of a legal corporation. The commu-nity holds the reasonable expectation that in return for its existence, a corporation or business will live up to the laws, ethics, and expectations of reciprocal participation and will function in all ways as a contributing member of society.

A less frequently noted phenomenon is that corporations are also "alive" in that they exhibit the characteristics of a living system. Life is more than the ability to adapt and be resilient; it also includes evolution. Living systems become both more complex and more essential through time. Ecological and biological systems not only adapt to their surroundings, they also transform them. They create contexts in which increasingly sophisticated networks of relationships emerge. This opens up expanding opportunities for the expression and development of their inherent potential.

Corporations, and the businesses within them, work more or less the same way. If they are to live and prosper, they find ways to remain connected to their origins while cultivating and then adapting to changes in the world around them. Their long-term viability has as much to do with how well they create networks of relationships with consumers and other companies and industries that advance the health of all. In the long run, all living things must contribute to a world of expanding life. The alternative is a world where life steadily dwindles away to nothing.

By definition, therefore, a corporate or business entity is responsible to more than just itself. It exists in a larger whole—literally, as well as within the legal and operating framework of business—and it is responsible to the whole of which it is a part. How it governs its own existence influences every aspect of the whole, and as a living system it is governed by the natural laws that govern all living entities. Responsibility is a function and benefit of being alive.

These observations apply equally to other kinds of organizations, including nonprofits and governments, where the customer is the constituency and the investor is the donor or taxpayer. Though this book speaks specifically to Responsible Businesses, the principles can be applied to any organization that wishes to operate responsibly.

The Responsible Business is itself a co-creative partner in ensuring the vitality and health of all the communities to which it belongs. It develops its capacity to play the role of partner consciously. It sees itself as responsible for getting smarter about contributing to the health and vitality of all the systems it touches. Nothing alive is neutral. All living beings either contribute value or receive it. The ones that endure are the ones that do both, even as the world changes.

The real challenge to becoming responsible is that most businesses erroneously see themselves as closed systems cut off from their environments—more like machines than organisms. Most businesses are unconscious of the real relationships that enable them to exist, and this blinds them to their responsibilities. Even worse, it blinds them to their opportunities.

A Responsible Business embeds an understanding of relatedness into all of its decisions, actions, and evaluations. This enables it to take responsibility for the body of the whole, including the global community and the planet. When most people think of corporate responsibility, they are focusing on a business's effect on and relationship to stakeholders. A Responsible Business sees stakeholders as full partners and meaningful instruments for the evolution of healthier communities and more successful businesses.

I have worked with companies in the United States and abroad for thirty-five years as a resource for whole business regeneration, from boardroom to shop floor, including cultural transformation, leadership development, strategic planning, and systems design, and not once have I worked on "corporate responsibility." Yet the ethos of belonging to communities and ecosystems has pervaded everything I've done. Until all companies think this way, responsibility will remain a stepchild of the business world rather than its natural and necessary way of operating.

A human must learn to personally navigate the same questions about responsibility that a business faces. For humans, this is accomplished through socialization. From a young age, humans internalize the principles modeled by their families, spiritual institutions, and civil societies and tend to be pretty clear about where their personal responsibilities lie. For example, they generally understand that they have a responsibility to contribute to family and society; they realize that benefiting a few while doing harm to many is irresponsible; and they know that they must be accountable for their own actions in spite of how others may be acting. These are entry-level ethical understandings and not subject to much controversy.

Adults understand that their responsibilities apply in multiple domains. Their families, friends, work, civic engagements, and financial choices provide different challenges and opportunities for responsibility, and they use guiding principles to make responsibility practical in each of these arenas. It is nonsensical to insist on being responsible at home but irresponsible at work, and insofar as there are fundamental conflicts in the values applied in these different arenas, individuals will feel torn and self-contradictory and society will suffer. One of the pressing challenges of the present era is to bring personal, social, and business responsibility back into alignment and harmony.

EVOLVE CORPORATE RESPONSIBILITY BY EVOLVING BUSINESS RESPONSIBILITY

Businesses are the most powerful situations from which to shift a corporation's practices. A corporation is often made up of a set of businesses, each with its own market focus, functional departments, and unique workplace culture. Even when there is strong central leadership and infrastructure, a corporation achieves it ends through the efforts of each of its businesses individually. Product development, supply chain improvement, and financial planning and tracking are usually carried out at the business level.

In organizations that have become systemically accountable, principles may be developed at the executive or board level, but businesses are where those principles are put to work. Responsibility is a practical skill, not a utopian ideal espoused by others. The courage to make responsibility work day-to-day can happen only at a business level. Responsibility looks different in each business, and businesses move at different paces and generate different results. Many successful responsibility efforts are started in business units and then taken later to the corporate level.

Corporatewide responsibility programs are often slower and less effective than transformations grown from the businesses outward. It is difficult to keep corporate-driven efforts from fragmenting because responsibility programs are usually generic, designed to be universal in their application, and are therefore separated from the activity of running a business. Working from the level of a business to achieve responsibility overcomes this fragmentation by generating customized responses to actual challenges.

THREE FORKS IN THE ROAD TO RESPONSIBILITY

The different options for how to work on business responsibility can be illustrated in terms of three distinct approach levels, each with increasing potential for systemic effects.

THE RESPONSIBILITY PROJECT

At this level, a company generally assigns a specified group and leader to undertake projects that establish standards, planning, and evaluation for various aspects of the business (such as resource use, waste management, philanthropic and community relations, and other important arenas). In general, this level of work is based on generic standards, monitoring and adjusting actions in order to be responsive to these standards or goals. Currently, corporate responsibility activists are working very hard to get people to adopt even this entry level of responsible thinking.

THE RESPONSIBILITY PROGRAM

At this level, companies become more proactive and comprehensive. For example, they undertake development of sustainable products, knowing that they are in a reciprocal relationship with the environment. They can see that "what goes around comes around," and they pursue a variety of initiatives designed to rebalance actions across the company to neutralize environmental and social effects. They may commit to products that are fair traded, carbon neutral, and environmentally benign. They recognize that it doesn't work to become responsible in one part of the organization while failing to do so in other parts. Advanced practitioners are addressing the entire supply chain, working to ensure sustainability at every step of the sourcing, manufacturing, and even recycling of their products. Best practices are borrowed and built.

THE RESPONSIBLE BUSINESS

When a business understands that its actions can actually improve and evolve healthy systems, it has reached the third and highest level of responsibility. Responsibility becomes fully integral to the way all business activity and thinking is conducted. The intention of such an approach moves significantly beyond being neutral or benign with regard to effects on social or ecological factors. The Responsible Business's workforce operates simultaneously at different levels of work: first responsibility becomes embedded in business strategic thinking and models of doing business, then it becomes increasingly embedded into all operational activities and decisions. At the same time, every person in or associated with the business works to evolve all of its stakeholders to a higher level of responsibility. Because all planetary systems are evolving, including human systems, the actions of human beings and human institutions matter. The Responsible Business understands this and consciously accepts the role of partner in the coevolution of communities and living systems.

The Responsible Business works at the project and program levels but it initiates and guides from the business level. The Responsible Business always asks, "How can our actions positively affect the society we live in and the planet we live on while creating a great market?" It sets direction based on the evolutionary effects it wants to produce. It establishes cross-functional ways of working to pursue this direction. Groups or teams work within the corporation to establish and deliver on particular pursuits, focusing and operationalizing the direction, but no initiative is ever allowed to lose connection with the corporation's external performance indexes for a better society and planet, better service to customers and consumers, and greater financial effectiveness.

For the business working at the third level, responsibility has moved from a peripheral concern to the central organizing principle. One of the great shortfalls of responsibility programs is that they are so often satellite endeavors, isolated from the ongoing nature of the business. This means that they have to constantly justify their business return. It also means that their objectives are too isolated and narrow to serve as a source for business innovation because that responsibility becomes both costly and relatively unproductive.

By contrast, the Responsible Business embraces its role as a coevolver of human and natural systems and achieves deep innovation throughout the company in service to its customers. Because it focuses on those things that bring greater meaning, value, and health to individuals and societies, a Responsible

Business never struggles to connect responsibility and profitability. Responsibility becomes the source of financial return and allows a corporation to work in a singular and unified way, without distraction or justification. To quote Amory Lovins's observation about sustainability, "The essence of [responsibility] strategy is to make it an issue for your competitor—not for your own company—because you've already made [responsibility] an integral part of your business."[1]

Although more and more companies and business leaders aspire to work at the highest level, the field of corporate responsibility is still young, with plenty of room for companies to distinguish themselves. This book is intended to describe how the Responsible Business is created, maintained, and evolved. My hope is that it may also renew the passion that entices people into business in the first place.

A FRAMEWORK FOR THE RESPONSIBLE BUSINESS

Some years ago I developed a framework to describe what it means for a business to work in a systemic way. The framework identifies five windows through which businesses view their activities and represent a business's key stakeholders and how they can become systemically integrated. Although many businesses view these stakeholders as isolated from one another, the framework provides a basis for seeing them as one interconnected system.

Because the framework is made up of five interconnected points, it is referred to as a *pentad*, a term borrowed from ancient Greek geometry to represent a multidimensional figure with five dynamic and interactive aspects that move in tandem and can only be understood in terms of their relationships. I use the pentad to extend and order my thinking about the relationships that businesses manage at all levels of operation. It suggests a quintuple rather than a triple bottom line (see Figure I.1).

In the pentad framework, the *customer* or consumer is the first and foundational stakeholder. The second stakeholder, the *co-creator*, refers to all the people and organizations who contribute to the creation of a product or service, from raw material suppliers to employees and contractors. The third stakeholder is *Earth*,

Figure I.1. The Stakeholder Pentad Framework

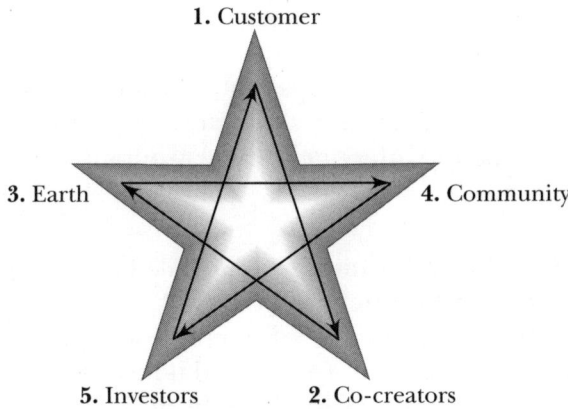

1. Customer

3. Earth

4. Community

5. Investors

2. Co-creators

the original source and infrastructure without which human activities would be impossible. The fourth stakeholder is *community,* the human inhabitants of all those places with which a business needs to partner in order to source its materials and workers, manufacture its goods, sell its products or services, and recycle or store its waste. The fifth stakeholder is the *investor,* without whom a company's dreams would be difficult or impossible to realize. A Responsible Business is designed to simultaneously serve all of these stakeholders through its way of doing business every day.

The pentad can be used as an instrument to shed light on five critical characteristics of a Responsible Business. The first two aspects have to do with stakeholders. A Responsible Business is developed from

1. A deeper understanding of the stake each stakeholder has in a better life for the end user.
2. An enlarged definition of capital that takes into account the investment made by each stakeholder—what the stakeholder puts into the game as ante. This is more than money and includes an emotional component.

The remaining three aspects have to do with the business itself. A Responsible Business must adopt

3. More creative thinking about the product or service that will produce the desired experience for each stakeholder, keeping in mind that the product is not the experience but the source of the experience
4. A way of conducting business that best serves its stakeholders
5. The ability to develop these characteristics within all five stakeholder groups and integrate the five groups into a single living system

The pentad enables a business to link stakeholder capital to the desired stakeholder experience and to link product development and operational design to the satisfaction of the multiple stakes involved in any business enterprise. And it has enabled businesses to do this work without ever losing sight of the whole.

From Add-on Responsibility to Full-on Responsibility

The MIT Sloan School of Management and Boston Consulting Group conducted a survey and interviews in late 2009 and found a large degree of consensus regarding the potential business effect and importance of sustainability and responsibility across all types and sizes of business.[2] The research further confirmed that there are stirrings of activity among those who have until now considered corporate responsibility outside their scope, but it found a material gap between intent and action at most of the companies examined. On the one hand, more than 60 percent of the respondents in the broader survey group said that their company was building awareness of its sustainability agenda. On the other hand, most of these companies lacked an overall plan for reconciling a broader approach to sustainability with their need to maintain delivery of performance results. Many of their actions were defensive and tactical in nature (for example, project and program based), consisting of a variety of disconnected initiatives focused on products, facilities, employees, or the greater community. Although these efforts might be impressive on some levels, they represented only incremental changes to businesses, which have created a "worst of both worlds"—sustainability that doesn't really make much difference and fails to contribute in a fundamental way to business strategy. Business leaders need a more systemic approach.

The MIT Sloan School of Management research reveals that sustainability will become increasingly important to business strategy and management over time and that the risks of failing to act decisively are growing. But how to achieve such strategic integration remains elusive. The report culminated with the conclusion of executives interviewed: To achieve such integration, companies will need to develop (1) new capabilities and characteristics, including the ability to operate on a systemwide basis and collaborate across internal and external boundaries; (2) a culture that values long-term thinking; (3) capabilities in the areas of performance measurement, process redesign, and financial effectiveness and reporting; and (4) skills in engaging and communicating with external stakeholders.

ABOUT THIS BOOK

This book offers an approach that goes beyond corporate responsibility as it is currently perceived and practiced. It is intended to help any business or organization develop a structured process for becoming systemically responsible. It supports the development of systemic thinking capabilities and actions, and it provides a framework that will help readers introduce this integrated approach into their own organizations. Used rigorously, it virtually ensures the ability to understand and work on systemic effects and approaches, not only to improve sustainability but also to improve all business activities.

The systemic approach described in this book is designed to support leadership or management that wants to embed responsibility into its way of doing business. It is a way of working that can be applied to any scale or type of business—from Fortune 100 corporations to small, privately held entrepreneurial enterprises. It has been successfully applied to the arenas of consumer products, line manufacturing, chemicals, and the high-tech industry in the United States and in global companies.

This book is organized into four parts. Part One describes what a business looks like when responsibility underlies everything it does. It illustrates what it means to be holistic, rigorous, and systematic in working with key stakeholders within a business, whether or not it moves across the boundaries into a larger corporation. The pentad framework is explored through stories from companies that have used it to create profound results.

Part Two illustrates the path to becoming a Responsible Business. It shows how the systemic framework can be used to describe an organization that can see and act systemically. It helps readers understand how to create actionable plans for working responsibly and effectively on strategy, product development, sales, operations, supply chain, distribution, and human resource development.

Part Three describes why working nonsystemically on parts of companies gets them in trouble. A variety of problems can present themselves, including distracting variances, inconsistency in message and effects, and even unintentional irresponsibility. Green-washing is a deliberate attempt to deceive others about a company's responsibility record, but sometimes an honest company may green-wash unintentionally out of ignorance.

Part Four explains how to measure stakeholder return and effectiveness at responsibility. How does one create significant performance indicators that illuminate the systemic benefits for each stakeholder? This is one of the greatest challenges to building support for efforts to become a Responsible Business. Most companies assess value from within their own perspective rather than take the perspective of the stakeholder. The key to helping stakeholders see themselves as invested in a company's success is to measure value in their terms.

Part Four also offers some thoughts about the future. It looks at how leaders can advance their organizations from Responsible Businesses to Responsible Corporations. It examines some of the emerging new legal and financial structures for businesses in addition to alternative models for influencing investor responsibility and building community collaboration.

About the Epilogue: many of my early readers suggest you read the Epilogue first because it presents the imperatives that underlie Responsible Businesses. So for once you are reading a book that invites you to skip to the end if you like!

About the Author

Carol Sanford is founder and CEO of InterOctave, a global consultancy working toward creating Responsible Businesses. Carol helps build clients' capabilities for developmental leadership and self-organizing management systems. Results of her involvement include strategic thinking that engenders nondisplaceable and ethical market positioning for truly value-adding offerings and creates an innovative ethic that permeates all aspects of business operation. An alumnus of the University of California at Berkeley, she has been a lecturer on business, urban planning, and economics in many universities, including MIT Sloan School of Management, Stephen M. Ross School of Business at the University of Michigan, and Haas School of Business at the University of California at Berkeley—with a deep attention to practices of conscience. She is a keynote speaker regularly at global conferences including in 2009 to 2010, "Middle East Forum on Sustainability and Climate Change," the Competitive Institute's "Global Conference on Economic Cluster Development," and the British Columbia "Forum on Food Fuel Fibre Policy." Carol was used as a consultant to the launch of a Colgate-Palmolive business strategy that included work in government collaborations with South African townships surrounding the elections forming the new nation from 1994 to 1996. She also worked on restructuring the Colgate-Palmolive business design in nine nations to enable integration into the European Common Market. In the Middle East she was an expert resource on building value-adding industries and green economies, creating collaborations with business and government to link sustainability with responsible economic, industrial, and business development. In British Columbia, Canada, Carol worked with the provincial government to innovate approaches for integrating sustainable economic and business development with natural resource management. She has worked with traditional businesses such as DuPont and P&G, technology-based companies such as Intel and Agilent, and new responsibility-focused businesses such as Seventh Generation. She currently lives in Seattle.

THE RESPONSIBLE BUSINESS

PART ONE

THE RESPONSIBLE BUSINESS: REIMAGINING BUSINESSES OF THE FUTURE

One of the challenges resulting from the popularity of new and innovative companies is that they leave ordinary companies feeling that approaching such is too big a jump to make. But it is not as hopeless as it seems. The detergent business at P&G, Lima, was a unit inside the more rigid and traditional structure of P&G—a hundred-and-fifty-year-old company—and it was composed mainly of established employees. Yet the team there was able to change its way of doing business and in the process became innovative and responsible. Their success, by their own account, paved the way for more than a hundred other businesses to take on similar change efforts, some tackling decades- and even generations-old business cultures and work designs.

The chapters in Part One explore the metaprinciples and practices that established, often staid companies employ to achieve successful retrofits and offer ways other established companies can learn from them, as well. Chapter One introduces some remarkable businesses and business leaders. Their stories will unfold throughout the Part One as I describe the unique ways in which Responsible Businesses evolve over time.

Chapter Two considers the meanings of *stake* and *stakeholder* and describes the unique stakeholder groups that make up a business's universe. In particular it focuses on the human innovations and natural resources that stakeholders bring to businesses and ways in which they are key to evolving a Responsible Business.

In Chapter Three I walk through the geometry of the stakeholder pentad, a framework that reveals the living system web of dynamic relationships among stakeholders—the essence of the Responsible Business. The pentad framework is an instrument that any business organization can use to understand itself and guide its development in reimagining and embedding responsibility.

Chapter Four describes *value-adding*, a key concept underlying the successful transformation of responsibility lived at the P&G detergent business. Using the pentad framework results in a shift to the *value-adding perspective*, which views the world as a complex of living systems working together to create value significantly beyond the concept of value-added.

Chapter Five demonstrates how any business can make the Responsible Business pentad work for them and offers case examples based on successful transformations at the businesses introduced in Chapter One. Working with the pentad reveals the principles and practices that underlie the vitality of older companies as they transform. I add one example of a start-up that used the same path to innovative responsibility from day one.

STORIES FROM THREE CONTINENTS

Boldness in business is the first, second, and third thing.
H. G. BOHN

Over the years I have had the good fortune to work with some extraordinary business leaders, helping them discover and pursue a variety of paths to growing Responsible Businesses. Each of the following stories introduces some remarkable people and demonstrates how a business, when it takes responsibility for the health and evolution of the whole, actually increases the equity of stakeholders. Each story illustrates the effect of being responsible on one of the five key stakeholders: customers, co-creators (employees, contractors, suppliers, and so on), local communities, the planet Earth, and investors. In later chapters, these stories will be filled in and elaborated on to show how a Responsible Business works to integrate all of its stakeholders.

Each story focuses on a particular business, although one ended up affecting an entire Fortune 500 corporation when the leader eventually went on to become CEO, president, and chairman of the board. Some of the businesses are large, some small; some public, others private; some local, others global.

HERBAN FEAST: CARING FOR CUSTOMERS

BJ Duft, founder of Seattle catering company Herban Feast, is widely celebrated by his customers and community for his environmental ethic, his commitment to small local farmers and businesses, and his dedicated and creative staff. His award-winning green business stands out in a city known for green businesses. But it wasn't always that way.

BJ started Herban Feast as a young entrepreneur with a conflicted sense of how to manage a company. He came out of the hotel industry, and all his reading and training emphasized the need to focus on managing costs and reducing waste. During the company's early years, BJ and his chefs managed for better costs and efficiencies first. They believed that only once this vital bottom line was addressed could they become creative and unique.

BJ is by nature social, engaging, and funny—the kind of perfect host who really ought to succeed in the catering business. He is interested in people's unique qualities and life stories. He peppers his own conversation with personal stories and seeks to bring his authentic self to his relationships. But the traits that make him so likable have also made it dispiriting for him to restrict his time and energy to efficiency issues. The cost-saving requirements of the catering industry have seemed to deny the expression of his creative and gregarious nature. Furthermore, they also put severe limits on his ability to be successful.

In general, the catering industry is dominated by two types of players. At one end of the spectrum are large hospitality companies, especially hotels, that offer package deals that include accommodations, meeting space, food, and other amenities. At the other end are individual homemakers or chefs who rent a kitchen and find work by word of mouth. Caught between are midsized operations like Herban Feast.

Catering is competitive and caterers can easily end up competing against each other to keep prices low. Even in the relatively high-end market of weddings, catering and food tend to be an afterthought organized by wedding planners or the hosting facility. Tradition holds that the distinctiveness of a wedding comes from the bride's dress, the decorations on the table, the site, and the party. Food contributes little more than a major line-item expense to be managed.

Operating within this context, Herban Feast was a modest success: a good, solid, but unexceptional caterer competing on price and good service with hundreds of other caterers in the Seattle region. BJ's clients were attracted to his warmth, but beyond that he was hard pressed to offer anything especially distinctive.

As the company grew, BJ became increasingly uncomfortable. Similar to other caterers, he had problems with turnover and staff discipline, which made it difficult to field people experienced enough to handle large events. He came to fear growth because he wasn't sure that by himself he could keep up with his business as it and the events it catered grew larger and became more complex.

BJ also wasn't getting media attention because nothing made him stand out from anyone else. He couldn't figure out how to create a public identity strong enough to make people want to tear out the story in the magazine or newspaper. It dawned on him that a company that isn't doing something creative won't get invited to do events where creativity is called for.

In one of our early conversations, BJ and I talked about the essence of his company. We discovered that his original inspiration to create Herban Feast was the idea of authenticity, in food and in relationships, and the desire to provide people with eating experiences that would nourish their bodies and lives. He made a decision to stop focusing his energies on minimizing waste and maximizing efficiency—an uninspiring vision for any company—and instead to dedicate himself to creating truly memorable and meaningful events. Each wedding, meeting, and party was to become an authentic source of joy for his clients and for his entire team.

BJ reconnected to the idea that his customers provided the meaning and reason for his business. Through deepening his relationship with them, he realized what he most wanted his business to be: creative, expressive, and a source of beautiful food and unique service. He understood that his customers, especially those who came for special events such as weddings and retreats, were looking to him to create meaningful experiences. They wanted stories that they could remember forever, ones that reflected images of their best selves. His company was being called on to write, cast, and perform plays that celebrated its clients' lives.

This insight about the company's relationship to its customers also transformed BJ's relationship with his staff. He had struggled with people's failures to follow through on instructions and their apparent inability to think for themselves. None of his staff seemed to love their work, and that was evident in their lack of energy and spirit. BJ couldn't see that these diverse problems had a single source. His company had its eye on the wrong thing. By shifting focus away from standards and controls and toward the lives of his customers and staff, BJ brought Herban Feast to life.

BJ and I collaboratively engaged with the staff in an exhilarating conversation about the lives of their customers. Soon after, one caterer had a concrete experience of the transformation that can come only from seeing through the customer's eyes. She was working with a particularly difficult wedding party who were making exceptional demands. They wanted special snacks and drinks while getting ready and seemed to forget that the folks in the building were caterers, not personal attendants. The caterer reported feeling at her wit's end about how to get her list of things done before the dinner started in the next room.

As she carried in a glass of juice (not her job) she heard the bridesmaids in the hall being chastised by another member of the wedding party for their impatience with the bride. Then she heard something that changed everything. One bridesmaid asked the others, "Well, how would you feel if you lost your mother just four months before the wedding you had been planning with her for a year?"

This moment made a huge impact on the caterer, who couldn't imagine simultaneously planning her own wedding and losing her mother. As she told her colleagues later in the debrief, "Everyone has a life we don't know about." The bride had not included this telling detail in her interview, but the incident educated the caterer who overheard it. She became a champion for listening for what is left unsaid. "Work with a caring ear," she advised her colleagues.

BJ's employees no longer represented a continual source of risk. They became improvisational collaborators. They were no longer food servers; they were storytellers. Herban Feast became the best improvisational theatre group in the region. Preparing for each event, one or more of the staff would learn about and open up to the clients, inviting them to share their dreams, their stories, and who they were trying to become. This intimacy enabled the Herban Feast crew to empathize and adjust their "performance" to create a perfect fit. Everyone participated—from kitchen help to waitstaff to parking valets—all aiming to create a whole, authentic, and meaningful experience for everyone involved in the event.

As a result, Herban Feast has become the most visible and sought-after caterer in the region. BJ is regularly featured in magazines and television interviews, and his company's excellence, authenticity, and innovation inspire audiences. Herban Feast's "green" weddings and events have made it the caterer of choice for a growing clientele who wish to live their values without compromising the quality of their celebrations. And BJ has evolved in his role. His team shares his vision, and he remains connected to them in their work.

KINGSFORD: CREATING COLLABORATIVELY

In 1985, I began working with Will Lynn, president and general manager of Kingsford, on a major effort to transform the company. Kingsford, a business within Clorox, makes charcoal and related products for backyard barbeques.

When we began our work, Kingsford was facing the enviable problem of rapid growth, which had created some real challenges. The company had outstripped the capacity of its manufacturing facilities. It was hiring new people, trying to bring them up to speed quickly, but this created serious safety problems. In the process, it had lost control of standards and quality as it tried to catch up with demand. It relied heavily on outside technical and management expertise.

Kingsford represented one-third of the people at Clorox, but by almost all measures it delivered a poor return compared to others in the industry and the rest of the company. Two years later that situation was reversed. Kingsford had halved its workforce while doubling its revenues. Even more remarkable, it had closed half of its plants without disrupting the lives of its workers and their communities. The company ensured that every laid-off worker was able to move on to an equivalent or superior job.

Seen from the outside, this transformation appeared miraculous. Kingsford's corporate headquarters were in Oakland, California, and its manufacturing was based in Louisville, Kentucky. But most of its plants were sited in backwater communities, in poor regions such as Appalachia and the rural South. Many workers lacked high school educations and some couldn't even read. Their work was labor intensive and dirty. Both management and workers called the chemical process of making charcoal "black magic."

The parent company behaved as though this poorly educated workforce could never learn to manage the business. The leadership of Clorox regarded Kingsford as if it were an ugly and embarrassing stepchild, useful around the house but certainly not invited to attend the ball. Its managers were thought to be ordinary, not worthy of promotion or investment. This was in contrast to the "extraordinary" managers at Clorox.

But Will Lynn refused to accept the stereotypes about his workforce. His connection to people was legendary. Will could tell you about everyone he ever worked with, employees and contractors—where they were now and what they were doing. For him, this was easy; he loved and was amazed by watching people grow. He saw the job of mentoring an employee as a lifelong commitment, whether or not a person still worked for him.

Will was dedicated to discovering and developing the wisdom hidden in every member of the Kingsford workforce. He repudiated the idea of imposing generic standards and worked instead to bring out each employee's unique contribution. He led by raising aspirations rather than by telling people what to do. He believed Kingsford had no problem with willingness on the part of its people. The issue was capability.

Hiring consultants to tell workers what to do was no way to create real change. He had observed that when Kingsford hired outside consultants to address its problems, the improvements went away when the consultants went away. The company had unintentionally cultivated its own dependency: change processes had no staying power without a consultant to lead them.

Will knew that he needed to grow people's ability to think like business owners. He felt that every employee should be able to stand in the president's shoes, understand the business as a whole, and make whole decisions based on defined products and profit-and-loss reports.

One day he had a conversation with Rod Lorimer, vice president of manufacturing for Clorox. Earlier in his career, Rod had been connected to the pioneering program at P&G's Lima, Ohio, division. This influential program had redefined the role of people in manufacturing, seeing them as sources of creativity rather than as self-operating extensions of machines.

Will suspected that maybe there were lessons from P&G that could be applied at Kingsford. Rod cautioned him: "It takes a pretty courageous leader to take on what they did in the detergent business. Most managers haven't got it in them. But it will make more difference than anything else you've ever done!"

Rod insisted that Will ask himself some challenging and unorthodox questions: Did he believe every person in his organization could grow and contribute significantly beyond their current level? Could developing his own and everyone else's critical thinking skills really make a difference? Was personal development something that belonged in the workplace as part of making a better business?

Will didn't disagree with the premises behind the questions, but he could see that what Rod was describing was different from any undertaking he had led before. He worried about whether he could pull off a change of this magnitude with a poorly educated workforce. He wondered whether the culture of his company would tolerate it.

Will understood that if he started changing the culture at Kingsford he couldn't stop. The process would build so much momentum and so much inspiration that stopping would leave his organization in a worse place than if he had never begun. Still, he knew from his conversation with Rod that those who had been willing to take this approach had generated an enduring legacy by creating some of the most innovative work systems in business.

Almost immediately the positive changes began to show up. Managers who had been little more than administrators suddenly started to reconceptualize the business they were in—from making charcoal to enabling great backyard barbeques. Within months they were exploring potential relationships with "picnic partners" such as Frito-Lay and Kansas City Masterpiece, and within a year they were talking to grill manufacturers about how to deliver a better barbeque experience. They learned to make swift and accurate assessments of which ideas were going to work, reducing product ideation testing from a two-year to a six-month process. They became experts in acquisitions and divestitures as they clarified what really fit with their new strategies. They discovered that running a business could be fun, creative, and improvisational.

The agility they were developing allowed them to try out multiple moves to find the ones that would work. Egos and conflicts that had previously slowed them down seemed to evaporate. Within six months Kingsford had introduced dozens of new ways of working into all parts of the business, and they found that people were hungry to join in.

Within a couple of years, a transformation had occurred throughout the entire workforce and in many of the supplier operations as well. It was becoming increasingly difficult to distinguish factory managers from their workers. Factories looked more like jazz orchestras, with every player helping compose the music as they performed it. Workers were initiating product development from the factory floor and recruiting research and development (R&D) to help them rather than the other way around. Operators and salespeople redesigned deliveries so that they could be customized to meet the specific needs of a given retailer. Workers organized themselves to promote their own development—everything from literacy programs to learning the science and technology needed to run the business.

Meanwhile, departments such as sales and R&D had dissolved their boundaries. Salespeople sat in the R&D labs and reported on what they were hearing from customers. Marketing managers were recruited from across the organization to plan their product launches. Suppliers were part of innovating new technologies and processes. The company was quickly becoming one integrated business team. They applied the systemic frameworks they had been learning to everything they did, making it easier and easier to communicate across all departments. As Will put it, "It used to be that you had to go up in the organization, then across, and back down again. Now you have operators calling up PhDs to get a technical question answered. Salespeople call up the guys loading the trucks. They're all just people now, trying to make this business work."

The result? In five years Kingsford had grown from a regional to a national brand, controlling 60 percent of a growing market. A business within a corporation had been able to instill a responsible culture and significantly affect its parent company. Will's efforts had paid off.

COLGATE, SOUTH AFRICA: LOCALIZING IDENTITY AND DESTINY

In 1992, Colgate's commitment to the turbulent communities in South Africa helped transform not only the company but also the new nation it was part of. Two years before the elections that created a new South Africa, the fledgling nation's economy was in a shambles. Workers were staging massive strikes and companies were routinely responding by shutting plants down. Violence was escalating among tribal factions in the townships. Transportation vans, with fifteen or twenty workers crammed into vehicles designed to carry ten, were regularly booby-trapped or prone to fatal road accidents. As if this were not enough, conditions of near war disrupted supply, distribution, and financing.

Colgate, South Africa, whose primary businesses were personal care and household products (such as toothpaste and detergent) for middle-class urban consumers, worried about its operations in such an unstable environment. Similar to all major U.S. companies, Colgate Corporation was assessing the situation on a daily basis and felt it needed someone on the ground who could wisely steer the business through a time of extreme change. For many Colgate workers, home and work environments were deteriorating. Bombs were a daily occurrence in neighborhoods and on vans that served as buses. Colgate wanted to make sure they could maintain a viable business, create a safe workplace, and offer support to the workforce.

At the same time, businesses were coping with a changing political environment. Managers in large companies were primarily white Afrikaans or English, but a new constitutional mandate required management to reflect the population, which was

98 percent black African. Most companies were terrified of this. They believed it was impossible to develop a management class from an uneducated workforce. And what a management class it would have to be, one capable of dealing with a crisis situation far more challenging than anything most managers would ever have to face.

The situation, in other words, was virtually impossible. Enter Stelios Tsezos, a high-energy Greek visionary who had led a successful developmental change process for Colgate Europe under other difficult circumstances. At that time Colgate, which operated in nine countries and twelve languages, was being forced to integrate in response to the emergence of the new European Common Market. This could have meant closing plants, consolidating operations, and other profound changes. The change process was initiated with company representatives from across Europe at a conference in 1991, in Compiegne, France. On the opening day, the room crackled with tension and longstanding rivalries.

Among its more powerful peers, the Greek company, led by Stelios, was considered the poor country cousin (an assessment that even the Greeks shared). But within three or four months it became clear that the Greeks were quickly outpacing all the other Colgate companies in terms of learning about and transforming their businesses. Then they did something no one expected. They began to share everything they had learned. The Greek contingent's intention was to keep everyone moving forward at the same rate. They systematically defused competition across national boundaries. Soon, they were being described by the leadership of Colgate Europe as the "cradle-of-business civilization." In time, Colgate was led by the Greeks to surpass other companies in every market in Europe, including P&G, who had originally pioneered this change work!

Stelios is a Fulbright scholar, born in Greece and educated in the United States, and an Athenian to the core. Most of all, he is a citizen—of his Athens, Greece, Europe, and the rest of the world. He has enormous presence and is fearless in his pursuit of a more civil and caring world. He has always encouraged people to see their role as lifting everyone in the community together. When I visited the Colgate factory in Athens with him, he would stop and talk with people who were running lines and ask what he could do to help them do their job. His most characteristic question was, "What are you thinking you could do to make this business perform better?" He was always challenging himself, challenging his friends, and challenging his workers.

Stelios's experience dealing with large-scale systems and cross-cultural, crossbusiness complexities in Europe made him uniquely qualified to tackle the challenges as general manager for south-eastern Africa, but particularly in South Africa at that point in its history. He had been sent to South Africa to handle a very specific task for the company: restructuring manufacturing operations and improving low profitability. Even from the beginning Stelios could see that he wouldn't be able to fulfill his mandate if he narrowed the focus to restructuring and efficiency. He quickly decided to redefine his task and asked me to join him in carrying it out.

Stelios was simultaneously committed to the country, to the workers, and to Colgate's success. He believed that the national company should do everything in its power to help the struggling people of South Africa. He could see that at Colgate, South Africa, there was animosity among blacks and between blacks and whites, bad relations in the management team, isolation from local communities, and badly structured manufacturing operations. Many of these workers were too poor to afford the products they manufactured. They faced violence at home and on the factory floor. Stelios was not a politician, but he understood that without skilled leadership in the townships, the violence would likely continue, putting the fragile new nation at risk.

At that time, Nelson Mandela was calling for councils in each of the townships to develop dialogue, reduce intertribal conflict, and grow the capacity for self-governance. The urgency of the mandate was immediately apparent at Colgate, where the workforce comprised six different tribes. Even on operating lines with only fourteen workers, conflicts broke out. The workers lacked the basic ability to talk through differences. "How," Stelios wondered, "when fourteen people around a line can't work together, and when forty operating lines in a facility can't work together, is it going to be possible to get hundreds of thousands of people in a township to work together?"

Stelios and I knew that the South Africa effort needed to be far more holistic and all encompassing than the targeted mandate he had been given by Colgate. His commitment to workers was both personal and deeply felt. Even during the worst violence, when it was extremely dangerous to enter the black townships, he never missed a funeral of one of his operators or their family members. This was his way of demonstrating an important commitment to the communities. People in the townships saw it as an acknowledgment of their abilities and a recognition that they would lead Colgate and South Africa into the future. Though Stelios believed he could replicate the crosscultural successes of the European effort, he was unprepared for the desire of South Africans for change—a hunger that allowed them to produce in nine months the results it had taken two years to accomplish in Europe.

He immediately initiated community-building processes within the company, believing that this would enable workers to transfer what they were learning back into the townships. He asked black operators to lead projects and trained them to lead others on the team—some of whom were white. He walked into meetings frequently and asked people to reflect on what they were learning from one another. A large number of workers from all six tribes approached him for help with bringing what they were learning in the company back into their communities. Thirty or forty people began meeting with us after work at each of the plants. Some of these workers and community members were serving on Nelson Mandela's township councils. The content changed—company work during the day and community work in the evening—but the processes were the same.

It was inspiring to watch Stelios at work. He always crossed boundaries and divisions. He involved the entire company by having researchers, marketers, and operators working together. While others engaged one tribe at a time, Stelios believed that the way to break down divisiveness was to encourage people to come together to address common purposes in the business and the community.

During previous efforts in Europe or the United States, I was accustomed to coming back to a business after six weeks and finding that everyone had been too busy to think about—let alone implement—the lessons and insights created during the prior visit. I would have to revisit and deepen material over five or six visits for it to really stick, and people often complained that I gave them too much content to handle. The South Africans, however, always complained that I gave them too little! Each time I returned, they had applied what they had learned the last time to everything they could imagine.

Not only did the South Africans implement new processes immediately but they also understood the holistic nature of the approach. "Try it on everything!" was their motto. This was one reason they were able to move it out into the townships so quickly and successfully. They no longer segmented their lives into home and work but began to see them as integrated wholes. These workers quickly grasped that for the township to become successful, the company needed to be successful, and vice versa.

Colgate's financial managers in New York feared they would never see a profit in South Africa again. Imagine their shock when the South Africa operation doubled its profitability during the first year. Strikes, which were universal in South African factories at the time, never occurred at Colgate's plants, and within six months the management team was 98 percent black. None of this was accomplished with quotas. Instead it was the natural result of drawing out, lifting up, and developing the inherent capacity of people to lead and create. A combination of rapid growth, which created more roles, and the departure of some who left because they didn't wish to participate, resulted in businesses where 95 percent of managers were black Africans. The legacy of that work endures in South Africa even today and has brought new hope and ideas to the Colgate Corporation about what a systemic approach to responsibility can accomplish.

Seventh Generation: Regenerating Planetary Systems

Seventh Generation was founded on the idea that business ought to be able to do well by doing good. Begun as a catalog company offering nontoxic household and personal care products, it soon found its standards compromised by its manufacturers. In addition, its margins were too small to drive its own aspirations and to support the few nonprofit organizations whose work to improve the world it sponsored.

Seventh Generation sold its catalog and set out to improve returns by regenerating the company's mission. Their strategy was to take control of the formulation of a set of products with high potential for environmental toxicity, transform them into non-toxic products, and let others sell them. This improved their leverage with regard to manufacturing and distribution and increased their returns.

The strategy has won Seventh Generation wide recognition and respect as a successful and influential pioneer in the arena of green products. The company has been so successful, in fact, that a number of large and powerful companies are looking to follow Seventh Generation's lead, bringing ecologically benign products to market. A lack of focused competition in its formative years allowed the company to thrive, developing a freewheeling "anticorporate" culture. But the rapidly evolving conditions it was now facing caused the company to do some serious thinking about its origins and its purpose, which is why they invited me to work with them.

When I met Jeffrey Hollender, the founder of Seventh Generation, he was frustrated by internal contradictions that seemed inevitable for a business dedicated to what might be regarded as work more appropriate to the world of nonprofits. Earlier in life he had founded several nonprofits but had come to the conclusion that the best way to create change was through business. He observed most nonprofits limit their work to pieces of the puzzle—each pursuing a different cause. He believed that in business he could get his hands around the whole of something.

Jeffrey is driven to make a positive contribution with his life. This desire to make a better world is fundamental to who he is and it influences every aspect of his company. It accounts for Seventh Generation's rapid growth in the nineties, as well as its strong movement toward sustainability and social responsibility. His deep commitment to authenticity in everything he does and his humility and willingness to admit mistakes result in a total dedication to transparency and honest disclosure. Seventh Generation was an early creator of corporate responsibility reports and a pioneer in publishing all of its ingredients on its labels. Because customers who buy its products are buying care for Earth and safety for their families, the company places a great deal of emphasis on deserving their trust.

As Jeffrey and his team began working together with this new approach to business thinking, it became increasingly apparent that Seventh Generation had failed to develop comparable emphasis on nourishing Earth (a surprise to anyone who knows them). Jeffrey and his team began to articulate two critical pieces that were missing from their thinking. First, their focus on reducing toxicity in products and the manufacturing process masked the question of what is needed to *create* health for people and the planet. As Jeffrey recently put it, "I've spent twenty years figuring out how to do less harm. Now I realize that the real question, a question I don't yet know how to answer, is how to do something that is genuinely healthy and healing."

The second issue had to do with the company's commitment to contribute part of its profits to nonprofit organizations engaged in worthy environmental and social justice work. Their donations, 10 percent of the operating profits, were made without sufficient evaluation of the relative effectiveness of the causes they chose to support. Some members of the organization even challenged their corporate philanthropy group on whether Seventh Generation contributions were generating beneficial results for the business or creating additional challenges. They feared that there was no way to know if the company was fulfilling completely on its promises and really helping or if it was actually letting people down.

Even as a respected ecological company, Seventh Generation faced similar challenges. Jeffrey was quick to admit that "Seventh Generation still uses materials that are not as green or sustainable as we desire with regard to finished product results. We consume nonrenewable fuels to ship materials and products. Our packaging ends up in landfills." Like most companies with philanthropy programs, its contributions back to communities and the planet are dwarfed by the primary economic activities that cause social and environmental problems in the first place.

As they looked hard at the contradictions, it began to dawn on the Seventh Generation team that the truly leveraged opportunity was to turn manufacturing, product development, and distribution into an integrated, regenerative process that could actually improve the health of communities and ecosystems. The company has since dedicated itself to a new purpose: to design household and personal care products and develop business processes that promote human and planetary health in a profitable way. If they can carry it out, this purpose will solidify their leadership position in their market, even as others seek to outpace them.

To illustrate the kind of regenerative work they are now pursuing, the company has dedicated itself to finding ingredients that contribute to environmental and social health. For example, it has eliminated the use of synthetic fragrances and replaced them with organic essential oils. These are healthier for customers and workers. Their production is carried out by small specialty farmers and businesses, which are often deeply rooted in local cultural traditions.

Ironically, one of the strongest restraints to successfully pursuing the new purpose has been the company's culture. From its outset, Seventh Generation has been sensitive to the needs of consumers and customers, kind to its employees, and dedicated especially to protecting children and young mothers. It has successfully attracted people who want to demonstrate an alternative to business as usual. But when I first met the Seventh Generation co-creators the company had not yet proved that a group of committed nontraditionalists could meet the thorny challenges of socially responsible business and were not just enjoying a socially responsible hobby. And still today an increasingly competitive environment is testing Seventh Generation's principles.

The team at Seventh Generation has positioned itself to work on the next phase of its evolution. They know that their credibility and influence on how business is conducted will come to nothing if they don't survive and flourish as a business. They know that moving from doing less harm to actually creating a healthier planet will require them to take on questions for which there are currently no answers. They will need to exercise an entirely new level of rigorous discipline in their thinking and practice, move beyond familiar prejudices, and embrace the possibility that business can serve as a source for transformation.

E. I. DuPont: Engaging Shareholder Value

Chad Holliday, who retired on January 1, 2010, from his position as CEO, chairman of the board, and president of DuPont Corporation, was one of the most sophisticated leaders I have ever known when it came to managing the delicate diplomacy required for large-scale organizational change. In particular, he used dialogue as a powerful instrument for growing shareholder consciousness, and he had the patience to take the long view.

I met Chad in 1980 when he was the head of strategic planning for DuPont. We were at a "Strategic Thinking Series" designed by Charles Krone, who developed the work systems and business design for the transformation of P&G's detergent business in the 1960s. The leaders of that effort had all left P&G in order to share their discoveries with other companies. By that time I had become a part of the team.

When we debriefed after each of the monthly sessions in which Chad was a participant, we would invariably say, "Chad will run this company one day." Though he was young, he was that good.

Chad was brought up in Tennessee, and he credits his parents for the disciplined thinking and strong conscience he always brought to his work in DuPont. With his respectful Southern gentleman manner, he tactfully challenged all ideas presented before accepting anything as true. He was rigorous in the way he engaged with DuPont's challenges; in addition, he educated himself on new ways to think. This never changed during the years I witnessed his move up the ranks, across functional roles, business groups, and nations.

Early on, Chad started making noises about the need to pay attention to the environmental effects of DuPont decisions and actions. He introduced changes in manufacturing procedures in each new business he headed, from Intermediate Chemicals to Fibers Groups, first in the United States and then in Europe and Asia. He was subtle but determined. I worked with many business teams under Chad's leadership and watched them become more systemic as a result of the questions he asked and the way he engaged. In all that time, he never talked about corporate responsibility or sustainability. He just kept using the principle *Do what is right* to question and redesign work and production systems as well as product development. As a by-product, the effects on Earth and communities were reduced and new relationships and partnerships were built.

When Chad became head of DuPont, we all expected him to implement this way of working across the company, changing everything at once. But change in a system of the scale and complexity of DuPont, we learned, is not as straightforward as one might think.

For example, early in his new position Chad arrived at the annual meeting to discover that the company was faced with two lawsuits from different shareholder contingents. One was from a shareholder group asserting that he was wasting money on attempting to reduce carbon emissions. It commanded him to cease such efforts. The second asserted that the company's practices were creating global warming and he needed to act to reverse such effects. This intractable situation illustrates the nature of the challenges Chad faced from day one.

Chad realized that one of his greatest opportunities for change was shifting shareholder understanding. He felt that shareholders were too disconnected from the effect of corporate decisions and he made shareholder education central to his strategy. He knew that butting heads with his board was not going to shift their understanding or perspective. It would only reduce dialogue and increase resistance. So instead he launched a campaign to educate not only his own shareholders but also the investment world as a whole.

He knew that what was driving his shareholders was not limited to his own company but part of a much larger set of assumptions about corporate governance, so part of his strategy was to use his influence as the head of a Fortune 100 company to evolve those assumptions. For example, Chad helped design the UN Global Compact—a voluntary initiative for multinational corporations focused on learning, dialogue, and partnerships—and took a position on its board. As part of that effort he helped develop the "Global Compact Governance Framework" and "The Ten Principles," which articulate agreements that guide global corporations' efforts to hold themselves accountable.[1]

Although participation in the UN Global Compact was voluntary, companies that signed on agreed to a mandatory disclosure framework, the "Communication on Progress" (COP). Participants were required to communicate annually on their progress with regard to human rights and environmental responsibility, first to their own stakeholders and then put the results on the Global Compact's Web site. This voluntary program enabled businesses to account, in their own words, not only for what they were doing but also for how they were progressing. This emphasis on progression has been a key factor in making the program an effective source for corporate change.

In a similar strategic move, Chad advocated for supporting rather than fighting regulations intended to promote corporate responsibility. He reasoned that if something is the right thing to do and companies are avoiding taking it on for fear of eroding a competitive position, then regulation can level the playing field. Everyone would make the same investment at the same time in what is right and no one would be left at a disadvantage.

At the same time that Chad was working to transform the field of corporate governance—the means by which companies interact with their shareholders—he was also working to transform DuPont. He believed that transparency was a meaningful and effective way to bring about change and to educate all of a company's stakeholders. Toward this end, he set up a set of advisory boards for a number of DuPont businesses. In the case of the biotech business, he recruited a broad range of members for the advisory board, including a priest, the leader of an environmental nongovernmental organization (NGO) from Mexico, and a diverse group of scientists, ethicists, and medical experts. In particular he sought out activists who would challenge the company, and he strongly encouraged them to make their case. In a recent conversation in which we were reflecting on our experience together nearly thirty years ago, Chad pointed out, "They [activists] can make you very uncomfortable at board meetings, and that is what we wanted. It makes the company better."

This process of increased transparency served to educate investors on the effects of their decisions. It also had the effect of educating the DuPont leadership, which made deeper and more systemic understanding pervasive throughout the whole company.

It forced management to question the usual business practices and get people reflecting with one another. To keep the process open and transparent, the advisory boards put up reports on their own Web pages, including independent assessments of company practices and reports on how management was addressing environmental and social issues.

Dissenting opinions were not only respected but also encouraged. "This is the only way to get outstanding people to come on board. They are given full access to all business leaders and work in the company," Chad insisted. This practice resulted in open and deep dialogues about issues that management might not think to raise on its own. "There are risks in such transparency but the increased intelligence across the company far outweighs the risks," he observed.

Over several decades, I saw Chad successfully lead increasingly larger business units, guiding an unusually conscious practice of management. In our recent conversation I asked him, "How have you developed your own conscience?" He said it was something he learned early in his career. "Without much effort, it was possible to see the value in doing it right the first time and the pain of not. You cannot fix your issues at the end of the pipe. This includes the social and environmental systems that DuPont's businesses affect. The process must be designed right from the start."

Early in his tenure as CEO, Chad recognized a critical distinction between debate and dialogue. Up until that point he had believed that public debate was a good way to demonstrate that companies could take care of the environment and make money also. Debate, he reasoned, was a good way to educate people and promote change. He participated in a couple of such debates, chaired by the editor of the *Financial Times*. At the end of both, he was convinced he had lost soundly. This was not a viable means, he decided, to educate people. That led him to establishing the various councils previously described.

The principle Chad had uncovered was that complex subjects do not lend themselves to a polarized, either-or discussion. They require dialogue, an ongoing deliberative process that builds an evolving understanding in all parties. Education and transparency are far more effective than debate at creating the accord and collaboration needed to address seemingly intractable challenges.

Today Chad acknowledges that transparency of the sort he practiced at DuPont is not welcomed by many companies. Like other retired executives, he sits on boards of several Fortune 500 and private equity companies. "In many places it is still a tough sell," he told me, "but with the Internet making everything accessible, I believe transparency will eventually happen to companies, with or without their conscious decision to take it on. So why not lead it?" he offered.

PANNING FOR GOLD

Five recurring themes or principles enabled each of the businesses described here (and many others as well) to go beyond corporate responsibility and become Responsible Businesses.

1. *Reality:* Evoke caring by connecting everyone in the organization to the real lives of its stakeholders. Eliminate dependence on the abstract data generated by market research and customer-feedback mechanisms. Use customer and market champions to connect to reality.
2. *Systemic Effects:* Define responsibility in terms of consciousness of systemic effects rather than as best practices and programs. Systemic effects should be the only measures of success.
3. *Systemic Wholes:* Combat fragmentation by working systemically. Fragmentation is the enemy of ecology, social justice, purposeful motivation, and market and financial success. It is overcome by working with wholes, not parts: whole businesses, whole people, whole watersheds, and whole systems.
4. *Self-Direction:* Redesign work to evoke self-developed people doing self-directed work that is self-evaluated within the context of business strategy. Hierarchies are artificial, while self-organization is the natural state of life.
5. *Capability Development:* Develop internal and external stakeholders through personal development and education in systemic approaches. Unlike training, this mind-set builds critical thinking skills and is the fastest way for companies to become a Responsible Business.

CONCLUSIONS

Oversimplification is the biggest risk in writing about living processes. It can be all too easy to give the impression that a set of successful practices can be transferred from one situation to another. Ways of thinking and working must be regenerated—brought to life again—in each new time, place, and set of circumstances. The purpose of these stories is to illustrate how this approach plays out differently every time it is applied. Even within the same company, systemic methodologies need to continuously evolve.

A Responsible Business operates in the world of the real and the living, not in the world of abstraction and numbers. The stories contained in this book are invitations to other organizations to become more real. Removed from their living context, the creative actions they depict become mere practices, abstract and dead. Recipes and best practices destroy meaning. They substitute generic instructions for self-discovery, which arises from the unique dynamics and circumstances of living organizations.

Thus I invite the reader to remember that each story's pattern is more important than the practice it depicts. Each story is intended to illustrate, inspire, and stimulate, not to be copied.

 Free download: For interviews with some of the business leaders described in these stories go to the free downloads section at www.The-Responsible-Business.com.

CHAPTER TWO

STAKEHOLDERS AS SYSTEMIC COLLABORATORS

The teachers are everywhere. What is wanted is a learner.
WENDELL BERRY

Each of the stories in Chapter One illustrates the importance of one of the five key groups of people connected to every business, its activities, and the value it endeavors to create. These groups are known as *stakeholders,* and together they form the central focus of this book. As a group, they reflect the whole for which a Responsible Business takes responsibility.

THE MEANING OF *STAKEHOLDER*

To understand the idea of stakeholder, let's review why societies allow and encourage businesses in the first place. Businesses are chartered to serve the common good by producing something of value that others seek but are unable to produce for themselves. In the case of consumers, the value might be goods and services. In the case of communities, it might be the social stability and the quality of life that accompanies sustained economic activity. Stakeholders are those who have an interest or *stake* in this production of value. Business aggregates a complex set of stakes, raises the value, and returns that value back to each stakeholder.

The modern meaning of *stakeholder* has a convoluted history, diverging since WWII from historic uses. In pre-Columbus days the word referred to a disinterested third party who held the stakes of gamblers when they were engaged in a game. In its modern usage, a stakeholder refers to anyone who has an interest in an issue. In English law, when one person hands something of value to a trustworthy other, knowing that he can't be certain whether or not he'll get it back, he is said to have handed over his stake. For example, when a grain farmer entrusts his crop to an auctioneer, he expects to receive back fair payment minus the auctioneer's fee, and thus each participant has a stake in the outcome.

The farmer in my example expects the auctioneer to understand his intention, the nature of uncertainty involved, and to exercise diligence in helping him realize the value of his crop. The auctioneer has a stake in playing this role and thereby performing a service that the farmer couldn't readily perform himself. The current meaning of stake—having a material, ethical, or other interest in an outcome—has become broadly accepted, especially when discussing corporate governance.

Stand in the Stakeholder's Shoes

To honor a stake requires understanding and valuing it from the perspective of the stakeholder. It requires engaging in a relationship that is reciprocal: one receives the use of the stake and in return one adds value to it. But that value needs to be in a form that is relevant to the stakeholder. Too often, in lieu of providing real value to stakeholders, companies offer self-serving interpretations of what they are returning and expect stakeholders to be satisfied with what they can get.

Let me give you an example from my own life. Recently I noticed that the airport shuttle I regularly use had started referring to me as a *guest*. When I asked the driver why, he told me, "We want you to feel at home in our vans." I said, "So you're telling me you want me to be happy in your world." He smiled and nodded, "Yes."

When I replied, "I'm not interested," he looked shocked. So I asked him, "What if this were about you coming into my world and helping me there?" He clearly had no idea what I was talking about. To help him out I asked him, "What do you think I'm thinking about when I get on this van?"

He answered, "Whether the temperature is comfortable, whether the price is fair, whether I broke anything when I loaded your luggage." I laughed and said, "Well, those are great. But after traveling all day, I really only see you as the fastest track to getting me home to my own bed." I knew I wasn't making much headway in getting him to think about the shuttle service from my perspective. Sure enough, when he dropped me off he said, "Thanks for your support; we've been having a hard time."

I wanted to tell him, "I don't ride the shuttle to support you." I walked into the house reflecting that our entire interaction had been about him and his company. He had been trained to offer euphemisms such as *guest, support,* and *appreciation* to mask his company's failure to actually understand its role in facilitating my life as a traveler.

This happens all the time with stakeholders. Employees are called *associates* and community organizations are called *partners,* but the change in title doesn't actually represent a change in relationship. This language is self-serving and irritating because the companies that use it still have themselves at the center of their universes. They're short-sighted and self-absorbed. The only way to truly honor a stake is to have a deep understanding of what the stakeholders are investing in and what fair return they are counting on.

STAKEHOLDERS AFFECT RESPONSIBILITY

Everyone needs other people to underwrite their dreams. When others share aspirations and invest in them, a kind of alchemy takes place. The resources needed to grow a person, a project, or a business become available. Involving more people provides access to a greater diversity of experience and ability. Additional resources provide cushions that allow exploration and discovery, which lead to creativity and innovation.

Enrolling stakeholders means not having to do everything oneself. By assembling an appropriate portfolio of partnerships, a company easily and effectively secures what it needs rather than searching, in a hit or miss way, for resources or intelligence.

Stakeholders supply a critical component of reality building. By placing stakes on a dream, they create possibilities and responsibilities. Businesses become appropriately beholden and enter into reciprocal relationships with their partners.

Entering into a stakeholder relationship requires both consciousness and transparency. When a relationship is based on these values, then all parties are enabled to take responsibility for its success. A relationship not based on explicit values and understanding can place the investment at risk for all concerned. A business has a responsibility to ensure that what stakeholders think they are investing in is in fact what they are investing in, and what they expect to receive back is consistent with what the business believes is the right thing to do and a promise it can fulfill.

The economic crisis of 2008 taught these values, if nothing else. People invested in financial instruments that they didn't understand or in many cases did not realize they were investing in. Each new tier of investment had a stake in the underlying health of all the investments that came before it. However, each new set of buyers of increasingly aggregated portfolios and investments had no knowledge or ability to care for the lowest stakeholder in the ladder—in this case subprime mortgage holders. People lost any sense of connection between the top and the bottom and no longer understood the effect of their choices, even on themselves. Mortgage holders were at a radical distance from the top of the ladder—the investment bankers—so it became nearly impossible for these distant players to understand, let alone maintain stewardship for, one another's stake. Without educating everyone involved in the implications of the choices, the stakeholder relationship functions without agency or consciousness. Caring is disconnected from choices. No one is in charge and no one takes responsibility.

A Responsible Business consciously recognizes all the stakes that have been invested in it and works to increase value for all the stakeholders. This is its singular purpose. For a Responsible Business, the living entities—ecosystems, communities, and individuals—that it affects are not externalities; they are part of the *body of the whole*. A Responsible Business holds a significantly expanded view of what constitutes its body and soul.

Similarly, a Responsible Business does not produce waste, which I define as an output that cannot be put to beneficial use in another cycle. Outputs must always be inputs of value to a subsequent process. Waste occurs when the cycle of life stops and material (or energy) can no longer be transformed to a new or higher use. A good way to think about waste comes from the study of ecological systems. Ecological design practitioners often say that nature does not produce waste; human waste is merely an underused resource. For a business that operates consciously as part of an open system, all processes produce usable surplus. Any business that produces waste is either engaged in a value-destroying activity or failing to integrate its surplus into the system of stakeholders in a form that they can put to use.

FIVE KEY STAKEHOLDERS AND THEIR STAKES

From my observations and work with businesses around the world, I believe that there are five distinct stakeholder groups, each with a unique nature, that give a stake to a business in exchange for achieving the value they hope to realize. Although the concept of the triple bottom line has been important in opening up what a business takes into account, it may also obscure the systemic nature of stakeholder connections.[1] Taken together, the five stakeholders represent the whole context or universe within which a business operates. To grow an increasingly successful and healthy business—the Responsible Business—it is essential to identify, understand, and develop all stakeholders. These are initiatives that go far beyond merely keeping them informed or measuring the business's effects on them. They can move a company from triple bottom line to *the quintessential top line*, fully developed responsibility in all areas of work and relationship.

The five stakeholders are *customers, co-creators, Earth, communities,* and *investors*.

CUSTOMERS

Customers include consumers, distributors, and in some circumstances clients and constituents. Customers use a company's output and make their own value from it. Most companies tend to think of them as *buyers* of products and services, but when customers are truly understood to be stakeholders, they are seen as *integrators* because they integrate products or services into their personal or work lives. The success of any business depends on how well that integration occurs. A business is important to consumers to the extent that it anticipates and serves what they are attempting to create through their lives. This goes far beyond simply "giving them what they want" and looks toward what they would want if they could imagine themselves supported in pursuing their deepest values.

Customers continuously seek the means to achieve and extend the fulfillment of their dreams and the material bases for their physical lives. Their stake is defined as the ability of a business or institution to advance and enrich life. Far too often, businesses forget that their core reason for existing is to serve the customer's ability to live a good, deeply fulfilling life.

Herban Feast, the Seattle catering company introduced in Chapter One, has grown increasingly skilled at serving its customers and in the process has grown a strong stakeholder constituency. The company has fully adopted the philosophy that no two clients are alike and no two events are alike. To achieve this resonance, Herban Feast's intake process engages each client in a conversation about who they are, including their values and dreams. Together they identify those values and qualities that will make the event a distinctive and authentic expression of the client's life and aspirations.

CO-CREATORS

Co-creators include everyone who is involved in creating the product or service for the customer, including full-time and part-time workers, contractors, and suppliers along the entire chain of production all the way back to the original sources of raw materials. When I describe these stakeholders, I focus on the idea of creation rather than the narrower concept of employment to underscore the extensive and diverse web of contributors to a company's offerings. Businesses can easily forget that all these people also have a stake in the success of the offerings and consider them the expression of their own creativity. All co-creators seek opportunities to contribute value, not only to secure their livelihoods but also to discover meaning for themselves. Without co-creators a business cannot fulfill its agreement with consumers to deliver products and services.

The actual stake that co-creators hand to a company is their personal uniqueness. They fear being reduced to cogs in impersonal machines. Since the 1960s work has been structured to favor efficiencies over the expression of creative urges. Businesses have instituted everything from quality-of-life to employee-participation to team-based-improvement programs as a way to improve efficiency, but none of these programs actually tap into and provide opportunities for the realization of the creative stake that has been put in play. Companies that encourage co-creators to stretch and grow in the context of helping the business are supporting the development of whole human beings.

Unfortunately, the structure of work since the advent of the assembly line has made it increasingly difficult for individuals to experience themselves as co-creators. And assembly lines are not limited to manufacturing; they can be found in any retail, finance, and service organization that creates standards to make everyone alike and every action replicable. At the most fundamental level, the task of a co-creator is to participate in the development and transformation of raw material into a form that serves the aspirations of the customer. Thus, they act as intermediaries and matchmakers between the material and the end user. Of course, a co-creator needs to be conscious of this role to be able to play it effectively.

The concept of the *supply chain* was created as a way to simplify and segment a more systemic idea. When reengineering was popularized by Michael Hammer and James Champy, they separated the product-creation flow into two parts, supply chain and market chain.[2] *Supply* became the cost end of the chain and *market* the revenue end. Thinking in terms of a supply chain actually destroys understanding of the co-creative process, negating or minimizing the contribution of those who work earlier in the process of moving raw materials toward product. Their contribution tends to be seen as insignificant except in terms of cost and quality. Yet these upstream suppliers also have a stake in the creation of the final product and therefore have creativity and value that could be brought to it.

One of the accomplishments at Kingsford was the shift from seeing employees as workers, whose actions were dictated by management, to including them as powerful, creative participants in production and business innovation. Kingsford invested in the development of every employee, enrolling them as part of an extensive reconfiguration of work processes, and enabling them to undertake the improvements that they could see needed to be made. Every employee understood the overall direction and aims of the business and was able to contribute creatively within that context. Kingsford actively acknowledged the stake its employees entrusted to the company and became an environment in which everyone was a creative source.

EARTH

Earth is the primary supplier and the final recipient of everything produced by human enterprise. In spite of several decades of education and action to reduce the harmful effects of business activities on the planet, most companies still consider it a stretch to think of Earth as a stakeholder. The idea is simply too abstract. For me, Earth is a way of symbolizing living systems interconnected in a seamless web of life and contributing to the evolution of the planet as a whole.

Anything alive—single cells to vast ecosystems—is in motion, continually processing the energies that it requires to sustain itself. When this processing stops, life also stops. Living systems secure their place in larger systems by contributing value. As they process energies they do more than just maintain themselves. They also help the larger whole to maintain and evolve itself.

For example, squirrels love acorns, and when an oak forest produces a bumper crop, they excitedly collect and stash them. Squirrels inevitably lose track of some acorns, and these lost seeds, neatly planted, grow into trees. The oak forest feeds the squirrels as a way of recruiting a crew of squirrel tree planters. Both squirrels and oak trees are adding value, for one another and for the forest as a whole.

Humans and the businesses they create are also living systems that are part of the larger living systems of Earth. When businesses work with nature's resources, they incur an obligation to follow the natural principle of contributing value back. Unfortunately, current business practice results in the opposite. The value of resources is depleted, often producing destructive by-products in the process.

A classic case in point is petroleum, a scarce, nonrenewable, and expensive resource. In June 2001, as part of a strategic planning process, a team of scientists, managers, and production leaders assembled at the DuPont Corporation determined that durability is what makes the petroleum molecule unique and therefore is its essence. It also makes petroleum a problem when it finds its way into oceans and landfills. It never goes away. For this reason, the team recommended that petroleum should only be used for products of great durability or ones that can be recycled forever. Through products made of nylon, DuPont has found ways to demonstrate its understanding of petroleum's essence by moving in the direction of perfectly recyclable petroleum-based products. W. L. Gore has also found ways to realize the essence of petroleum with Gore-Tex and related products. From an essence point of view, it makes little sense to burn petroleum because burning destroys its real value.

This example illustrates how Earth's stake in human activities is generally misunderstood. People often characterize Earth stewardship as "doing no harm." But Earth actually has a stake in the full participation of all species in an organic, ecological dance that evolves each to a higher level of contribution. Kat Anderson reports in *Tending the Wild,* her thesis on the role of indigenous peoples in healthy ecosystems, that Native American cultures have understood this for generations. They have been full participants in creating healthy ecosystems that are often mistaken for natural "wilderness."[3] Anderson observes that forests did better when tribes played active roles in their management and development. In the same way, Earth expects business to produce increasingly robust health and vitality for all living systems, including but not limited to human systems.

In a backhanded refusal to take responsibility, people argue that humans can't know what health and vitality mean for another living system. But this is no more legitimate than saying we can't really know what the stake of our customers or employees is. Humans have an inescapable responsibility to ensure that the planet receives an appropriate return for the investment it has made in us. It is actually the business of business to fulfill this aspiration on the part of the planet. A business assumes responsibility for Earth's stake when it brings together resources in a synergistic way to produce higher-order value than those natural resources would have produced independently. This requires understanding the working of each of these resources as part of a system.

Here is another example. Seventh Generation felt it was important to use only natural fragrances in its products because artificial perfumes are unhealthy for consumers and the environment. But it also wanted to go beyond being "nonharmful" and proactively ensure that the entire fragrance production process was beneficial. So they worked their way back to the growers, ensuring not only fair trade but also growing and distilling processes that produced healthy soil before they committed to buying and embedding a fragrance in a product. The program has been so successful—30 percent annual growth since 2009—that the company plans to spend the next few years extending it. They have committed to answering the question, "How do we ensure that Earth is healthier as a result" for every raw material that they purchase and develop. And they have proved that they can grow financially through serving customers uniquely and Earth sustainably.

COMMUNITIES

Communities are the social context within which businesses operate. A community may be as small as a neighborhood or as large as a nation, depending on the scale and effects of a business. To work in a systemic way, a business must take into account the effect it has on all of its communities. Anchoring itself to the stories, interests, and concerns of specific communities helps a business become concrete and accountable in its decision-making process.

Companies often treat communities as the generic suppliers of raw materials, workforce, material and social infrastructure, and as regulatory environments that allow the activities of the company. Sometimes they treat them as customers, but this overlooks the unique character of a community, its traditions and history, and misses the opportunity to see communities as partners and sources of creative potential.

Similar to customers, communities help determine whether companies stay in business. They tolerate and welcome certain endeavors and they disallow others. Communities stake their trust in the quality and local relevance of the economic activities occurring within them: the nature of goods and services produced, the quality of jobs created, the stability of the economy, and the reliability of the tax base. In addition, most communities are dependent on businesses to sponsor cultural life.

For example, the city of Detroit introduced and developed the concept of mass production that drove middle-class wealth creation for most of a century. The city has long been known for its innovation and leadership, but in recent decades, Detroit's leadership failed to engage the region's distinctive creativity and its position was lost along with the financial stability of a major industry. Efficiency, not innovation, became the focus, and leadership waned. The entire region has collapsed as a result and now experiences the highest unemployment rate in the nation, one of the highest rates of foreclosure, and extensive failures among the many small businesses dependent on the big three automobile makers.

By contrast, at Colgate, South Africa, Stelios Tsezos placed particular importance on growing the stability and health of the communities his company was part of. Because his work coincided with the birthing of a new South Africa, Stelios committed to developing the capability of black Africans to move rapidly into upper management. At the same time, he worked with the leaders in the new township councils formed by Nelson Mandela to provide governance among diverse and even warring tribes. These two efforts supported and reinforced one another as an overall leadership development initiative. Colgate was the only company not to experience a strike during that three-year period, a clear indication of how greatly it was valued as a member of its communities.

INVESTORS

Investors are the fifth key stakeholder group in a Responsible Business. From my perspective, they get the least attention. This is ironic, given that conventional business wisdom generally considers investors to be the most important stakeholders. An extensive body of law protects their interests and most companies work diligently to ensure increased dividends and growth in earnings. Accounting systems report on the effect of business decisions, and annual reports and communication to analysts are primarily directed to investors. So in what sense could investors be considered neglected?

Investors are not developed as stakeholders, and undeveloped, unintegrated investors are a great impediment to the Responsible Business. By undeveloped, I mean that companies are not helping investors see themselves as part of larger wholes and making them aware of their effects. In the current business paradigm, the supposed needs of investors drive much of the decision-making process. For this reason, developing investors is a highly leveraged way to transform many destructive practices.

The current way of working with investors—or with taxpayers or philanthropic donors in the case of governments or the nonprofit sector—fosters the opposite of enlightened engagement. Showing only how actions affect them personally emphasizes self-interest alone. When self-interest is the primary and perhaps only filter for investor decision making, the conventional company is forced to justify its actions based on extremely narrow and at times self-destructive criteria. Well-informed, responsible investors become part of a contextualized decision-making process.

Investors are both the least developed and most affected stakeholder group. Bringing them back into a coherent and systemic set of relationships with other stakeholders is critical to building a Responsible Business.

CONCLUSIONS

Business is based on a set of stakeholder agreements that must be made explicit and transparent if business is to play its role in creating a better world. These agreements have two sides. First, the stakeholder agrees to loan the business some part of its life energy, expecting the business to work on the stakeholder's behalf to grow the value of that energy. Second, the business agrees to use the invested stake to accomplish its own ends.

For customers, the stake is the fulfillment of purpose in their own lives and work. For co-creators, it is opportunities to work collaboratively on making creative and meaningful contributions. For Earth, it is the new life that can arise when human activities make habitats more complex. For communities, it is the ability to pursue a vital and viable future that harmonizes economic, social, and educational activities based on their distinctiveness. For the investor, it is the enduring value embodied by brand equity and customer loyalty that is ensured by the principles and practices of the business. When a business can see and integrate these stakes, it begins to access the full potential of the resources available to it.

 Free download: To print a colorful graphic display of the stakeholder system go to the free downloads section at www.The-Responsible-Business.com.

CHAPTER THREE

GEOMETRY OF THE RESPONSIBLE BUSINESS

A problem cannot be solved by people who are concerned with only one or another of its parts.
MASANOBU FUKUOKA

The inconvenient truth is that we share this planet with the rest of creation for a very good reason—and that is, we cannot exist on our own without the intricately balanced web of life around us.
PRINCE CHARLES

The five key business stakeholders are connected in interwoven dynamic relationships. Stakeholder groups are nodes in a dynamic system that connect and influence one another. The key to becoming a Responsible Business is to learn how to understand and work creatively within this system.

To understand this definition of stakeholders matters because the world we live in is made up of interconnected and mutually influencing living systems. For example, if consumers don't buy, then employees lose work and shareholders lose their investments. Or if employees refuse to work or severe weather interrupts delivery of an essential raw material, the available supply of goods to consumers is interrupted. Businesses are in open and permeable relationships with their environments, far less isolated and far more integrated with their stakeholders than most people imagine.

With the advent of globalization, businesses have become increasingly aware of how powerfully affected they are by dynamics beyond their control. They have begun consciously to experience themselves as open and alive systems. This is why since about the mid-1990s and the explosion of the Internet, the idea of stakeholders has gained acceptance in the language of business. The meaning of the term *stakeholder* continues to evolve, from "disinterested party" to "one who has an active interest and expects to benefit from a venture."

In order to get a true picture of such an alive, complex, and evolving business, one must be able to think not only about its activities but also about the interactions with and among its stakeholders. This can quickly become an overwhelming task, which is why I use a framework—a graphic means for depicting relationships within a whole—to help understand and manage the complexities of the system of business stakeholders.

SYSTEMIC STAKEHOLDER FRAMEWORK

When I work with the pentad, I move from point to point along the connecting lines that form a star, just as the Greek mathematicians did. The lines represent a structure inherent in the relationships among stakeholders that enables them to be in harmony. As will become increasingly clear, it is important always to begin with the customer—the people who will actually buy a business's products or services—and then to move to co-creator—the range of people and services a business employs in order to provide its products and services to customers. Continuing to move in order, I go from co-creator to the third point, Earth, the living source of energies and raw materials. The next step is to go from Earth to community, the local people and institutions who allow and are affected by the presence and activities of a business. Finally I move to the fifth point, investor, the people who supply the financial capital needed for a business to evolve (see Figure 3.1).

Currently there is a raging debate within the business community about which stakeholder is the most significant to overall business success. It completely misses the point because all five stakeholders work as an indivisible whole. A walk around the business books table at any major bookstore is a walk around this pentad. Writers about business base their books on their

FIGURE 3.1. THE STAKEHOLDER PENTAD FRAMEWORK

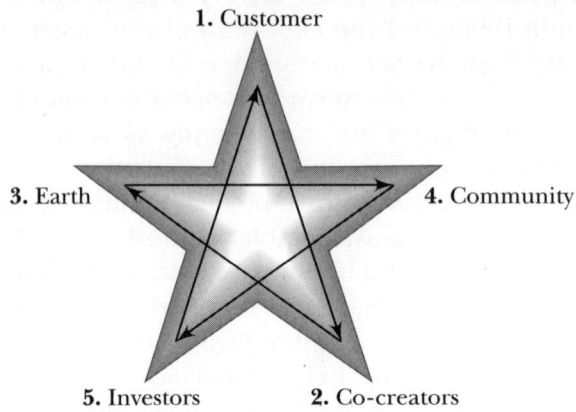

1. Customer

3. Earth   4. Community

5. Investors   2. Co-creators

professional expertise, the windows through which they have come to view the world. These windows create fragments. They show only parts of the whole, sometimes one stakeholder, sometimes another.

For example, an author or executive who holds a position of authority and experience with regard to marketing is likely to see customers as the only important stakeholder. The CEO or president who reports to a board of directors will tend to see the investor or shareholder as key. An environmental journalist will tend to define Earth as critical.

Rather than focus on which is the most important stakeholder, the business community would do better to understand *all* stakeholders as necessary aspects of a coherent whole. Unfortunately, business practice tends to undermine the ability to do this. Management of the relationship with each stakeholder group is typically assigned to a different vice president, and consultants tend to specialize in serving one or another of the stakeholders. Very little in existing business practice supports working on the system as a whole. I have used the sequence of thought embedded in the pentad repeatedly to support businesses generating a complete and accurate view of the world and from that to discover new business potential.

The Logic of the Pentad

Over the years I have noticed real differences in how companies think about and work with stakeholders. The majority of people begin thinking about stakeholders by making a list. They weigh or prioritize this list based on an environmental scan, by taking stock of how things are moving, how actions might affect them, how rules are changing, and how market conditions or tastes and trends are evolving. An environmental scan tells companies when they may be required to respond as the world around them changes, but this has the unintended result of promoting reactivity and limiting understanding.

Some animals, rabbits for example, become aware of nearby predators only when they glimpse them in motion. A rabbit may be sitting in a very dangerous environment, but until the fox moves it's invisible. A company that tracks its stakeholders by scanning its environment reminds me of a rabbit. It looks at parts and pieces and is able to respond only when something moves. But why act like rabbits when we have the capacity for foresight, insight, and holism, kinds of vision that penetrate beyond immediate sensory information?

Many companies characteristically emphasize certain stakeholders. For example, some companies are market-driven, others stockholder-driven. This narrowness of focus always eventually leads to imbalances—at times even dramatic damages—in their relationship with other stakeholders. For example, if a community is not considered, it may eventually bring a lawsuit or demand increased regulation, which cost time, money, and loss of good will. Walmart has faced these kinds of actions in many of its communities and continues to pay a price in the form of a damaged reputation. When imbalances occur, companies must react quickly, and even when they do, it may take them years to reestablish balance.

By contrast, I have also observed a small number of companies who regularly succeed with their stakeholders. They are less reactive, more even-keeled, and less likely to be engaged in complicated balancing acts. Interestingly, they also tend to be high performers with regard to multiple dimensions of corporate responsibility, though this isn't necessarily a focus for them. I have thought a lot about them and I often ask them what they are doing that is different. Amazingly, they usually don't know! Most of them attribute it to luck or to having really good, highly skilled managers responsible for potentially problematic stakeholder relationships.

Finding this pattern across all the businesses that regularly succeed with their stakeholders led me to the pentad as a way of integrating these thoughts. When I tested the framework I found that it made sense to everyone who worked with it for a time. Business people would begin to assess their company's effectiveness based on the order described. A business that starts at the beginning with the lives of its customers looks very different from one that starts at the end with investors. The pentad reveals very quickly why businesses find themselves in trouble, and for those who choose to work with it, it yields multiple creative insights.

For example, the first time I introduced the pentad to the core team at Seventh Generation, lights went on: "We started in the middle, with the planet! We aren't connected in any deep way with our customers as a basis for our values!" Though they had invested heavily in their ethic of transparency and building trust, they had never stopped to think about what it was like to *live* the life of a customer, even though they themselves were typical users of their company's products. The minute they backed up and made that connection, all kinds of creativity were unleashed. For example, the customer with severe allergies to most other household products was a highly invested stakeholder with a strong motivation that only incidentally had anything to do with the planet. Thinking about the life of this customer helped them see the importance of extending their line of non-perfumed products and using only natural essential oils in the remainder.

As a result, the relationship with co-creators—employees and suppliers—was transformed. Everyone from chemist to consumer relations representative shared a mental picture of the problems with a life filled with perfumes. They extended their sense of being champions of Earth to being champions of customers and could readily see how the two were connected. The creative teams became self-managing by focusing on what served specific consumers, and as a result many of the problems that managers often face were resolved, including formula mistakes, difficulties with promotions to markets, and invoicing issues.

Another example that illustrates the profound insight that can be generated from engaging with the pentad comes from Molly McNealy, a manager who headed U.S. Bank's information technology (IT) group. Within the culture and language of U.S. Bank, her group was seen as serving other bank employees, known as *internal customers*. Molly realized that the idea of an internal customer was a barrier that prevented her group from seeing themselves as co-creators working together with U.S. Bank's other departments to serve the same external buyer. Now the work of her team was to understand the bank's real customers, the depositors and borrowers.

Watching Molly work with her group helped me recognize how often this problem crops up for groups that are subsidiary or serve as support within a company, for example, IT departments. Helping them connect back to the true customer unleashed all kinds of creative energy and inspiration. At U.S. Bank it led to redesigning work reports, which made it easier for salespeople to communicate choices and results to likely consumers. Time between questions from sales teams and answers from IT all but disappeared when the IT team put themselves in the shoes of customers who were waiting for information to help them make big decisions. Excellent performance became personal, a way of making a meaningful difference in the lives of other people. As Molly says, "We became annoying to contractors because we wanted to talk about how what they did would affect our bank customers. In the past they had been used to answering only technical questions. Our advocacy for real customers made work far more meaningful and demanded more of us, and we in turn demanded more of our contractors."

In another example, Craft Warehouse, a chain of stores in the Pacific Northwest, serves the creative self-expression of its customers. After encountering the pentad framework, it set out to dissolve the artificial boundary between buyer and salesperson, helping each employee connect deeply with customers and thus the community. Each department created customer engagement activities that built excitement over time. For example, the quilting department invited local quilting groups to participate in a storytelling project that would capture local, community, and family histories through quilts. The store exhibited these quilts along with the stories and invited the community in. Craft Warehouse made a significant contribution to the life of its community by engaging in its business from a community investment perspective rather then as conventional philanthropists. In the process, the store became a lot more fun to work in, shop in, and live next to, and it turned into a local gathering place for crafters. Sales increased, immediately improving return to its owners. Employees were transformed from management problems to creative leaders and invested themselves in the success of their customers' projects. In appreciation, local craftspeople became invested in Craft Warehouse.

Businesses build systemic understanding when they use the pentad to describe their relationships with their stakeholders. This understanding leads to higher-levels of creative thinking and a constant upward spiral in the quality of relationships, which is the essence of a Responsible Business. The opposite is true when businesses approach stakeholder problems nonsystemically. Relating to stakeholders as if they existed in isolation increases the odds that businesses will stick with old patterns and that they will become static and increasingly chaotic.

INTEGRATE STAKEHOLDER INITIATIVES

The pentad is a way of understanding stakeholders who work together to create a system. The following story illustrates how working with the pentad develops systemic understanding. It describes a shift in stakeholder relationships at one DuPont facility.

A company with a history that extends beyond two centuries will have ups and downs. I was involved with DuPont from the early 1980s until 2008 and was fortunate to work with a number of leaders as they moved up to senior positions in the corporation, including presidents of different holding companies around the world and Chad Holliday, who became chairman, CEO, and president of DuPont Corporation during that time. One of the most challenging periods occurred at a critical moment when the

United States was awakening to some of the environmental implications of its past industrial and economic actions.

The story began on a day that was so hugely and theatrically bad that in hindsight it's comical. I was scheduled to work with Dick Stewart, vice president and site manager for DuPont's enormous Chambers Works Intermediate Chemicals site in Deepwater, New Jersey. Chambers Works produced some of the most environmentally challenging chemicals manufactured by DuPont, everything from Freon to sodium cyanide to the lead intermediaries for gasoline.

I found Dick in his office, with his head in his hands. He explained the police cars and fire trucks I had passed on my way in: Greenpeace activists had handcuffed and chained themselves between the railroad tracks and water tower to protest the effect of DuPont's products on the environment. Then he handed me a letter he had just received from a major customer who, for the second time, had received a railroad car of contaminated materials and was threatening to change suppliers. And with a gallows flourish he pointed to a flip chart with the heading "Union Negotiations" and a banner in red letters: "Strike Scheduled for May 4." Five days away!

It was obvious he was overwhelmed, and I just waited as he spun out the implications of these dynamics. We'd only begun working together a short time before and I eventually offered to come back at a later time. But he said, no, if any time were right to begin learning to think differently about his business, this was it. "I feel like a circus performer who's constantly having to keep a set of plates spinning. When I don't get back to one in time, they all crash."

As one of DuPont's best and brightest, Dick had been given its "mother ship" to run. It was clear that he was facing a classic leadership challenge. He had assigned different vice presidents to be responsible for each of these stakeholders—community (including activists), customers, and employees—and they were dealing with them as segregated and isolated groups, each with distinct problems. It may have been a coincidence that they were all showing up in the same week in his life, but I doubted it. The fragmented nature of his approach made it almost impossible to avoid a systemic collapse.

To enable Dick to think about his business as a system, we began to look at his vice presidents and their responsibilities not as separate plates to be juggled but as an improvisational jazz quintet. From a shared musical structure, they needed to elaborate distinctive voices and ideas. Instead of seeing stakeholders as segregated and isolated, we worked to imagine them as a single audience, all listening with different ears for different aspects of the music. Dick enjoyed music, and this was a metaphor that worked for him.

Out of that meeting, a host of transformative initiatives was born. One of the first of those initiatives was a major effort to transform the Freon business, a primary target of the Greenpeace demonstration. Dick knew that Freon, which was manufactured on site, was contributing to ozone destruction. As a refrigerant, it also played a critical role in delivering and preserving reliable food supplies around the world. Its use was expanding rapidly in China and India, whose growing populations and affluence meant huge new demand for refrigeration. Dick knew that it was only a matter of time before it was outlawed in the United States, but banning Freon here would be a relatively insignificant gesture in terms of global destruction. Because DuPont was aware that Earth is a stakeholder, and because DuPont is a significant player in the refrigerants industry, Dick resolved to lead a global effort to find an alternative.

Starting at the beginning of the pentad, Dick thought deeply about what the customer really needed. He realized that it wasn't Freon they sought. It was preservation, particularly of food, until time of use. At the same time, customers needed air, water, and soil, all of which were being threatened by the destructive side effects of Freon. Dick brought in several members of his team and began a rigorous examination of Freon's larger effect on the whole life of the customer. This gave his team the basis for engaging the total resources of DuPont's Intermediate Chemicals Group. The leadership team went beyond the corporation's internal employees to recruit participation from scientists and suppliers across the industry. Dick wanted to connect everyone to this new image of the total life of the customer. Dick's team knew that they had to do more than just find a replacement refrigerant. They also had to build understanding and participation in the chemical industry throughout the world. They figured out that their commitment was to fire the imaginations of manufacturers around the world and draw together a global coalition of co-creators.

Just two and a half years from that day in Dick's office, DuPont introduced the new refrigerant with one of the first open source processes for materials manufacturing. Rather than seek a patent, DuPont published its formula and groundbreaking technology in order to move the whole world quickly toward Freon replacement. This offered the company no direct proprietary business advantage but instead was seen as an expression of its global responsibility. However, by engaging the creativity of the entire workforce, putting them in service to the whole life of the consumer, DuPont had managed to generate proprietary manufacturing processes that would make it an effective manufacturing competitor without undermining the innovative capacity of other companies and countries. This was the work of a Responsible Business.

The tangible return came in creating a healthier alternative to existing cooling agents. But additional returns came in good will and global credibility from DuPont's work with community stakeholders. They actively involved regulators in the process to ensure that the new product exceeded current and emerging community aspirations. Needless to say, the regulators were surprised and delighted. DuPont's leadership within the global chemical industry was strengthened. Also, in the process to transform the refrigerant industry, they worked closely with many governments, and these relationships, along with their strength in managing risks, led them to new contracts with governments and industries around the world.

One of the most interesting and significant parts of this story was DuPont's invitation to Greenpeace to become a primary co-creator. By committing to Earth as a stakeholder, DuPont was able to enlarge its circle of co-creators and thereby to increase the intelligence it brought to its work. With its community organizing and public relations skills, Greenpeace was able to foster deep understanding within communities of the importance of replacing Freon. They helped make it personal for people. To this day, DuPont sees Greenpeace as part of its co-creative product development team.

Finally, Dick's systemic work with diverse stakeholders had a positive effect on investors and share price. Shareholders were now associated with a product that they could feel good about, one that reflected well on the company in the eyes of the public and was unlikely to face sudden environmental or regulatory challenges, enabling it to produce a steady return. It also influenced the way of doing business for the corporation as a whole.

CONCLUSIONS

Stakeholders comprise a living system because each is dependent on the others. None is isolated; together they are all part of one body and each either supports or undermines the success of the others. As a system they evolve the potential of each stakeholder and of all of the stakeholders together. Outside of a synergistic system, stakeholder potential is significantly diminished.

Each of the companies whose stories I've told imaged its stakeholders as though they were always sitting at the table when business decisions were made. In fact, team members were often asked to take on the voice and perspective of each stakeholder, bringing them alive in planning and operational meetings. All kinds of mutually beneficial relationships became apparent. Planning generated a host of new ideas about how to serve and connect stakeholders. In a Responsible Business, responsible actions evolve organically from the systemic engagement with all five stakeholders, which is an inevitable consequence of the appropriate use of the pentad.

 Free download: Want an easy, one-page reminder of the Responsible Business's key principles? Go to the free downloads section at www.The-Responsible-Business .com.

> CHAPTER FOUR

BE VALUE-ADDING, NOT VALUE-ADDED

Companies are living systems. They flourish according to the very same principles that foster sustainability in nature.
TACHI KIUCHI

There is nothing so useless as doing efficiently that which should not be done at all.
PETER DRUCKER

The pentad is a powerful instrument, but it can easily and unintentionally be misunderstood and misused. The fragmenting worldview that is now the default mode in business tends to treat each of the pentad's stakeholder groups as a "thing"—a box or category for pigeonholing individuals and institutions. In reality, each of the points on the pentad refers to a living process, a particular way of seeking to improve the world. For example, customers generally buy products not because they want to own them, but because they have aspirations, intentions, and plans for their lives and the product serves these in some way.

To use the pentad productively requires shifting from a *thing-based* to a *process-based* way of viewing the world. This might be described as looking for relationships among a series of events rather than focusing narrowly on one. It requires seeing the world in terms of what I call a *value-adding perspective*, where the world is made up of living systems, all of which are working with the larger systems they are part of to create more value. A tree helps the forest become a forest. The forest helps the atmosphere maintain conditions that support life. People apply their creativity to making products, services, or systems that will improve life for those who buy them. Customers incorporate products into lives that serve families, workplaces, communities, and the world at large.

To think about a value-adding world requires visualizing work as a story that unfolds through time and offers multiple opportunities to add new value. This story is always characterized by at least three simultaneous levels of value-creating activity. At the first level, individuals or organizations work to improve their capability to create. At the second level, they improve their collaborations or partnerships with others in order to increase the value of what they are creating. At the third level, they work to ensure that the value is increasingly relevant to the value-creating activities of those they serve.

As a simple example, imagine a tennis shoemaker. The shoemaker is continually applying creativity to get better at making a shoe to serve a specific kind of athlete. The tennis player will buy a shoe matched to her specific game and skill level because it helps her pursue the value that she is trying to create, in this case playing a better game every time. Without a wearer and a context, the shoe isn't inherently valuable. Its value lies in the contribution it makes to the tennis player's value-creating process in her own game of tennis.

Prior to the industrial era, it might be said that products or offerings were made for some person and not for the "shelf." Although the Industrial Revolution democratized the ability to consume, it also severed the living connection between maker and consumer. The industrial worker no longer had direct experience with the consumer's life or a concrete image of the product's contribution to enriching that life. The worker experienced a diminished sense of fulfillment in the work, and the consumer experienced a diminished sense of personal relevance in the product.

The concept of value-adding came out of the historic change process at P&G, Lima. It was the brainchild of Charles Krone, a key designer of the transformation of P&G's work systems. The team set out to regenerate the values of the craft era within a modern industrial process by conceiving all of its work through the lens of a value-adding process. The design of the factory, the work process, the products, the packaging, the marketing strategy, the hiring systems, and even the organization were all informed by this perspective. For decades, the detergent business at Lima was one of the most studied systems in the world, and a value-adding process view was foundational to its success as a business and as a force for change within industry.

VALUE-ADDED IS NOT VALUE-ADDING

The term *value-added* came into use as a result of the success at Lima. A professor of business administration at Harvard University visited the plant and was told about the *value-adding* process as it was practiced there. He claimed that this was a big part of the success at Lima. Unfortunately, he failed to grasp either the meaning of the concept or its correct title and so began using the term *value-added*. He missed the richness of the Lima experience and instead described *value-added* in narrow financial terms as increasing one's margin through a specific act in the refinement of materials and processes.

The deep flaw in the concept of *value-added* lies in its assumption that value comes from production of an offering rather than its use. If value is derived from the making of a product, then that implies that value can be added at a single point in time and that the creation of that value can be repeated over and over again. This solipsistic point of view (whereby I see the world revolving around me) completely misses the fact that the creation of value depends on continual improvement in how well and how holistically the product serves the user. Craftspeople understand this firsthand.

Viewing the stakeholder pentad through the perspective of a value-adding world brings the stakeholder groups and their relationships to life. One can see the purposeful activities of all of the stakeholders, the connections among them are discernible, and the ways that a business activity will contribute to or subtract from their aliveness become apparent. By contrast, a value-added perspective looks at each of a business's activities as an opportunity to increase financial return rather than an opportunity to enable ongoing value-creation for stakeholders. The effect is deadening—for the business and its stakeholders—rather than enlivening, and it is bad business practice.

ENERGIZE CARING THROUGH VALUE-ADDING PROCESSES

By adopting a value-adding perspective, a Responsible Business significantly improves its ability to perceive and understand what actually matters, namely, how its actions will create value in the lives of its stakeholders. This enables a business to consistently generate beneficial effects and eliminate negative ones.

More important, a value-adding perspective allows the business to become an ally and source of support for its stakeholders, enabling them to more successfully generate the value they seek to add to the world. In other words, a Responsible Business leverages or amplifies its impact by helping stakeholders live as responsible and creative contributors to their communities and ecosystems. In this way, the process of value creation extends beyond the activities of the business to become ongoing and evolving in the world.

For example, when Anita Roddick's The Body Shop set out to work with village women in South America and Africa, it helped them create networks of value in their lives: securing a livelihood for themselves and their families, increasing the viability of their villages, ensuring the continuance of culturally significant products and artisanship, and growing the health of the agricultural and natural ecosystems that were the source of their products. By carefully selecting and supporting its supplier networks, The Body Shop created an amplifier effect from its purchasing. While Roddick was at the helm, she brought a value-adding approach to doing business.

Businesses are microcosms that reflect and create the societies in which they are embedded. The people who make up a business are citizens and human beings. Their lives are shaped by the way they live away from work and the way they are at work. The boundaries of a business, in other words, are largely imaginary. Life constantly flows between what is outside and what is inside— businesses are open systems. So a business's character—how it behaves, how it maintains integrity, how it lives up to its promises, how it engages with its people and its world, every action it takes no matter how large or small—affects the character of society. Responsible Businesses understand and embrace the critical role they play. They actively assess themselves as communities of citizens, asking, Do our ways of working and our outputs create the conditions for families, neighbors, communities, and the planet to work in lively and life-enhancing ways?

FIVE STAKEHOLDER IMPERATIVES

To work successfully with a stakeholder's value-adding process, a company needs to understand stakeholder *imperatives*, the essential effects-in-use, which are the effects that products have in the lives of people who use them. For example, dishwashing liquid's effect-in-use is to prepare dishes for the user's next meal. It does this by making them clean, which is its outcome. Imperatives are often implicit rather than clearly understood and articulated, and part of the value-adding process is to bring them to light and to life. This is necessary if stakeholders are to be fully engaged and to perceive businesses as their allies in realizing their life aspirations. The following are some guiding ideas that help portray stakeholders in terms of their imperatives and define business relationships that are genuinely value-adding to stakeholders and their world.

VALUE-ADDING VIEW OF CUSTOMERS

Customers and consumers are fully alive. They nurture dreams and aspirations and they engage in personal processes for adding value to what they care about. That an individual is female, Hispanic, forty-two years old, and has discretionary income tells one nothing about her dreams and potential or how to help her realize them. That requires an act of creative imaging. To *image* is to form a vivid, reality-based mental picture by projecting oneself into the workings or processes of a living entity—in this example, into a woman's life and her motivations. A business that conceives of its job as helping a consumer become the best at who she can be will secure a nondisplaceable role as a partner in her life. (This thinking, by the way, applies as equally to the partnering between institutions or businesses as it does to the partnering between individuals.)

Unfortunately, the buyer or customer traditionally has been understood through market research, consumer feedback, and demographic analysis. All of these methods are abstract; they generalize from discrete bits of information and they focus backward, trying, as the proverb says, to steer the train from the caboose.

In his most recent book, *The Age of the Unthinkable*, Joshua Ramo offers a "new theory about how to think about the world"— including business. Ramo, who is managing director at Kissinger Associates, co-chaired the Santa Fe Institute's first working group on "Complexity and International Affairs" and is a global leader for the World Economic Forum. In his examination, data- and research-based approaches have a fatal flaw. They lead people to think they understand more than they actually do. He points out that although internal factors actually have greater effect, they do not lend themselves to data-based examination. He further argues that data defeats empathy, a critical quality in a complex and rapidly changing world, because it distances people from the living reality of what they are studying.[1]

A business that intends to be responsible for the value-adding process of customers will need to *give life to their lives*; that is, it will need to give them the ability to lead meaningful and fulfilling lives in ways unique to them. This is the imperative or expectation (usually unconscious) that the customer places on the businesses they choose to buy from. Therefore, the product or service offering of a Responsible Business aims to do three things.

Enrich the Lives of Customers, Their Worlds, and What They Affect
Truly creative businesses recognize and respond to their customer's deepest longings, often before customers themselves have become aware of them. To do this, they seek to understand the lives of their customers as they are actually lived—without the filters of assumptions or the abstractions of marketing research.

Because it is a common human failing to want to be handed answers instead of having to work for them, businesses will rely on customers (or more often some surrogate research firm) to interpret their lives for them. This is why they so often fall back on market surveys and research rather than do genuine work to create an internalized understanding. With rare exceptions, customers can't articulate what would actually improve their lives, a fact that growing numbers of innovators understand and are using to change the game for themselves and their customers.[2] For example, until the CD player or iPod was brought into existence, no one thought of asking for one. Insight and appreciation are the value-adding responsibility of any company that wishes to make itself nondisplaceable in the lives of those it serves.

P&G's Lima team knew it was critical to connect to and feel stewardship for the actual lives of their customers. Through a rigorous reflective process, they differentiated distinct buyer groupings and articulated the value each of these groups was trying to create in the world and in their lives. By imaging people they actually knew, they discerned that some buyers wished their laundry detergent to preserve the *bright colors* of their clothes and others cared more about *fiber durability* and detergents that could make fabrics last longer. P&G varied their products to support these differing aspirations. According to their own research, the Lima team's product development and marketing strategies more accurately reflected the desires of the customer and delivered a higher return on investment than divisions that used demographic market research. P&G has recently returned to a simplified version of this approach, visiting consumers in their homes to identify buying patterns. However, this connects co-creators to the buying habits of a market niche, a poor substitute for the work that was done there forty years ago, and it yields correspondingly less powerful results.

Create a Better Life Than Competing Offers from Other Producers or Companies

In the modern, global, competitive world, many companies look sideways at competitors to figure out what to make, what to charge, and even how to go to market. If they saw through the eyes of the customer, they would realize that she is not comparing competing products to one another. The buyer is comparing each to her own life, measuring it in terms of how it will enrich and facilitate what she's trying to accomplish. Without anchoring its decision making in the life of the customer or end user, a company will find itself operating with a "value-subtracting" worldview. Instead of offering something unique, such a company only seeks to best the competitor's interpretation of what customers want. Every time a company copies another company, it moves further away from the reality of the customer, and value is lost.

Be Reliably There and Reliably Distinctive in the Face of Hazards and Opportunities

A customer who has come to trust and count on a product will feel understandably betrayed or annoyed to find it unavailable, delayed, or discontinued. This is particularly true if the product was "exactly right" in an era when products look pretty much alike and none quite fit the bill. What consumers really want is something that feels like it was made for them, as though someone had really *seen* them and given them something wonderful that they can count on. And if they can customize it to make a truly perfect fit in their lives, they will no longer even see the other options on the shelf.

A company that creates that kind of experience creates enduring customer loyalty. But beyond that, it also creates for itself real responsibility to its customers. When a company has perfectly matched its customers' lives, any failure to deliver the product creates a void that can feel deeply disruptive. What a wonderful two-edged sword! A company faces every kind of opportunity and hazard, from disrupted supply flow to new and exciting materials. But if it wants to hang on to its hard-won customer loyalty, it had better see its decisions through customer eyes.

Differentiate a Value-Adding from a Value-Added View of Customers

At a superficial level, a number of approaches to customers seem similar to what I'm describing. In one approach, companies observe people in their homes, interviewing them with regard to the function or task that the product or service is intended to enable. In every report I have ever seen, these marketing groups looked not at the life and the living of the consumer, but at the doing of the task that used their product. For example, one might imagine a research team watching how a vacuum cleaner works in a research lab or consumer's home and focusing on how well it's cleaning the carpet or floor. By focusing on the functional dimension of the task, they would fail to even ask about its real value, what it contributes to life. It is hard to build a system of products or portfolio of offerings from this limited examination.

Another approach that also distances businesses from real people works with predefined archetypal categories. Archetypes are a set of metaphorical images that are believed to represent all the categories into which humans can fit. The concept comes from a psychological model developed by C. G. Jung for counseling humans to better understand themselves and their approach to life.

Market researchers look at customers through the perspective of the archetypes to see where they fit. The intention is good; archetypes show the differentiation among people. But because the system is prefabricated, it tends to prevent businesses from immersing themselves in life as experienced by the customer. It creates a lens that limits what can be seen by focusing what is to be sorted. Working without prefabricated categories is critical to being able to imagine people living their lives. Truly understanding customers is accomplished not by asking them but by envisioning them actively engaged in life and seeing what differentiates their choices. The process reconnects people to living buyers instead of dead data.

A similar problem arises from the use of avatars, an increasingly popular practice with Fortune 100 companies. An avatar is a synthesized or virtual personality used to test product offerings and services. This approach creates two hazards. First, as with the archetype, the avatar becomes the lens through which the customer is seen. Second, an avatar can never awaken the shared sense of meaningful contribution to the lives of others, which is the basis for awakening craftlike caring and responsibility on the part of all co-creators.

The problem with relying on these various methodologies to sort and categorize customers is that they tend to keep companies disconnected. In *Wired to Care,* Dev Patnaik and Peter Mortensen describe the disconnecting tendency of many businesses: "Decision makers end up with simplified data that lacks any sort of context. They deal with information in the abstract with no experience of the context for themselves personally. [This creates a] . . . disconnection from the customer and they end up relying on so-called authorities (e.g., the researchers) who are anything but. Empathy for the people you serve can make the abstract grounded and connected to real people."[3] In fact, Patnaik and Mortensen tie the success of IBM, Harley-Davidson, and many other household brands directly to their work on and attention to creating caring cultures and practices.

In his groundbreaking book, *A Whole New Mind*, Daniel Pink predicted the coming importance of empathy as one of six core right-brain aptitudes. He called them *six senses* because they represent for him a new way to connect with the world. He described empathy as the ability "to imagine yourself in someone else's position and intuit what that person is feeling . . . to feel with their hearts."[4] All these authors are pointing to the same thing. Data blocks understanding and caring. It encourages making decisions from abstractions. Without caring, work gets made up of functional tasks to be checked off a list or measured on an index of customer satisfaction, supplier ranking, sustainability goal, philanthropic donation, or shareholder forecast. Work is never about anything real.

The challenge is to replace practices that distance and disconnect with ones that evoke empathy, caring, and creativity. Without this, a Responsible Business is not possible.

VALUE-ADDING VIEW OF CO-CREATORS

Co-creators are participants in the flow of work carried out to create an offering; for example, employees, suppliers, contractors, and distributors. Entire professions have evolved that are dedicated to bringing co-creators back into the business equation, drawing from the fields of psychology, ecology, sociology, and ethics. In the process, they have generated best practices for different aspects of co-creator relations, including fair trade, supply chain sustainability management, and human resource systems or programs.

Unfortunately, all best practices, no matter how well documented, have a tendency to make the creative processes of individuals, families, and organizations feel generic, banal, and as if everything is the same by design. Best practices are a substitute for innovation and relevance. In the same way, the supply chain concept offers a machinelike and lifeless image of what is really a complex and layered creative process.

If one envisions the cycles of transformation—from Earth-based raw material to ingredient, from ingredient to formula, from formula to product, and from product to factory, office, or home—it becomes evident that a great variety of human caring and value-creation is possible at each step. This variety arises from the nearly unlimited diversity of human natures, cultures, Earth-based resources, products, and uses. Although the overall direction of human commerce since the industrial revolution has been toward manageable uniformity, the desire from customers contin-ues to be for a perfected, distinctive, and customized fit. The key to reconciling this contradiction lies in harnessing the creative potential of the co-creators.

What is imperative with regard to co-creators is to *reveal their essence and express it in meaningful ways in their work.* Essence is the true nature or distinctive character that identifies or makes some-thing what it is. It is the aspect of a person or thing that is continuously present from birth or origination, in spite of the layers of socialization or artifice that get laid over it. Mihaly Csíkszentmihályi, a Hungarian professor of psychology at University of Chicago, found in his research that humans who feel "in the flow of life," at their most creative and grounded, are in touch with a sense of their true self.[5] This is the state from which they make their highest-quality contribution, and it is invaluable to a company.

Yale psychologist Paul Bloom, in his excellent new book, *How Pleasure Works,* also emphasizes the importance of essentialism, which he describes as the instinctive belief that everything in the world has an underlying reality, true nature, or essence. He links essence to the ability to experience pleasure.[6]

Essence is related to but different from the concept of strengths, as developed by Buckingham and Clifton in *Now, Discover Your Strengths.*[7] Their work on strengths has made a differ-ence in the lives of many, especially young people and organizations. Unlike essence, a strength is not unique and may be shared. A person can become functionally strong in certain areas through adaptation to circumstances. Essence, however, is inborn and related to being. It is not a set of functional skills. It makes one distinctive—like no other. It does not have to be articulated to be drawn on. As Dr. Seuss said, "Today you are you, that is truer than true. There is no one alive who is youer than you."[8]

A Responsible Business designs work systems that evoke expression of essence from all its co-creators. A Responsible Business therefore aims to pursue three purposes in this arena.

Enable Co-Creators to Increase Value to the Lives of Others

It is a basic human characteristic that work becomes meaningful when it is seen to make a difference in someone's life. It becomes even more meaningful when it arises from the worker's essence. For example, imagine an Egyptian farmer who grows organic cotton for the European market. Distant though he may be from the world of his consumers, his task becomes more meaningful and the need for innovations that improve quality more apparent when he envisions the family that uses the towels and sheets for which he grew the fiber. Without this living image, his work is judged only against standards and goals provided by a series of intermediaries. It's hard to find any real meaning in that.

The same is true for an employee at an accounting firm, preparing someone's tax return. Most such workers are connected only to a work plan that specifies their task and deliverable. The "deliverable" that would excite them and ignite their capacity to improve their work would be an understanding of the *liberating* effect they could be having on a real customer. She hasn't had to spend her own time and effort filing her tax return, she needn't worry about not having met IRS requirements, and she may receive a larger than expected return for which she's planning a special use. People need to see the connection between their daily tasks and the difference they make.

Unfortunately, current work design methods chop up service into a series of discrete functions, links in a chain whose relatedness and meaning are fully understood only by the more encompassing view of someone further up in the hierarchy. But the meaning that work can provide only comes when each and every worker is able to create the mental bridge that links their contribution to the life of the final user.

Call on Each Individual to Develop Unique Potential in a Way That Complements the Working of a Team

Since World War II, business managers have increasingly thought of teams as the best way to organize work. There has been a corresponding plethora of advice generated on how to work with teams: high-performance teams, quality-of-work-life teams, cross-functional teams—I'd be here all day if I listed them all. At their worst, these team processes can be dehumanizing, such as when the team is designed to enable any member to play any role, essentially turning people into interchangeable parts. Even the best of these approaches fail to understand what teams are really about, namely, that what most evokes someone's creative spirit is the opportunity to bring something unique to a task and know that it made a huge difference.

It is often said that recognition is critical to performance in an organization. Actually, very little recognition is needed if work has been structured in a way that allows others to see one's essence and understand one's role in the bigger picture. A European dockworker once described to me the effect of actively engaging with the Carrefour warehouse workers who unloaded his trucks. "I never realized that I had an influence on their job performance. Now that I'm back here doing my end of the job, I feel a lot more determined to find ways to support their success."

Reveal and Enable the Worthiness of All People Through Fostering Their Creative Expression

It is a common misperception that people working in a business, large or small, base their decisions on self-interest. Based on this misperception, companies try to motivate people with personal rewards. But like most mammals, people are social and have a strong need for community bonds. Stories of altruism tap into what Daniel Goleman calls *emotional intelligence.*[9] People want others to be treated not only fairly but also generously, especially when they are part of the same creative team or process. They want each individual to be developed, encouraged, and supported in their efforts to be an increasingly better version of themselves.

When an organization punishes, ignores, or sidelines any member of a team, it has a debilitating effect on the entire team.

By contrast, companies that design work to support the growth and development of all co-creators, assist them in overcoming shortfalls and limitations, and provide opportunities to stretch beyond their last accomplishment are consistently rated among the one hundred best places to work.

The key here is that the company does it for everyone, not just those at the top of the evaluation ladder. A Responsible Business works tirelessly to ensure that every person and entity from beginning to end of the creative process is deeply engaged and developed as a part of a creative community. Even suppliers and distributors and installers, who are usually seen as outliers to the basic work of the company, must be seen as co-creators worthy of the same commitment. They, too, have a need for meaningful work and creative opportunities and a wise company will seek to develop their unique contribution in service to a shared customer.

Let me offer an example. Seventh Generation distributes more than 20 percent of its consumer products through Whole Foods Market. If Seventh Generation looked at Whole Foods Market only as a distributor, it would have been easy to focus on the ongoing negotiation over Seventh Generation shelf space and Whole Foods Market margins. Instead Seventh Generation chose to look deeply at this key co-creator and found that the essence statement "expression of freedom" seemed to underlie Whole Foods Market's work practices and market positioning. Whole Foods Market valued freedom of choice for customers, workers, and suppliers and worked hard to create a knowledge-able workforce who could support customers in making informed choices.

This value coincided with Seventh Generation's value for transparency and authenticity and led to the development of an in-store, interactive, learning program specifically for Whole Foods Market. Seventh Generation representatives provided education for Whole Foods Market customers about the uses and production of household products, including help and information about competing products. The aim of this effort was to expand customer knowledge about the effects of cleaning products on health. The program was appreciated by customers, helped Whole Foods Market improve its market basket return, lived up to Seventh Generation's value of transparency, and led to significant growth in sales for its products. But to do this, Seventh Generation had to change its view of Whole Foods Market from only a sales channel to a meaningful co-creator of an informed decision-making process for their shared consumer.

Differentiate a Value-Adding from a Value-Added View of Co-Creators

Businesses seeking to be more responsible pursue a variety of well-intentioned approaches to engage and provide meaning for their co-creators. Some will seek fair trade or Leadership in Energy and Environmental Design (LEED) green building certification or pursue carbon-neutral objectives, hoping to awaken people's enthusiasm and passion by involving them in worthwhile programs. Others focus on the human resource side. They create programs for working moms or parents, extend health benefits, offer massages in the office to reduce stress, and form committees to improve the quality of work life for employees—all worthy ideas in and of themselves. But these approaches rarely, if ever, engage the co-creator in what really matters, the life of the customer. A Responsible Business approaches the development of its co-creators from a value-adding perspective.

VALUE-ADDING VIEW OF EARTH

Earth is made up of many living systems interconnected in a seamless web of life. Although they are complex living wholes, ecosystems have typically been understood in terms of their manageable parts. For example, foresters tend to think about trees; hydrologists think about water; soil scientists think about soils; and wildlife biologists think about bugs and bunnies. Yet all of these are just dimensions of a single and integrated whole.

Companies and communities that wish to understand their ecosystems tend to rely on interpretations and measurements provided by government agencies. Or they turn to not-for-profits that monitor particular aspects, such as rivers or air quality. Environmental impact statements, among the most comprehensive instruments for assessing ecosystems, are lengthy reports with dozens of sections that fragment the environment into its constituent arenas. Corporate responsibility reports typically sort projects based on their focus: water efficiency, carbon savings, air quality, and so on. This fragmentation makes it difficult to do a full accounting of a company's or product's effects and offers no way to document, let alone encourage, multiplier effects. In almost all cases, these narrowly defined and targeted interpretations fail to deliver an understanding of an ecosystem as a whole. They lead people to mistake ecosystems for Humpty Dumpties and imagine they can repair them by pasting together broken pieces.

This fragmentation extends to include the way that humans are seen in relationship to Earth. Much of the modern world has been hampered in its ability to understand living systems by the strong bias that separates humans from "the environment." Even when humans are considered stewards and caretakers, they are seen as separate from the environment they caretake. How can humans come to see themselves again as a part of Earth? It is only from considering themselves part of an ecosystem that humans can accurately see it as a whole.

What is imperative with regard to Earth is to help *evolve the unique potential of natural living wholes*. With regard to their relationship to Earth, even the most conscientious businesses tend to stand at their own boundaries and look inward. That is, they ask how their internal actions affect "that out there." The first shift a Responsible Business makes is to stop seeing itself as separate from the larger context of which it is an everyday part. It redefines the whole that it is working on and within. Therefore, a Responsible Business will aim to do three things.

Start from the Essence of Materials and Their Role in Living Systems

All materials originate in Earth and play some role in life. When integrated into the ongoing metabolic processes of living systems, these materials play a beneficial role. But materials can also play a negative role when they are overharvested to the point that living systems are weakened, oversupplied to the point that living systems are polluted, or altered in ways that living systems are poisoned.

Besides the light it sheds on product design, one of the powerful reasons for investigating the essence of a material is the insight it yields into the role that material plays in nature. This allows a business to adopt practices that take full advantage of the material while integrating it with biological processes, thereby eliminating any potentially harmful effects.

For example, when DuPont, Canada, shifted its focus from production efficiencies and the bottom line to working on an understanding of the essence of hydrogen peroxide as a bleaching agent, they were able to displace the highly polluting use of chlorine in the Canadian paper industry. At the same time, because hydrogen peroxide is much less caustic to the fibers from which paper is made, it not only improved the quality and integrity of the paper but it also allowed paper makers to use a broader range of fiber sources and thereby better manage forest and farm resources. Refocusing on essence opened the door for helping an entire industry to better integrate with its ecosystems.

Operate as a Conscious Member of Ecosystems

There is a difference between doing less harm to ecosystems and belonging to an ecosystem. When the aim is to do less harm, thinking focuses on how to meet, agree to, or define best environmental practices. For example, a business that has committed to becoming carbon neutral will seek every opportunity to reduce carbon release or carbon exploitation. It gets very busy with programs to eliminate carbon waste by means such as promoting employee use of public transit or hybrid vehicles, conserving energy in building design and management, reducing energy use in manufacturing processes, or working up- and downstream to reduce embodied energy, or energy cost, the amount of energy consumed in the creation of a product. Some companies go to great lengths. Seventh Generation provided $5,000 financing for any employee who was willing to convert to a hybrid electric car. But no matter how much money a company is willing to spend on conservation, best practices don't support evolution, and evolution is what living systems are concerned with.

By contrast, a living entity that participates in an ecosystem plays a value-generating role and secures its species' place in the whole. The richer an ecosystem becomes, the more opportunities open for new species and new life. In an interactive, dynamic, and creative process, the whole gets healthier when each of the subsystems fulfills its role. As with any other species, human beings have a role to play in expanding the opportunities for evolution of the ecosystem. Through playing that role well, humans secure for themselves not just their own survival but that of an ecology within which they are an integral working participant.

Seventh Generation set a direction for itself to innovate and provide offerings at the interface of a healthy planet and people in their homes. To do this successfully, they realized that they would need to discover how that interface operates in particular places. A detergent that cleans well and biodegrades well in a rain forest will not do the same in an alkaline desert because soil and water chemistry, climate, and communities of organisms will be completely different. A detergent, like all other cleaning agents used in a place, must also be able to integrate with local hydrology, building living water from the cleaning process. Seventh Generation understood that it would have to stop thinking of cleaning and Earth-care as generic and isolated processes and commit to specific ecosystems.

Improve the Productive Working Processes of Ecosystems

Just as employees have an essence and a unique contribution to bring to their work, so do ecosystems. Each ecosystem is unique, and each is part of a community of ecosystems to which it adds value. A forest contributes nutrients, shading, and purified water to a river. The river, when it empties into the ocean, contributes fresh, nutrient-laden water to coastal estuaries. The estuaries provide habitat for fish that eventually make their way back up the river to die in the upland forests and fertilize the trees. Once one understands the distinctive workings of an ecosystem and the contribution it makes to other ecosystems, one can ask what role humans play in ensuring the ecosystem's ability to make that contribution.

To improve an ecosystem requires that one understand its essence and anticipates changing conditions and hazards in the larger environment. The effects of global climate change will almost certainly place strong pressures on natural systems, forcing them to adapt in response. This will have huge effects on human communities and businesses because of changes in the natural resource base on which they depend. In addition, ecosystems are stabilizers, and as they become more chaotic and unpredictable, so do floods, droughts, and radical temperature swings. All of these things put pressure on both natural and human infrastructure and interrupt the pursuit of "business as usual."

Every community is faced with major changes at the ecosystem level. The challenge is to translate changes into opportunities for a better future by assisting ecosystems as they attempt to adapt. Ecosystem changes have the potential to radically alter or disrupt fundamental infrastructure and material flow on which businesses depend, so infrastructure needs to be reconceptualized and reconfigured to support the resilience and stability of ecosystems. Responsible Businesses make this integral to their strategic planning. Businesses will thrive in the new normal if they shift from thinking of these changes as risk management factors to understanding them as opportunities for ecosystem enablement.

For example, rivers change their course and form over time. Human communities have expended much effort trying to engineer controls to this natural process. As climate instability increases, these engineering solutions become more unstable and the costs to businesses, communities, and human life escalate. A better solution would be to allow river systems to operate according to nature and evolve human infrastructure and economic activities over time to align and evolve with them.

Equally important, ecosystems are linked to other ecosystems so that the outputs of one become the inputs of another. As ecosystems become disrupted, they can set off a chain of disruption in connected systems. The Chesapeake and San Francisco bays offer useful examples. Each of these was once an almost unimaginably productive estuary. They supported vibrant fishing economies and helped maintain the world's ocean fisheries. This enabled them to develop into dense population centers and economic powerhouses. However, pollution and human development have caused the collapse of the underlying ecological systems, contributing to global collapse of fisheries.

Sea-level change is already causing the communities surrounding the bays to look at how they will need to change urban forms and practices. Many of the ideas currently under consideration are defensive: sea walls and other flood control measures. However, more visionary thinkers such as Helen and Newton Harrison have proposed using climate change as an opportunity to reconfigure settlement patterns, returning function and health to entire river and estuarine systems in the process. Such reconfigurations could allow these bay ecosystems to once again play their roles in the planetary systems that once depended on them.[10]

Creative companies are already looking for ways to transform the emerging needs of ecosystems into business opportunities. A growing number of farmers and ranchers have evolved practices that allow them to use grazing and cropping as tools for land and watershed restoration. An increasing percentage of their income flows from the ecosystem services that they provide. Ecological foresters have also become increasingly sophisticated in their ability to harvest timber and other products in ways that improve forest health. But the majority of businesses have barely scratched the surface of this fertile entrepreneurial arena. Addressing it offers the potential to secure themselves an increasingly central role in the economy of the future, the good will of the public, and the loyalty of customers.

Differentiate a Value-Adding from a Value-Added View of Earth

Businesses are taking many different approaches to protect ecosystems. There is no lack of intention or effort toward sustainability, but these endeavors continue to be isolated and compartmentalized.

One of the most widespread and comprehensive efforts currently underway is carbon footprint reduction. Many companies have committed to accounting honestly for their net carbon effect. If the net is not zero, they either make commitments to reduce or they arrange with others to sequester carbon on their behalf.

Another popular approach works on a sustainable supply chain. Businesses endeavor to ensure that growing, harvesting, and transporting processes for all the materials and products they use are sustainable according to a limited definition that includes carbon neutral, nontoxic, nonpolluting, and harmless to wildlife. As currently practiced, sustainable supply chain planning fails to address the whole of an ecosystem. Instead it limits its purview to the plot of land or square foot of building space where raw materials are extracted and processed. So although this approach may contribute in various ways to harm reduction, it certainly doesn't contribute positively to the health or evolution of living systems.

An emerging phenomenon is the creation of alternative brands, products, and services, such as Green Works, a line of environmentally friendly products created by Clorox. One might hope that such lines would turn out to be transition products, part of a larger strategy toward corporatewide sustainability. Sadly, they are more often than not simply an attempt to capture market share, another case of green-washing. Even if every product became environmentally friendly, industry would still have failed to take into account the evolution and health of ecosystems in their design, production, and distribution. Products might become environmentally friendly without ever becoming ecologically friendly.

When Earth provides part of its assets to a producer, it becomes an investor in that producer's future. It expects an increase in the resources it has available in the future. But this is not how Earth is viewed; at best, it is seen as a kind of storeroom. A business goes to the storeroom to get the parts and materials it needs to do its work. If it's a sustainable business, it knows it needs to replace the materials it took—a zero-sum game. Such a perspective offers no potential for increase, especially to Earth. Earth is alive, creative, and can be enlisted as a powerful partner to the business—as long as its imperatives and potential are respected and served.

VALUE-ADDING VIEW OF COMMUNITIES

Businesses typically develop their understanding of the communities they operate in through surveys, polls, or demographic information. They tend to work with citizens in much the same way they work with customers, segmenting them into political, ideological, or demographic groups. Just as with customers, this kind of analysis gives companies a superficial and abstracted picture of the community and its members and misses entirely the reality of their lives.

Reinforcing this tendency toward abstraction, businesses tend to have a distorted view of a community's relationship to them. Communities are often seen only in terms of their regulatory or permit-granting role, as an unpleasant but unavoidable reality. Or they are experienced as a collection of interest groups that have to be mollified or defended against. Sometimes they are seen as philanthropic opportunities, places where a company can practice good corporate citizenship.

But communities are living entities with coherent cores, and when properly engaged they can be powerful allies in creating healthy businesses and economies. Despite their apparent self-contradictions and irrationality, communities actually operate from deep currents of intelligence and common purpose. This commonality comes from a variety of interacting influences, including culture, history, language, climate, ecosystems, and yes, even the water they drink. In short, it is the sum total of all these elusive qualitative characteristics that cause people to choose to live in a given place. To understand and work with communities, one must learn to listen through the noisy hubbub of discord for the deeper strains of harmony that come from connection to place.

The relationship between Responsible Businesses and their communities is layered and complex. Looked at from one perspective, each community is distinctive and therefore has something unique to contribute to its people and its businesses. This uniqueness can encompass natural resources, infrastructure, cultural perspectives, and local skills and aptitudes. A diversity of talents broadens the palette of choices available to a business seeking to establish operations and recruit co-creators and resources. It also increases the likelihood that a business can seek and find an optimal fit between itself and a community. Just as monocultures are bad for nature and boring for people, mono-cultural communities actually reduce the possibility for business creativity and diversification.

This leads to a second perspective. It is ultimately in the interest of businesses, even inside very large corporations, to adapt their operations, facilities, and product offerings to reflect and support the differences in the various communities where they do business. Cookie-cutter chains are just as deadening to communities as best practices and standardized procedures are to co-creators, a criticism that is frequently leveled at big-box stores moving into new communities.

At first, this idea of adapting to each new community may seem counterintuitive. Standardization of products and facilities around the world have allowed many companies to generate explosive growth and maintain uniformly high quality. However, this standardization has cost communities their uniqueness and the creation of "geographies of nowhere," to quote best-selling author James Howard Kuntzler.[11] Just as customers benefit from product offerings that can be customized to perfectly fit their own purposes, so communities benefit from business operations that fit with and enhance their unique characters.

The resolution to this apparent paradox can be found in the stakeholder pentad. By unleashing the creativity, self-organization, and self-accountability of its co-creators, businesses can tap precisely into the local intelligence needed to adapt to local circumstances. This is particularly well demonstrated by the workers of Colgate, South Africa, who built their communities and built the company as a seamlessly integrated activity.

Even Internet companies, which characteristically think of themselves as placeless, are linked to communities in multiple ways. They have places of origin, often centers of technological innovation like Silicon Valley, whose local cultures imprint themselves on their founding visions and business philosophies. They have supply chains and co-creators, everyone from software engineers and graphic designers to the folks who make the products sold on Amazon.com, who live in communities. And they have customers who are trying to integrate their products and services into their daily activities. The Internet has the potential to be a particularly powerful tool for differentiation and continual adaptation, but to access that power, Internet companies need to develop a consciousness and a way of thinking about communities as stakeholders.

Given all this, it is imperative that businesses *help every community develop itself from its essence.* Within its communities, a Responsible Business will aim to do three things.

Design Human Systems to Contribute to the Evolution of Uniqueness and Health in a Given Place

Communities are made workable by the creation and operation of hundreds of human systems, mostly designed to improve day-to-day living. These range from utility infrastructure to social services, from urban planning to schools. All of these systems are intended to contribute to community life, but they can just as easily degrade it. Even when built with the best intentions, highway systems can increase sprawl, urban renewal can destroy community character, and business recruitment programs can undermine local entrepreneurship.

No community will ever be identical to another. Each is characterized by a unique story of how it came into existence, what its essence is, and what it has the potential to become. This story is a key to understanding the community as a living entity and knowing how to translate that entity's unique characteristics and potential into design. A growing number of communities around the world have discovered ways to tell this story, stepping back to see the patterns that connect their economic, cultural, and settlement histories. They have become articulate about the essence or identity of the place they live, creating the basis for working together to develop its potential. This often awakens strong commitment to preserving and evolving that essence with regard to every aspect of how the community governs and grows itself.

When the little town of Paonia, Colorado, engaged in value-adding process work with Living Education and Developmental Economies Group International, it discovered that local businesses, schools, and even ranchers shared an unexpected common resilience and that this resilience was reflected not only in the community's current life but also in its history: a significant part of their business activity and revenue was tied to educating others.[12] They had become quite innovative in developing attractive educational programs linked to life in that community, everything from training solar entrepreneurs to teaching country cooking to ranching vacations to creating one of the nation's most progressive homeschooling programs.

In fact, it became clear to residents as they reflected on how their community had evolved over generations that the vocation of Paonia was as a "learning valley." From this revelation, it was possible to create new business incubators and schooling systems, improve existing businesses, and establish a place-based brand for the town. Because it comes from within, the learning valley idea has generated a new spirit for the town as well as a guiding direction for its economic planning efforts. It still has a long way to go to embed this thinking into business recruitment, development, and marketing efforts, but it is making progress.

There are three reasons why a Responsible Business should work with its communities to develop essence-based understandings of who they are. First, it is both responsible and practical to develop the distinctive and living character of a community as a dimension of doing business there. The absence of such work is what creates uprisings and protests in some communities when large new businesses or institutions enter. They are experienced as threats to the very being and identity of the community. A business has an ethical responsibility for ensuring that it is working in resonance with the uniqueness of a place.

Second, a business that understands a community well enough to harmonize and merge with its identity and aspirations will be better able to formulate acceptable and beneficial business concepts and proposals. Acting as a collaborative partner in community creation, a business achieves its objectives while extending a community's ability to benefit from its own uniqueness. As Starbucks has learned, when it can work with a community to tailor its stores to local needs and cultural styles, the regulatory hurdles are lower and much less costly and time consuming.

Third, communities that are anchored in their own uniqueness are much more effective at creating a branded identity for themselves, capable of attracting and sustaining a healthy economy and distinctive business sector. By linking business activity to the indigenous character of a place, a synergy develops. The natural and human resources are already present for a business to be able to innovate, grow, and flourish.

Portland, Oregon, offers a striking example. Portland's economic development has occurred around its unique ability to offer an experience best expressed as "life happens outdoors." Rather than chasing trends ("Become the next Silicon Valley!"), Portland has remained true to itself. This makes it desirable as a place for particular kinds of business and it attracts a diverse portfolio of companies connected to outdoor living. Makers of athletic shoes and clothing as well as some of the nation's most innovative bicycle manufacturers have found it a hospitable environment and a source of a knowledgeable workforce. Outdoor eateries flourish, as do artisanal microbreweries and local farmers. Each of these businesses benefits from and contributes to the distinctive culture of Portland, helping make it one of America's most desirable places to live. In spite of some of the highest taxes in the nation, businesses have no difficulty attracting workers because of the quality of schools and businesses and the cohesiveness around community identity.

Inspire Visionary Leadership Capable of Manifesting Integrative Solutions Through Time

In many communities, leadership tends to be politicized and divisive. Engaging a community in understanding its essence helps ground leaders in their commonality. They may continue to disagree, but they will recognize that they are using differing means to work toward the same ends.

Sam Adams, the mayor of Portland, says that he could never have run for mayor in another town because only in Portland did he really understand what he was leading. In his home city, the threads that weave the social and political tapestry are clear to him and he is able to pull together adversaries and resources to find integrated solutions for challenges too big for any single entity to tackle alone.

The role of the Responsible Business is to strengthen and enrich its working environment by calling for and providing this kind of leadership. Both business and community will be more effective and durable when they are willing to act from a shared understanding of what makes a community unique and healthy and what gives it a sense of purpose. This leadership work needs to benefit everyone, including the competition, because its purpose is to create a healthy business ecosystem.

Business has a unique perspective and set of skills to contribute to community leadership. A Responsible Business, grounded as it is in a value-adding approach, is able to foster and nurture the entrepreneurial spirit of community members young and old. It can also help a community achieve a distinct and nondisplaceable market position through growing a place-based and developmental economy.

Elevate the Overarching Principles That a Society Chooses to Be Governed by in All of Its Pursuits

Usually businesses try to persuade cities to downgrade or degrade their principles on the assumption that this will make it easier for businesses to function. The horse-trading can get intense when a business has real leverage, for example, when a city is trying to recruit a new source of employment.

A Responsible Business, however, will work to elevate a city's governing principles and create a matrix for health within which the business, along with all other living entities, can thrive. This philosophy understands that a business has an interest in the long-term well-being and evolution of the community in which it does business. Businesses tend to prosper in cities with strong education systems, broad community involvement, planning and decision making based on a core identity, and a culture of leadership that looks beyond terms of office or fluctuations in economy. A smart business becomes involved not just in who gets elected but in organizing and leading community efforts to develop a set of principles that can be used repeatedly across different planning and implementation processes.

An example is Kingsford, who understood that the quality of workers at its Burnside, Kentucky, plant was directly related to the educational standards and principles held by the community. The company engaged community and school district leadership in raising the level of educational opportunities and methods. It also made education a component of its own work practices, bringing teachers into the workplace and sending workers into the community as mentors. Kingsford introduced the idea of "development of character and opportunity to contribute" as a core educational principle. That is, the whole person—character, uniqueness, and contribution—needs to be developed, not just knowledge and skills. In this way, Kingsford helped evolve the level of curriculum and pedagogy throughout the community and was recognized by the State of Kentucky for its effort. The principles created for Burnside went on to became core to workforce development throughout federal and local programs in the region.

When Kingsford needed to close its facility in Dothan, Alabama, it adopted the principle that a company is responsible for community economic health not only when it opens a business but also when it closes one. It helped all employees who would lose jobs build capabilities that would enable them to move to a parallel or higher level in another company or to build a business that would have a viable place in Dothan's economic structure.

Because Kingsford accomplished this in a very visible way, it was taken up by the Chamber of Commerce and used to guide future economic development.

Differentiate a Value-Adding from a Value-Added View of Communities

There are lots of ways for businesses to give back through community engagement and philanthropic processes. These can include loaning an executive for a year to a nonprofit, sponsoring community or cultural events, participating in civic organizations, or contributing to planning efforts. Businesses may also create foundations through which they contribute percentages of their revenues to good work. These are all worthy and important endeavors, but they don't change the fundamental relationship between business and community.

By contrast, when a business understands itself as nested within a larger whole, a mental shift occurs. The community is no longer an *other*. Instead it is a bigger *us* through which work finds its meaning. The business has a distinctive role to play in maintaining and evolving community health. Community engagement is no longer segregated from the rest of the business, but central to it.

In the case of both ecosystems and communities, a value-adding perspective requires moving from thinking of business as a closed system to seeing it as open, alive, and in continual, reciprocally beneficial exchange. Rather than standing at the boundary of its organization and looking out at others, the Responsible Business nests itself into the living, breathing worlds of its communities.

VALUE-ADDING VIEW OF INVESTORS

Investors are generally divided into three groups: those who invest in the quality and value of the company, those who invest in the income-generating potential of the company, and those who hope to generate social or ecological benefits from their investment. Companies tend to ally themselves with one or another of these groups and make decisions, interpret success, and generate reports based on what they believe is most important to that nature of investor.

Currently, businesses attempt to understand their investors indirectly, either through their boards of directors or through the work of analysts. A value-adding perspective sees investors as living entities, individuals, or institutions with hopes, dreams, and aspirations, including but not limited to a financial return. It also recognizes that investors have restraints and worries and decisions to make, often with incomplete knowledge or understanding. From this point of view, businesses have a role to play in helping investors achieve their aspirations and providing them with information and experience necessary for good decision making. In other words, the business and the investor are in it together and need to support one another's development and capability so that both can succeed.

Unfortunately, in the current business culture it's almost as if the investors are seen as dollar signs rather than real human beings and institutions. They become disembodied, engaged through a generic understanding of the role of money. But money is not a stakeholder; it's an instrument. A business that wishes to add real value will look through the money to see the individual or institution behind it.

What is imperative with regard to investors is to *educate and engage real people and institutions in real wealth creation*. In its work with investors, a Responsible Business will aim to do three things.

Generate Durable Returns and Systemically Beneficial Effects

Through their wealth-generating activities, businesses fulfill the dreams and promises of all kinds of investors, from parents who want to build a child's college fund to governments responsible for managing employee pensions. To play this role, a business needs to live up to its promises with regard to returns and volatility. When it cannot, it needs to keep its investors informed early, often, and completely. For a company that truly understands the importance of its returns to the lives of its investors, the responsibility becomes very real, but for the Responsible Business, this is only the entry point.

More and more people understand that business is a powerful instrument for creating beneficial change in the world, and they are seeking to channel their investments toward the changes they would like to see. Yes, it's a means for them to generate personal income or wealth, but it's also an opportunity to leverage that wealth to help others. They invest in businesses with the assumption that good people are in charge and will act according to principle in their business, social, and environmental transactions. Many investment studies have documented the connection between investors' loyalty to a stock and their trust that management will maintain the qualitative equity of the business in the eyes of its communities and nation. For the health care giant Johnson & Johnson, management integrity is an overarching principle for maintaining high-quality, long-term investors. It expects its managers to evaluate every decision, including costly ones to the company, through this lens.

Progress the Industry's Capacity, Character, and Asset Value

The Responsible Business sees itself as a champion of its industry's integrity. Its future depends on public perception that it is a trustworthy, conscientious tender of investor assets. Bob Cannon, an advisor for accredited investors, said to me about the 2008 financial crisis, "Out of the financial debacle I assumed many companies would demand a thoughtful examination and revision of the financial industry's practices and procedures. I expected the question of character to be central to the conversation and that we would insist that they begin to manage our assets with the same care they would their own mothers'. Sadly—shockingly even—that's not what I'm seeing" (personal communication, summer 2009).

Leaders in the corporate responsibility movement have called for greater transparency and stricter regulation, but these are actually symptoms of the illness rather than cures. Regulation gets created when the public believes that it can no longer count on a company's values. Transparency can easily become a substitute for integrity when investors and even consumers are required to interpret corporate actions.

Instead, a business should hold itself accountable for setting, extending, and monitoring its own principles and imperatives. A board of directors' most important role is to establish the high ground and work with management to embed this in every action and decision at every level of the business. Transparency cannot be a substitute for this work.

Two influences—a competitive global environment and best practices—can undermine the cultivation of a values-driven company. Globalization has created a stiff competitive environment in which the drive to find what's new and innovative is not always tempered by a careful and reflective consideration of ethics. Best practices encourage companies to borrow what they see working in other companies, whether or not those practices are consistent with their values. Boards of directors and managers of Responsible Businesses are vigilant in their own assessment of principles and call on their colleagues and competitors to be equally vigilant.

Understand Divergent Forces and Leverage Resources to Create World-Changing Effects and Business Evolution

Most investors understand that companies are subjected to and affected by forces over which they have little direct control. From currency fluctuations to interruption of shipping because of war, any company that does business beyond its local neighborhood will feel the constraints of political, economic, and social shifts and disruptions. Investors assume that management and directors will guide the business through tempestuous times.

In *The Black Swan*, Nassim Nicholas Taleb introduces research to suggest that this is more possible than is generally assumed, if businesses can learn to see the world as it is rather than as they assume it to be. Expectations cause people to deny evidence that disagrees with the "facts" as they know them (all swans are white) and become blind to what is unexpected (black swans). Taleb argues that gray swans can also be predicted but this requires the development of critical thinking skills in order to see patterns emerging.[13] Boards of directors, if they are to be fully responsible to their investors and executives, will want to develop the habit of challenging their white swan assumptions and learn to predict gray swans.

These days, a rapidly growing percentage of investors are expecting even more of companies: that they anticipate and beneficially influence these larger fluctuations through effective application of resources to social change. Not only do investors not want to be associated with a green-washing label, many also have a genuine desire to use their resources in ways that create a better world and more stable businesses.

A Responsible Business sees itself not only as a fiduciary for investor money but also as a smart investor itself in the work of world change. For example, a company should be able to assess its contribution to the increase in tangibles such as high school graduation rates, community stability, or ecological health through its business and philanthropic activities. When undertaken intelligently and strategically, this work can contribute to the evolution of the business and its effectiveness. This has the advantage of leveraging investment by creating social as well as financial returns. These competing requirements for attention—an unpredictable, changing, and hazardous world on the one hand and impeccable corporate citizenship on the other—can be reconciled by anchoring all of a company's work in its essence and manifesting that in the world. A Responsible Business doesn't allow changing conditions or evolving community expectations to pull it off course. Instead, it uses these challenges as the raw material and creative opportunity for moving itself closer and closer to the unique value it brings to the world.

Differentiate a Value-Adding from a Value-Added View of Investors

The traditional way of engaging investors is to provide a steady and increasing return through growth, income, or both. The means for generating this return is to manage efficiencies for the bottom line or to acquire new markets for the top line. The focus in either case is the effect on the investor's financial return.

A Responsible Business that holds a value-adding view of investing will augment its operating principles. To gain financial returns, it brings a comprehensive and multigenerational perspective rather than the myopia of quarterly returns. Significant recent research, summarized by Jonah Lehrer, demonstrates that people can delay gratification if they can see a better payoff in the future.[14] A Responsible Business supports the enlightened self-interest of investors by providing the comprehensive reporting that helps them think holistically.

To describe its role within its industry, a Responsible Business brings a strong voice to collective industry accountability for its effects on society. This collaborative work is superordinate to simplistic competition and ensures the vitality and viability of the industry. Again, this requires an education effort to make it real to the financial conversation. To the subject of a changing world, the Responsible Business brooks no excuses for a narrow, nonsystemic focus. It insists on considering and being accountable for the effect of its decisions on global economic, ecological, and cultural phenomena. It refuses to see itself as a victim of forces beyond its control.

CONCLUSIONS

The stakeholder pentad has many layers. Just being able to see the flow of relationships is a significant improvement over seeing stakeholders as separate pieces. Understanding the value that each stakeholder aspires to attain by its involvement with the business adds another level of depth. The pentad offers a more coherent way to understand the world, overcoming the tendency to see it as made up of parts and pieces. The more one shifts to understanding the world as an integrated web of value-adding processes, the simpler it becomes. Stakeholder imperatives enable businesses to ascertain if they are truly responsible by judging outputs based on the effects they produce in the lives of stakeholders. This is the foundation for performance indexes that accurately indicate responsibility.

In the next chapter, I will explore how the business exemplars introduced in Chapter One found leverage points for change—places where seemingly simple actions affected multiple stakeholders, results were magnified, and the time needed for tasks was reduced. This leverage came from being systemically strategic.

 Free download: A visual depiction of the working of the stakeholder framework can be found at "VAP Imperatives" in the free downloads section at www.The-Responsible-Business.com.

CHAPTER FIVE

MAKING THE RESPONSIBLE BUSINESS PENTAD WORK

I don't think in terms of priorities, because all of the big problems and all of the solutions are interlocked.
E. O. WILSON

Working the pentad is a systemic means to create systemic change. It provides a simple framework for thinking about and managing a complex set of relationships as a whole. Looking at each of those relationships separately can become challenging or overwhelming. Viewing them as a system, however, reveals the leverage points where simple actions can have big multiplier effects (see Figure 5.1).

This sounds great in theory, but the real power of the pentad framework is demonstrated when it is applied to real businesses. The following stories show how it has worked in the real world.

REVOLUTIONIZING BUSINESS MODELS: RED HAT

Recently, I spent time with Paul McNamara, a former client who reminisced with me about the inspiring story of the founding of Red Hat, the software service company that took the open source revolution mainstream. In 1998, Paul was the fifteenth employee hired at Red Hat. His new job was to find business models that had made money from a free product and convince venture capitalists to invest in a company that gave away its software. He was

Figure 5.1. The Stakeholder Pentad Framework

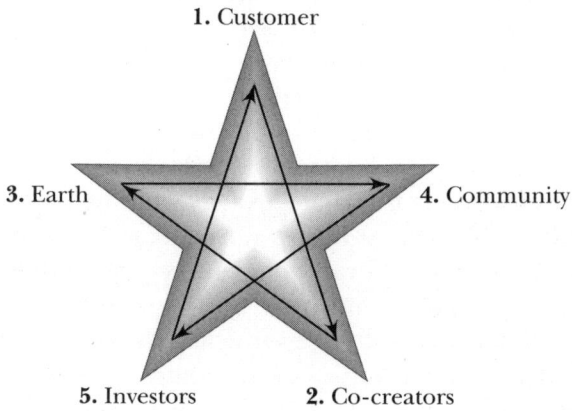

1. Customer

3. Earth

4. Community

5. Investors

2. Co-creators

also asked to engage the best people in the new open source industry, software designers who had been giving their expertise away for free. "The community of developers is the essence of free software," he was told. "And by the way, they don't do bosses."

The free-wheeling and idealistic culture of the open source community presented real challenges to creating a business organization. Paul had started his career at IBM, and his first step was to learn about the world in which this new business existed. He spent his first day on the job at the Linux Expo hosted by Duke University, ground zero for the open source revolution. All one thousand seats in the auditorium were filled and participants stood three to four deep against every wall waiting for the keynote speaker, the man who had invented the open source phenomenon. Paul was amazed at the electricity in the air. "It was like waiting for U2 to come on stage at Madison Square Garden," he told me later.

A man finally walked on stage and said, "My name is Linus Torvalds . . ." The auditorium erupted. Torvalds continued, and the room went dead quiet, ". . . and I am your God." The audience again went wild, shouting Torvalds's name.

In that moment, Paul knew he had entered a very different universe from IBM. This was pure passion—a community giving its extraordinary skills to create something that could be available to everyone. These engineers earned their livings at day jobs working on software design that within a few years would be replaced by what they worked on for free at night. They were the best in the business, and they were revolutionizing the field of computing just because they could.

Paul kept asking, "What's the business model? Free and brilliant? You can't build a business by selling what people could otherwise get for free." But that's exactly what he had been asked to do. By this time, several things were clear. The users and creators of open source software had always been the same, but suddenly a market was beginning to evolve to meet them. Business buyers were looking for software for which they could manage the code, and they recognized that free didn't necessarily mean inferior—shareware had paved the way for years. But they needed backup plans. What if they ran into coding problems or had trouble launching applications with their new software? Even worse, what if something threatened to take their business down for hours or even days?

These commercial customers needed a relationship with a trusted provider of Linux, the popular shareware operating system for personal computers. They needed someone who had both strong standing in the open source community and the ability to provide businesses with the support and services necessary for maintaining their software. Red Hat, in a *Eureka* moment, realized that it could supply the software for free and charge for providing high-value services. In an industry where bits and bytes of the software were usually considered to be the most valuable thing, Red Hat's new approach was nothing short of radical.

Red Hat began to offer software services and the market responded immediately with enthusiasm. The company began by offering 24/7 support; shortly after, it began to offer training, allowing in-house IT staff to become "Red Hat–certified engineers." It also came up with the idea of offering electronic services to customers: automatic upgrades, security patches, and system health monitoring. All the while, Red Hat's engineers continued to be coevolvers of Linux, contributing all of the code they developed for Red Hat Linux back to the Linux community.

Initially the idea was hard to sell to venture capitalists because the idea of open source was still hard for them to grasp. But the investors who finally got it have been very happy that they did. When Red Hat eventually went public in 1999, it became the seventh most successful IPO in the history of the stock market.

From the start Red Hat built a way to make its offerings work for customers, co-creators, and communities. Reciprocal benefit was inherent in the design. The company played with the idea that it could offer modified software, selling it as proprietary, but realized that this was inconsistent with the ethic and process of open source; freedom (and making it free) was the essence of both the product and the process. This created an entirely new business philosophy. The process was supercharged because it was part of a visionary movement to eliminate the software priesthood and democratize how things get created. The sense of mission surrounding the company and community meant that all were welcomed into the design and creative processes and the co-creators were both the community and the customer. This was a unique period in business history and Red Hat's stakeholders were at the center.

Red Hat is successful today because it did not segment and draw lines between stakeholders and try to manage them separately. It saw them as one entity and brought them together to create one of the most amazing businesses of the new century, one founded with a stakeholder integration ethic. It represents the wave of the future and requires radically new ways of thinking about the purpose of business organizations and how they work. Any company can create such a work culture if it follows the thinking offered in a pentadic approach to responsibility.

From Commodity to Nondisplaceability: Kingsford

Turning back to the Kingsford story, which I began in Chapter One, I want to fill in the details that illustrate how the company used the entire pentad to create transformation. This was such a rich, multilayered experience—it demonstrates beautifully what can happen when a company uses a comprehensive set of frameworks and processes to address every aspect of its operations in an integrated way.

As previously described, when Will Lynn took over Kingsford, its workforce was relatively uneducated, it was a regional brand sold in a relatively short season, and it was costly to produce with a limited return to the corporate bottom and top lines.

Will, who had been based in Kingsford's Oakland, California, headquarters, liked to barbeque. He was a good host and loved being outdoors in the California sunshine, serving friends good food and good conversation. But his new focus on improving charcoal made him aware that he spent more time fussing with his grill than being with his guests. He took pride in being able to cook to order, serving burgers and steaks at precisely the right level of doneness, but the grill and the charcoal just wouldn't cooperate. So when he began Kingsford's strategic planning, he was already standing in his customer's shoes.

Will also knew that he had to get his vice presidents to also stand in those shoes. Nothing fundamentally different was going to get created if they stayed locked into their marketing, manufacturing, and R&D mind-sets. As part of the requested radical new thinking, Will organized a company picnic with the Kingsford senior team serving, a sort of living laboratory for enacting and observing the barbeque experience. They set up a line of grills at a regional park near Sacramento and invited operators and their families from the nearby Elk Grove manufacturing facility.

This was more than just an in-house focus group. Will's vice presidents were carefully prepped to observe the living dynamics of the barbeque experience. They were asked to watch closely and at two levels: (1) "What is actually happening as I prepare, cook, serve, clean up?" and (2) "What is my inner experience of that work?" Understanding would come from reflection.

By carefully observing at these two levels, the management team was able to note how different people managed transactions between the food and the grill and the guests. They observed themselves trying to deliver a qualitative experience of family, outdoor living, and camaraderie that went far beyond serving good burgers. And they couldn't fail to notice that Kingsford's products were making it difficult to live up to that experience.

Through engaging in this rigorous mental exercise, Will's vice presidents were able to bring a conscious awareness to the experience as it was unfolding. Afterward, when they came together to work on strategic planning, the group was able to generate a shared image of the totality of the experience, including both its inward and outward dimensions. From the moment they started planning the event to the moment they finished cleaning up, their observations included the work flow, emotional responses, challenges, and payoff involved in creating a family picnic. This was a process of an entirely different nature than product testing, which would have been about observing the charcoal, and it put the group in possession of a new level of understanding and caring that could never have been generated through market research or focus groups. That understanding, along with the awakened consciousness that developed it, forever changed the working of Kingsford.

It's amazing, really, that simply paying attention (albeit very high-quality attention) to small everyday activities can have a transformative effect on a company and an industry. Yet the development of consciousness is precisely what makes the difference between incremental change and massive and total transformation. It seems nearly miraculous that Kingsford could go from an unprofitable regional brand to dominating more than 70 percent of the national market in two years, while at the same time moving its workforce literacy rate from 50 percent to 95 percent, but that's the natural outcome of a process based on shifting consciousness. The same concepts apply to very large, sophisticated businesses operating in the modern global economy.

ATTENTION PRODUCES INTENTION

Kingsford's leadership group now had a visceral and conscious experience of something so commonplace that they had never paid enough attention to it. For them, barbeque had become a living process, and this allowed them to generate creative insights.

First, the guy (even today in the world of backyard grills it's usually a guy) with the spatula in his hand was not simply trying to cook. He was trying to orchestrate a bonding and energizing group experience.

Second, he was taking on an archetypal male role—the pioneering, campfire-cooking outdoorsman or cowboy or hunter—and making it semigourmet, Wild West meets James Beard. The

Kingsford group called it "macho" and included in it elements of personal style, self-expression, honoring of guests, connecting to nature, and rugged manliness. At the backyard grill, a man's aspiration to elevate a picnic into a life-affirming special event became linked to his sense of what it means to be a man. No wonder it became a maddening experience when his tools failed him.

Third, if they were to support this guy in his aspiration to create the perfect event, then they needed to look at all the aspects. Even the best-formulated charcoal wouldn't be enough if the packaging created a mess, the grill delivered unpredictable temperatures, and there was no place to put a tray of meat or a bottle of sauce. They needed to provide him with a new bag, a new grill, and a new formula—that is, a product system, not just a product.

Inspired by this vision and direction, the team set out to enroll every co-creator, from the raw materials suppliers to the R&D labs at Clorox, the parent company; from the manufacturing line crews to the distributors. They were aided in their efforts by the fact that nearly all members of this value-adding stream had their own backyard experiences, good and bad. Still, it took some effort and education to get people to see how each part of the process played out at the grill, from raw material choices to formulations to production procedures to creation of packaging. Their challenge was to awaken the whole co-creative network to a new order of consciousness, and they used real and imagined picnics to do it. With an intensive education and reflective process, it was not long before they had sparked deep caring for the life of the consumer throughout Kingsford and beyond. As P&G's Ken Wessel reminded me, "Get people connected to how they're affecting real lives and they'll find a way to make those lives better."

For many years prior to this time, Clorox had chosen not to invest in Kingsford's people or equipment. These were, in their eyes, people who were "unskilled workers," and to get any improvement in return from such an investment would require too much capital. The Kingsford team was starting in the hole, yet they knew that to earn their workforce's trust they would need to make good on their promises to fund improvement ideas that were bubbling up. John Kabler, the manufacturing vice president for Kingsford, began to look for ways to scrape together small amounts of funding to get the process rolling. If someone could make a case for an improvement in consumer experience, product differentiation, or manufacturing process, John and his team found ways to make it happen. People often said that John could make money appear of out thin air. John's version was that it was a matter of priorities. Salespeople began to identify ways to better serve many of their long-neglected retail and wholesale outlets, so their ideas were implemented. These small acts confirmed that Kingsford respected its people and believed they could be a source of creativity.

Self-Accountability Drives Responsibility

The key to the work in this early period was that everyone from operators on the plant floor to executives was engaged and educated to contribute their ideas for improving customer success. At the same time they held themselves accountable for demonstrating the validity of their ideas. Co-creators were taught to reflect on the connection between their own work and the effects on the people who experienced the results. Up until then, managers in distant offices, sometimes thousands of miles away, had been responsible for making these connections. Now every person, regardless of role, was asked to take responsibility for downstream effects, particularly the customer's experience. Needless to say, it took some time for managers to shift roles, which required them to give up being intermediaries and delegators who spoke for the workforce in aggregate, and learn instead to act as Socratic questioners, helping every individual to think and act independently.

As Kingsford became more sophisticated and more self-organizing, it extended this process to its network of distribution channels. This time the operators drove the process, using marketing, sales, and R&D as resources. They went into all kinds of stores, from Costco to local mom-and-pops, and worked side by side with the people there. This gave them direct experience of the lives and challenges of the drivers, the warehouse workers, the shelf stockers, and the checkout clerks. From this firsthand knowledge and accountability, they developed a variety of innovations to serve distributors, including redesigned pallets and pallet-loading practices, packaging, and merchandising campaigns.

Making the company *customer conscious* sparked a quiet revolution. Without initially really trying to, the people of Kingsford dismantled the departmental and hierarchical barriers that had prevented them from working effectively together. They became an increasingly egalitarian organization, not because they set out with that goal in mind but because that was what was required. One's function, department, or level in the organization became irrelevant. The culture shifted to one of deep respect for the inherent intelligence and capacity of everyone on the team. By the time that work redesign was being implemented, everyone was involved in eliminating any vestige of the old assembly line model.

People organically organized their work around what advanced the company's contribution to its buyers. Self-organization allowed co-creators the flexibility they needed to respond to changes in the competitive environment and also made it easier for those who were caring for kids or elders at home. The union had sought more flexibility through bargaining but now it was emerging from the evolution of work systems. Just as Will Lynn had hoped, every worker learned to think like an owner. In the process, they also discovered new levels of dignity, self-respect, and meaningful contribution in their work and their lives.

This way of working changes not only a company and the lives of its workers, it also ripples out into neighborhoods and cities and eventually even to the nation. People who are part of an experience like the one at Kingsford know to their core that social justice and equity are workable and valuable. The Responsible Business doesn't work on social justice by creating a program. Instead, it enables people to work together reflectively on something they consider important. Equity and justice come into being as natural by-products of principles and aims, not departments. The experience is literally life changing for everyone involved, and they carry it with them into every other part of their lives.

The transformation of Kingsford's company culture didn't happen by accident. It was actively cultivated through a fundamental redefinition of the role and development of individuals in the organization. Kingsford did not follow a program to become a decentralized or democratized organization. Its aim was to cultivate and harness the creative energies of each individual in service of the consumer. But this had the effect of creating a self-organizing workforce.

Democratization of the workplace, another popular human resource program, is generally implemented outside the context of a customer-conscious culture and instead focuses on attempts to increase participation, access collective experience and intelligence, and move decision making down the ranks from managers to front-line employees. The limitation of this approach is that it invites people to help make decisions without evolving their thinking and personal capacity to do so. Better decision making requires a shared larger purpose and increased individual ability to make judgments about what will advance that purpose. In the absence of these conditions, and in an attempt to be inclusive, people tend to sink to the common denominators on which they can agree. By contrast, the Responsible Business sees individuals rather than roles, and this recognition enables all co-creators to self-identify the unique contributions they have to make to the customer's life.

CHANGE THE CULTURE, CHANGE THE GAME

Kingsford put in place a comprehensive education and engagement program to develop the company at all levels through the use of systemic frameworks, one of which was the pentad discussed in this book. Capacity for self-management was grown through working on critical thinking skills and personal and professional development in monthly events followed by weekly work sessions in smaller groups. Using a variety of practical systems frameworks, people at all levels of the organization were invited to look beyond their own jobs and address themselves to market dynamics and the life and evolution of their customers. The frameworks and Socratic process enabled them to reflect on their own thinking and improve the quality of their decisions and actions. They began to see that the integrity and thoughtfulness they brought to their tasks had the potential to influence the customer, society, and even the health of the planet.

This transformation of corporate culture developed over a number of years, fueled by the early success of Kingsford's strategic planning breakthroughs. It depended on four key processes.

1. *Education and business evolution.* People from across the organization as well as suppliers and contractors worked on business improvement by enhancing their own capabilities. They learned to notice and break habitual patterns of thinking, replacing them with patterns that promoted innovation and reflection. They worked on real opportunities in monthly events that crossed stakeholder boundaries.

2. *Core teams.* Each business organized a team that was chartered to take stewardship for the vitality, viability, and evolution of the business. The initial core teams were for BBQ, but eventually they spread to Hidden Valley Foods and Deer Park Spring Water, demonstrating the effect that one Responsible Business can have on others within a corporation. These core teams were responsible for managing the entity as an open, living system, looking at how what happened inside affected what happened outside and vice versa. They then worked to improve relationships across those boundaries.

3. *Resources.* Individuals stepped up to become resources, building their own capability to grow critical thinking and personal development in others. These resources were drawn from all functions and levels within the business and continued to carry out their work roles even as they grew into their new resourcing roles. They assisted with sessions to improve offerings and work design, helping people become more reflective, strategic, and self-managing.

4. *Work redesign.* Core teams and resources together redesigned every aspect of how people were managed and developed—from organizational structure to hiring to pay to acknowledgment. Their philosophy was developmental, emphasizing the inherent self-directing capacity of all people, and they set up structures, processes, and systems that encouraged and required self-organization toward a common purpose.

Education and Business Evolution

Will Lynn and his leadership team launched the education and business evolution process by introducing the workforce to the idea of working simultaneously on improving oneself, as a person and member of a team, *while* improving the business. They sought out participants who reflected all of the functions, perspectives, and energies that made up a business. They established demanding criteria for participation: a love of learning and change, willingness to engage with others in change, commitment to the business as a whole and not just one's "turf," a high level of tolerance for confronting existing patterns (including habitual ways of talking about business), excitement about personal development as a means to move oneself and the whole business forward, and, for those who had been involved in earlier change programs, willingness to get past the "been there, done that" feeling so that the real distinctiveness of this way of working could be experienced. All those who chose to participate agreed to make the effort to live up to these criteria.

The business groups met for two days every month, organized into product or service teams. After the first meeting, they could see they needed to add other perspectives in order to reflect accurately the whole of the value-adding process, so they recruited suppliers as well as more members from lower levels of the company hierarchy. Systemic frameworks and reflective processes were introduced and immediately applied to real business challenges and opportunities.

The invitation to think as an owner of Kingsford disrupted how people normally thought about planning, running, and evaluating a business. When they had been accustomed to identifying a task and objectives within a function, they were now asked to think in terms of multiple levels of interacting systems (for example, the business, the stakeholders, and the guy at the grill). This was both frustrating and exhilarating because what they were generating was genuinely new. One man reported, "I feel like you took a bicycle pump and blew my head up to three times its size."

Participants worked in cross-functional groups that were responsible not just for projects or practical objectives but for the growth of business across Kingsford. They were expected to apply this entirely disruptive way of thinking to that growth and at the end of each and every meeting to develop and move on ideas worth market testing. There were no suggestion boxes, only ideas and execution. These ideas included evolving charcoal formulations, new models for grills, and co-branding ideas with other companies. Not every idea was validated, but many were implemented straight away and others were diligently pursued over years until they came to fruition. Within a few months, participants' ability to generate usable ideas and leverage scarce resources had been so dramatically increased that they could no longer imagine working the old way.

Core Teams

Most of the people who participated in these early sessions went on to set up the next tier of work, establishing core teams for specific manufacturing facilities so that the rest of the people in the business could be involved. Each core team reflected all of the working aspects of that facility along with marketing, R&D, and members from the co-creator ranks. They met monthly to improve and evolve the businesses and facilities. The core teams did not replace management, which continued to be responsible for the ongoing work of the business; rather, the core teams looked at the unrealized potential of the business and sought ways to develop the capacity to realize that potential. To do this, they imaged themselves sitting on the boundary between the business or facility and the world and asked themselves what was required to ensure a healthy business and a healthy business ecosystem. Much of the innovation in co-creator relationships, as well as the integration of functions that had been isolated for decades, came directly from the work of the core teams.

One of these core teams, based at Burnside, Kentucky, could see that the pursuits they were taking on would require people to do a great deal more independent learning, self-managing, and self-evaluation, and that this meant they would need to be able to read or read better. The Burnside facility, including the core team, had a 50 percent literacy rate, so they initiated the first literacy campaign at Kingsford. They weren't imposing requirements from above; they were taking on a fairly terrifying challenge for themselves and committing to it as a group.

The core team talked over what would move them past their own fear into courage and agreed that three things must be present for a successful literacy program. First, they had to see how it would contribute to the business and not become just a training task. Second, they had to connect their families to the program so that they could understand the importance and the demands of the undertaking. And third, they felt it was imperative to do it with others and not in isolation. They also made sure that privacy would be respected by providing after-work classes and ways to enter classrooms unseen. Pretty soon everyone who could benefit was involved. This broad participation effectively broke the generational chain of illiteracy for hundreds of families in the region.

To make the literacy program work, the group needed to apply their learning immediately. They decided to start by writing and publishing a newsletter and agreed to report on both company and community news. Their publishing staff included some literate persons, and the group hired a teacher to help them learn to read and write. They created collaborative circles for writing, critiquing, and managing technological challenges (this was initiated prior to the era of computer self-publishing but they brought it online partway through the project). Their passionate commitment to communicating accurately and in impeccable English motivated them to achieve their literacy goals in a third of the time usually required. They involved their children in the editing and storytelling, giving them a powerful connection to parents as well as to the value of communicating and writing well.

The newsletter became an important and popular source for community information. It told stories about what real people were doing inside and outside of Kingsford, nurturing a sense of pride and of place. This community may never have been reflected back to itself in this way, and it was a powerful and uplifting experience. The wife of the governor of Kentucky nominated the project for a Toyota Community Action Award after going on a site tour when she heard the story from operators, their families, and community leaders. They won the award.

Although this initiative was both impressive and inspiring, it is important to remember that it was undertaken not from a charitable impulse to "improve the community," but to improve the business. It was a completely natural and necessary part of the work of the business, and it was the work of a Responsible Business. As a business initiative, it succeeded. Kingsford was able to integrate increasingly sophisticated technologies, chemical processes, and market relationships because it had an educated, articulate, self-organized, and self-directed workforce.

Resources

Within a Responsible Business, a resource is a person whose responsibility is to educate and engage others in thinking better. The core teams at Kingsford knew that their success was going to depend on their ability to develop such internal resources within the company. Resources work with individuals and groups to build capacity for critical, systemic, and reflective thinking capacity. They help people become better able to operate and contribute in a complex world. Resources orient people to their role within nested systems. In a Responsible Business, everyone has access to this level of master mentoring.

Typical responsibilities for resources include working one-on-one with leaders, helping them plan and lead events. In meetings, they frequently intervene with questions or calls for reflection when they see automatic patterns of thinking or inter-action. They help select the appropriate level and complexity of frameworks based on the level of challenge or objective. And they never let a team leave the room without engaging in structured reflection on how they have improved in this meeting and what they see as their next opportunity for growth. This emphasis on reflection might be expected to slow things down, but anyone who has ever experienced it will report that it eliminates politics, egos, and irrelevant crosstalk, enabling teams to accomplish significantly more in a given period of time.

At Kingsford, criteria were developed for the role of resource. To the existing criteria for core team members was added commitment to rigorous personal development and immersion in understanding developmental philosophy and practice. For all but one of Kingsford's resources (for whom it became a full-time role), this work became an integrated part of their existing day-to-day work. They spent two days a month in sessions, working on their own development, and devoted about a fifth of their time to the resource role. To a person, they reported that the time available for their primary job actually increased because their own ableness and reflective capacity grew at such a rapid rate.

Eventually, every function and every facility in Kingsford had dedicated resources. All projects and significant planning or evaluation efforts invited a resource to either join the team or participate when they met. Resources might be tapped for their existing functional capabilities or for their willingness to develop new capabilities through participation. Even the most senior leaders and teams worked with resources and benefited from the disciplined thinking and probing questions designed to develop their own capacity and results.

Work Redesign

Having initiated a number of market and product ventures, the core teams were increasingly aware that the way work was organized needed to be completely overhauled. Together with the resources, they set out to completely redesign work at Kingsford, a process that eventually involved everyone. The initial focus was on developing individuals as the basis for business improvement. They believed that each individual was unique and therefore had something distinct and useful to contribute to business evolution. The business strategy had by now been well defined and the team wanted individuals to initiate their own improvements in the way work was organized and executed to achieve its objectives.

It was time for Kingsford's structures, systems, and processes to support self-organizing and self-direction, enabling individuals and teams to work toward business ends without top-down direction. Given Kingsford's fast-moving new culture and its strategic mandate to cut the go-to-market time by two thirds, moving up, down, or across the business for a decision was simply too slow. People needed to use their newly developed systemic wisdom and critical thinking skills to make their choices from the perspective of business owner.

Recently, this idea has found more traction in new start-ups. Tony Hsieh, CEO of the best-selling shoe company Zappos (now owned by Amazon), observed at a June 2008 Amazon company event that if insects and animals created a business network, they would self-organize and take over the world. It's the only model that makes innovation ubiquitous. Kingsford knew this decades ago.

Make Promises-Beyond-Ableness

The first priority for work redesign was a developmental personal practice called *promises-beyond-ableness*. Every individual was expected to generate meaningful and significant ideas that would require them to stretch beyond their current capabilities in order to contribute to the overall strategy. They did not have to stay within the bounds of their current job or role, though as they began to step outside of that role they would engage others to gain alignment from the part of the organization they sought to affect. This is how the Responsible Business ties intelligence development and expression to pursuing and achieving business strategy and marketplace nondisplaceability.

These promises-beyond-ableness took the form of initiatives, projects, or targeted changes in work practices. Though these promises always came out of an opportunity or hazard about which the individual felt great passion, they also had to meet certain criteria. They always had to be rationally defended in terms of their relevance and significance to the corporate strategy and the effects on stakeholders. They had to include a rigorous plan for the time and resources required. They had to include systemic performance indexes that could be measured with regard to the effect on the market, the business, the team, and the individual. And they had to place a significant demand for personal growth and professional learning on the individual.

The resulting personal development plans specified the work to be done and set up "deliberative practices" intended to ensure success. That term has now been popularized in Geoff Colvin's highly useful and paradigm-changing book, *Talent Is Overrated*. According to Colvin, "Deliberative practice is characterized by several elements, each worth examining. The practice is activity designed specifically to improve performance, often with a teacher's help. It has to be engaged over a sustained period of time, with a desire for improvement, not a few days of repetitious practice. Reflection on results must be continuously developed with a teacher or mentor."[1]

Kingsford's mentoring resources offered developmental questions intended to improve the capacity of learners to reflect and grow independently. This took rigor and discipline on the part of learner and mentor alike. Critical thinking development was core to these personal development plans and was explicitly evaluated as part of the learning process.

Individuals had to justify their plans and the resources required to a self-chosen team, all of whom would be affected by the promise and its delivery. This helped extend accountability and support beyond individuals into teams, which often found themselves drawing together in pursuit of large, compelling promises. Along the way, individuals led timely evaluations of their accomplishments, their learning, and the understanding they were developing of the next phase of planning and action. Over time, individuals took on increasingly challenging and significant tasks, growing themselves and the contributions they could make. Through this process, workers were able to conceptualize and carry out transformations that affected the entire company. Promises-beyond-ableness were a critical factor in Kingsford's rapid and strategic growth.

A key aspect of each plan was predicting what was sought in terms of financial outcomes (improvements in earnings, margins, and cash flow). The predictions were based on changes expected in sales, market penetration, sourcing improvements, or production improvements. Generally the people developing and implementing these plans were not accountants. They were adopting accounting thinking as a means to increase their understanding of how the business worked as a whole, to dispel myths and the overconfidence that myths can produce, and to evoke their own curiosity and commitment.

Years later, I discovered that the validity of this approach had been demonstrated through research. In their book, *Made to Stick*, Chip and Dan Heath tell the story of Eric Mazur, a physics professor who came up with a learning approach called "concept testing." He asked students to make a public commitment to finding an answer. He found that the simple act of committing made the students more engaged in the dialogue and more curious about the outcome.[2] Committing also woke people up to gaps in their knowledge or understanding, which stimulated their curiosity. At Kingsford, any sense of failure was quickly overcome because people had set their own predictions and were curious to find where their assumptions had been off. It was a self-guided learning experience that stuck with them forever.

An exemplary Kingsford promise-beyond-ableness story is that of Bob Raynsford, a successful sales director at Kingsford who was particularly good at building relationships. Because he knew his customers so intimately, he was often invited to consult early on in new product offerings to provide perspective on their likely acceptance in different markets. From this experience, he knew how costly it was to develop a new product, market test it, and then take it to a national brand—and that the longer it takes the more costly it gets. Because he moved between functions, he could also see that what slowed things down the most was the lack of an elegant and integrative planning process.

Bob Raynsford committed to figuring out how to halve the go-to-market time for new product development. Though Bob had a well-developed capacity for one-on-one relationships, he had always shied away from coalition building. Yet it was clearly a capability the organization needed, particularly if it wanted to achieve its strategic objectives in the arena of developing products and taking them to market. And Bob knew that if he ever wanted to move on to leading whole businesses, he needed to develop those skills, too.

Together with Gary Lillian, another bright and creative contributor and a senior marketing colleague, Bob pulled together a cross-functional team that included R&D, distribution, and sales. Their task was to design an elegant process for moving rapidly from idea to profitable national product (or, alternatively, for quickly abandoning products that weren't going to be successful). They anchored their work to the increased success of their distributors by improving the ability to evaluate the "excitement-producing effect" of any newly introduced products. They applied the thinking processes they had learned in the business education meetings to the flow of activities from ideation to market success. By seeing in this systemic, value-adding-process way, they identified critical decision points, places where collaboration was needed to make good judgments. And they agreed on criteria for making those judgments.

In the past, these decisions had caused major internal conflicts because individuals or departments would advance and defend pet projects. Through reflection, they could see how their own past behaviors were doubling the time it took to make good decisions. They developed new principles and practices for group process, decision making, and technical procedure. Their time to market was reduced by 60 percent and they radically improved their ability to kill products early that failed to demonstrate potential for national success.

The increased speed and accuracy with which Bob's team could generate successful products represented a significant improvement for the distributors, who spend thousands of unreimbursed hours and dollars staging a product introduction. The team was able to achieve these results by starting from an understanding of the effects consumers were seeking from Kingsford's products, which yielded much better results than any focus group or market test. It enabled them to rigorously ask how each step from sourcing materials to shipping was likely to affect the consumer's integrated experience. This tripled their predictive accuracy and cut go-to-market outlays in half.

In addition, they learned to identify products in the incubator with high potential but no immediacy. These formed a reservoir of future offerings that could be introduced when market conditions evolved, filling the pipeline for years to come. Finally, Bob transferred this capability to other teams and individuals, a key requirement for any promise-beyond-ableness plan.

There is a postscript to this story. Bob Raynsford went on to use what he learned from his time at Kingsford, and from this and other promises-beyond-ableness commitments, to build a number of companies of his own, continuing to contribute to the field of holistic business thinking. This work has made him a very successful man, and he attributes it to what he learned at Kingsford. Like dozens of others who have gone on to found small but industry-changing companies, Bob radically expanded his capabilities through participating in cross-functional education teams.

DESIGN WORK FOR IMPROVISATION

Personal development planning, based on promises-beyond-ableness, was only one of a number of work redesign efforts at Kingsford. Hiring, discipline, pay, organization charts—everything that touches on how people participate in a business—was reconceptualized, restructured, or in some cases eliminated. (For example, incentive systems based on evaluations by a superior or peers were jettisoned.) The momentum of change and improvement was driven by the increasing self-management of the co-creators, who became better able to think like owners with each passing year.

Similar to business, the essence of improvisation is the ability to work with patterns and not just perform according to the lines of a script. Performers work together closely to create something entirely new. Ideas are thrown at them from unexpected sources and unexpected perspectives. They have to be willing to move "into" the request as if it were their own, connecting seemingly unrelated subjects into a meaningful scenario that evokes a strong response. To be creative, both business and improvisation require spontaneity and an ability to love the unexpected, knowing that the best ideas will emerge from the players themselves operating in the moment. It takes courage to make the miraculous.

I know firsthand how destabilizing an improvisational process can be. In my twenties in the San Francisco Bay Area, I spent five years performing with an improvisational theatre group, Left Feat. It was a training ground for staying awake and alive to what is emerging in the moment, and it taught me to always value the creativity that necessarily shows up when the dialogue, stage blocking, and lighting haven't been worked out ahead of time. I often carried a guitar on stage and composed lines to fit the scenario. The discipline of improvisation calls forth one's best self. It can be terrifying but it is profoundly effective.

Frank Barrett, a professor of Systems Management at the Naval Postgraduate School in Monterey, California, has called self-organizing processes like the one at Kingsford *jazz improvisation*. He is a jazz musician and describes a jazz ensemble as a diverse group of specialists who make fast irreversible decisions, are highly dependent on one another to interpret equivocal information, and are dedicated to innovation and the creation of novelty. They perform without a prescribed plan and without certainty of the outcome. They discover the future as actions unfold. Though it looks like chaos to an outsider, it is a highly disciplined endeavor that requires continual development and conscious attention.

Barrett's jazz metaphor fits Kingsford well. A group of diverse and uniquely proficient individuals dedicated themselves to creating distinctive, meaningful effects for their customers. We can see this at work in Apple, Google, Facebook, W. L. Gore, and many other innovative companies as well. In a journal article about the dynamics of jazz improvisation and their relevance to organizational design, Barrett offers seven characteristics that allow jazz bands to improvise coherently and maximize social innovation in a coordinated fashion.[3] All of these characteristics were reflected in the work at Kingsford.

- The team at Kingsford deliberately tried to break patterns, avoiding being mechanical at all costs. They extended themselves beyond what they could already do easily because personal and professional development was an important part of what they were seeking.
- They redefined mistakes as indicators for as-yet-undiscovered answers and approaches. They avoided performance measures that limited them from going out on the edge of their knowledge and experience.
- They worked with minimal structure to ensure maximum flexibility in the context of a shared desire to innovate.
- Tasks were not hierarchically assigned but distributed and constantly changing based on what was emerging and could be synchronized in the dynamic interplay.
- Reflection, the ability to self-observe in order to manage one's behavior and thinking, was built into each task. They constantly sought to discover how they got where they were and what shifts might generate different outcomes.
- They were more than colleagues—they were a community united by a shared practice of innovation. They met for breakfast or at the end of day. They wanted to be together to challenge their thinking and learn from and with one another.
- Each person was equally valued because they all contributed by means of their promises-beyond-ableness and their participation in various teams and dialogues. No honors were given to exemplary people because everyone was exemplary. To distinguish particular players would disregard the fact that they all took turns being both leaders and supporters.

What was critical to the personal growth process at Kingsford was the continuous development of the capability to think, reflect, and work as teams toward innovation. The Kingsford employees knew that building standards and measures that oriented the mind toward following familiar patterns was the death knell for growth. They held to a strong motto: *To grow the business, you have to grow the people.* They fostered skills in themselves and others that enabled highly creative improvisation and opened the way to rapid transformation.

AMPLIFY EARTH'S ROI

Through education, providing resources for the development of thinking, core teams, and work redesign, Kingsford's co-creators underwent a profound transformation, lifting the company even as they were lifted. In time, they began to extend their systemic view to Earth. In particular, they began to image and, eventually, to speak about their raw materials as alive, seeing the distinctiveness in each and the role it played in their formulations. They could start to experience their kinship to Earth and its resources. Operators captured both the science and the poetry of charcoal when they described the briquetting process with lively comparisons. "This one is like reeling in a big bass. He has to be brought in slow and steady. He'll get away from you if you rush him." They were expressing hard-won insights into the distinctive natures of their materials and the art of coaxing them into a superior product. This new kind of relationship with the materials triggered a series of innovations. The team became increasingly aware of the difference between materials from different suppliers now that they were no longer seen as commodities purchased only on the basis of cost. Several operators and managers teamed up to build their own retort, an oven used to manufacture charcoal, so they could better control the quality of material that was going into the briquettes—a major jump up not only in Kingsford's capacity but also in the scientific and technical capabilities of the operators. Up until that time, raw material was stuff they measured into a machine. Now they saw themselves as key actors in the realization of a particular material's potential.

One innovation led to another as teams took more systems into consideration. They realized that many of the things that were making the manufacturing process inefficient were also making it polluting. They figured out not only how to make the retort a closed system to reduce air pollution and material waste but also how to purify water as an integral part of the process. Because they realized that the use of charcoal briquettes can be a polluting activity, they created a new formula that would light without lighter fluid and burn more completely and cleanly.

Some of this work was done over two decades ago and went significantly beyond what anyone had ever accomplished in the industry. And it was done without government regulation or corporate mandate. The people of Kingsford had woken up to the fact that they were part of a living world through an intentional and rigorous education process. Teams began to extend their thinking and work into forestry practices and the link between healthy ecosystems and high-quality raw materials, a natural outcome of the application of systems thinking to daily work. Many of the leaders who left Kingsford went on to new roles where these kinds of questions could be raised and moved into new businesses.

Leave Communities Better Than You Found Them

As a Responsible Business, Kingsford was also evolving its understanding of the contributions that communities were making to its success and the responsibility it had in return to those communities. The business had improved so rapidly that nearly half of its facilities and contractors were no longer needed to meet its growth commitments, so it became evident they were going to need to close those facilities down. However, Will was unwilling to simply abandon those who had invested so much into his change effort.

A cross-company task force was established to figure out how to downsize in a way that left each community healthier. Beginning with the first facility closure in Dothan, Alabama, the task force developed ways to ensure that every individual who left—and the leaving process itself—would grow the local economic and social infrastructure.

Departing from more conventional corporate practice, Kingsford alerted the workforce at Dothan approximately one year before the facility was to be closed. All employees would help design an exit strategy that would leave them and the community better off, while helping the business meet its strategic objectives during that time. Members from the Dothan operation were added to the cross-company task force. Their first step was to develop the following principles to guide the transition:

- No person inside the company would leave until he or she had found an equal or better opportunity, in terms of both income and the potential for creativity.
- The transition would create new businesses in the community, filling voids in its current economy.
- The workforce's productivity and quality obligations would continue to be met or exceeded every day the Dothan facility remained open.

The task force worked with local community and educational institutions to determine the employment and business opportunities that existed in the Dothan region. Dothan residents wanted to buy more of their staples and services locally rather than drive long distances to a larger population center to shop. An in-house business incubator helped each individual start a business or find a job in a field that was personally compelling. The task force teamed with local community colleges to provide the training, certification, and experience the workers would need to pursue their plans. Reeducation was paid for, including books and child care during night classes. When start-up funding was required for new businesses, the task force worked with local economic development groups to set it up. They did whatever it took to make it work.

A conventional business perspective would assume that this was an unreasonably costly venture, but the opposite turned out to be true. Improvement ideas and a surge in productivity reduced Kingsford's finished product cost by 40 percent in the first six months—for a company that was closing its doors! The spirit in the place was extraordinary. People helped one another in ways they never had before because they felt they were in it together.

The professional development occurring through this process drastically changed the business landscape in this community. Suddenly the town had accountants when before there had been none. Shops that supplied and repaired farm equipment and supplies were now local. Day care and early childhood education centers were built that supported the new entrepreneurial spirit growing in local families. Most important, many of the departing employees became active in local politics and economic development. Kingsford had proved that even under the worst of conditions, a business can help a community grow and benefit by its actions.

Too often corporate downsizings break up families, increase unemployment, and destabilize a local tax base. But the Responsible Business understands its membership in a community system and dedicates every part of its business process to evolving that system. As Kingsford's story proves, the social returns are not just marketing copy—they are real and tangible.

Later, the Clorox board of directors was surprised to receive letters from virtually every member of the Dothan plant. Even more surprising were letters sent by community leaders, thanking them for closing their doors. The board sent copies of these letters to their investors and invited some of the people from Dothan to tell their stories at the annual meeting. But to the board's credit, they never used the Dothan story as a public relations tool. Instead, they understood and respected it as a part of their work and their responsibility.

It was a great honor to work with the people at Kingsford. Their strength of character made them exactly the kind of people I want as neighbors and friends. I have stayed close to many of them over the years, watching with joy as they moved into new positions, took on community leadership roles, and served as mentors to others with the aspiration to lead Responsible Businesses.

The next three stories illustrate how differently this process unfolds every time it is undertaken by a different business.

DEEPLY CONNECT TO YOUR CUSTOMER: HERBAN FEAST

When I introduced Seattle caterer Herban Feast in Chapter One, I talked about this business in the context of the customers as stakeholder. Everyone in the business knew that customers were important and they used event feedback forms to guide the server teams. Herban Feast's founder and co-owner BJ Duff didn't start out recognizing the stakeholder concept as a key issue, but when we were able to connect the company's essence to the customer's essence, a host of seemingly unrelated problems began to be reconciled.

I first met BJ when he was a participant in a strategic leadership program for entrepreneurs that I led at Antioch University in Seattle. BJ was committed to bringing a better management approach into his business but was stumped by how to engage his organization. As we began the class, his questions returned again and again to the people in his company and really basic issues like problem employees and staff turnover. He was clearly concerned that these issues compromised the business's integrity, preventing Herban Feast from fully delivering on its promises.

From hearing his story I knew that what was really missing was a strong connection to the life of his customers. But instead of answering his questions immediately, I decided to challenge him by advocating the idea that "you can't address your people problems until you have something you can deeply connect people to," a core strategic concept the class was working on from the outset. I had the participating business owners and leaders articulate their strategic focus and really dig deep into why they were doing business. "What," I pressed them, "were they trying to do better for their customers than their customers would or could do for themselves?" This work was iterative and ongoing as participants deepened their understanding of what creates a nondisplaceable business.

During the entire time we were working on nondisplaceable strategic focus, BJ continued to struggle with his human resource problems and his own frustrations as a manager. Meanwhile, at the beginning of every class as well as in all of our subsequent work together, we used critical thinking to examine real stories of real customers. We made a concerted effort to move past market and customer service clichés about quality, service, and price competitiveness. As this process helped him become more rigorous, BJ rapidly improved his ability to image the values and meaning a client (for example, a bride) wanted to realize, even if she couldn't necessarily describe them. He and the catering teams also got better at inventing ways that Herban Feast could uniquely help her achieve those values. He began to embrace this imaging of real lives as a major source of creativity and inspiration for the organization and to learn how to see the story that the client wanted to be able to relate after an Herban Feast event.

After one masterful event, he entered the class, walked straight to the whiteboard and drew two separate circles. One was the client and him, the other was his organization. He added a bold line dividing them. He announced to the other entrepreneurs in the program, "I'm terrible at helping my employees and suppliers see what I see! And so are my other salespeople. When a client comes to us to do an event, the sales team gets a vision of what it could be. It's an incredible source of excitement for the client and us. But that never really gets translated to the rest of the company." From that day forward, BJ stopped asking me how to deal with problems and started pursuing how to connect everyone to the vision and potential for each upcoming event.

Previously, the first step to engaging the staff around an event was to walk them through a form with specifications: number of attendees, menu, choice of place settings, and the many other details of a catered event. Even asking themselves what the ideal event would look like led them to generalities, not personalization. This approach evoked an automatic response and work was reduced to getting things checked off the list. The energy and spirit created in the conversation with the client stayed locked up in a few people involved in sales. Even the sales team would lose touch with that energy as they engaged with the next client. Their work was done when the checklist was handed off to be implemented.

Now, don't get me wrong. Herban Feast created fabulous corporate and life ritual events. Those checklists showed a high attention to detail and every promise was delivered on. But people's creativity would get lost in checking off "to dos" and scrambling to cover shortfalls. BJ hired the best people in the industry and they could leave any time they wanted. They needed more than checklists to inspire them to stay.

BRING DREAMS TO LIFE

After BJ's *aha* moment, Herban Feast completely transformed the way events were designed and created a reputation that allowed it to influence the entire industry in its region. Salespeople began to sit down with service staff to tell stories until everyone could join in with the client's dream. When that unfolding dream was alive in each of them, motivation was strong. They became determined magicians, working to bring dreams to life—so much more fun than checking items off a list. Every member of the team was a co-creator, continually looking for new and better ways to deploy Herban Feast's assets and exceed clients' aspirations.

On one occasion, I got to see the team's magic in action. The staff was gathered in the kitchen on the Monday after a wedding held in the peaceful setting of their own historic venue. Those who hadn't been there wanted to see the pictures and hear the stories. The bride had been deeply touched when she approached the altar and saw BJ, holding the leash of her big, goofy, and much-beloved golden retriever. He had really understood how much the dog was part of her family and it made the experience complete for her. Her husband, an amateur brewer, toasted the future with his own homemade beer. These kinds of loving touches would not even have been conceivable in an institutional setting like a hotel ballroom. Many of the small touches had come from members of the service team who felt personal responsibility for creating a wedding story that could serve as an enduring touchstone for this couple.

The group in that kitchen was not engaging in Monday morning quarterbacking. They weren't analyzing what went wrong, what went right. They were a family reliving a powerful event, telling stories to embed it into their culture. Each of them had exercised creativity toward realizing a dream and they all wanted to see know how it had come out. In the following week, they carried these stories back to the farmers, distributors, and other contractors who had helped make them possible and shared the gratitude and sense of connected community needed for that specific dream realization.

ARTICULATE AND MANIFEST ESSENCE

This transformation of Herban Feast's relationship to its co-creators and the value it was able to deliver to its customers began with articulating its essence as a business. I've mentioned essence in the context of people, communities, and even raw materials. Businesses also have essences, which are usually reflections of the essence of the founder. Often people can feel a business's essence, although they may not be able to name it, and this is what draws them to buy from it or work for it. Being able to articulate its essence gives a business strategic clarity and the basis for making systemic change.

To get at the essence of Herban Feast, I engaged BJ in deep reflection on who he really is and how he embeds that into his company and its way of doing business. Through dialogue, we discovered that core to everything BJ does is a desire to discover and express what's authentic. When he prepares a meal for a guest or for friends, he seeks to offer an experience of what's local and seasonal and chosen to appeal to them, rather than trying to impress. He's not chasing a trend; this is simply who he is. In conversation, he is genuinely interested in the life of his companions. He creates based on what is present and real.

Not surprisingly, he engages his clients in the same way as well as the local farmers, artisans, and provisioners who supply him. He wants to know personally the people he does business with and help them feel part of the creative process. This commitment to authenticity was an unspoken promise he had made to himself when he left the world of corporate catering. It was also the source of his anxiety when personnel problems were eroding the quality of what he expected to be able to deliver to his clients.

Because BJ is himself an organic gardener, with a home surrounded by unusual herbs and edible plants, he wanted his business to be as authentic in its relationship with nature as he was in his relationships with people. It was easy for him to move into an ecologically oriented catering business. After all, it's a short step from composting and using local materials in his garden to envisioning a catering company where nothing goes to waste.

These essence qualities were implicit, so much BJ's second nature that he was pretty much unconscious of them. His task was to make them explicit so that his co-creators could test their own resonance with them. He found that virtually all of the people who worked with him were drawn to his company because of its unflagging pursuit of what is authentic. Articulating essence allowed people to integrate their values into their work and fostered spirit and creativity in what had been everyday mundane activities.

DESIGN WORK AND OFFERINGS TO EXPRESS ESSENCE

The real, though not always conscious, imperative held by co-creators is that work should be an opportunity for them to reveal their own essence and express it in meaningful ways. For Herban Feast, the next step was to redesign its work systems so that the essence of each co-creator would be included in expressions of the company's essence. Monday morning reflections allowed the team to examine its progress on all three of these planes—realizing individual essence, Herban Feast's essence, and the essence of the client's dream. As a result, co-creators have become personally invested in the company's offerings, and turnover is no longer an issue. Where else would they have such an opportunity to offer more than what is on the purchase order?

In the annual survey of catering venues and services in Seattle, Herban Feast now repeatedly tops the list for its efforts to create a healthy planet and fabulous events. BJ didn't set out to run an ecological business; his natural way of working and thinking just made it inevitable—which is, after all, the way it's supposed to be. But the power of his intuitive ecological sensibility wasn't fully realized until his whole team could connect to the same deep drive. When Herban Feast explicitly stated its business objective, extending an authentic relationship to Earth by creating healthy living systems, the lid blew off. Suddenly everyone went to work on what had been in their hearts all along. Although they determined to have no waste from their events, the team had a much bigger goal in mind: to create healthy farms and local economies through what they offered in the business.

An ecological consultant was hired to educate the whole company as part of the change effort. His focus was on how to work toward a healthier planet and community through food service. When systemic thinking got added to this content, the stage was set for regenerative catering—making everything better while doing business. The education helped everybody, from sales force to kitchen staff, think about how their roles and their work could serve this purpose. How could menu planning make farms healthy? How could contracting improve the local economy? How could a server educate a business conference about better business practices? How could customers translate what they had experienced at an event into their lives at home? Before long, every item on the menu advertised the local farm or artisan who supplied the ingredients. Semiannual open houses introduced clients to the farmers, artisans, photographers, musicians, and everyone else who made up the Herban Feast community and enabled it to provide such a unique service.

At one point, the challenge of finding event facilities that fit their increasingly explicit values made it clear that it was time to find their own venue. They chose a location where they could work with other businesses toward shared objectives and shared events. They repurposed an existing building, a machine manufacturing operation from the 1940s, and stripped it back to the unfinished wood from which it had been built, revealing the authenticity of its materials and building methods. They remodeled it with local salvage from Second Use Materials, a Seattle company that had been in the Antioch course with BJ and subsequently sold him everything from vintage lighting to furnishings.

Weddings remain constant even in economic ups and downs, and as Herban Feast becomes more and more successful, it exerts a stabilizing influence on the market for products from local farmers and artisans. It occasionally rents the buildings of neighboring businesses as a backup space, promoting them in the process. It educates its clients about suppliers, encouraging them to buy from local organic and sustainable sources. Its work with local artisans and service providers helps improve the sustainability of their practices. Through its usual buying processes, Herban Feast helps suppliers to develop distinctive product offerings, proactively ensuring the unique ingredients that allow it to continue to offer fresh, authentic, and compelling menus. Though Herban Feast has no sustainability department, officer, or program, it has become so integrated that everything and everyone is responsible.

BJ has now added a new restaurant in West Seattle to his list of endeavors and he is applying the lessons learned at Herban Feast to a new venue. I'm lucky. I live in Seattle and I get to sample the marvelous menus and cheerful service he offers. I love to recommend Herban Feast to my friends, but these days people beat me to the punch.

MISSION-DRIVEN MEETS FUTURE-PROOF: SEVENTH GENERATION

My collaboration with Jeffrey Hollender, the founder of Seventh Generation, began with a planning process to clarify the company's strategic direction and strengthen its ability to live out its purpose as a Responsible Business. One of the biggest challenges of mission-driven companies like Seventh Generation is to avoid backsliding on their mission as they grow. During a period of four years, Jeffrey and his strategy team redefined the business, strengthened its extensive network of partnerships, and produced an average growth rate of 30 percent a year. Seventh Generation was already a major leader in the world of sustainability and social justice. Jeffrey and his team worked together to chart a course that would move its responsibility commitments to the next level while ensuring an enduring future.

THREE DIMENSIONS OF A WINNING BUSINESS STRATEGY

The need for deep strategic work was apparent. Jeffrey was generating new business ideas almost weekly. A company of Seventh Generation's size could not possibly keep up with him. What was needed was to harness his inventive mind and unleash the talent and dedication of his co-creators. So from the beginning I offered three critical dimensions of a winning business strategy.

Start from Essence

As with so many other examples in this book, Seventh Generation's business strategy needed to be grounded in its essence. Every company needs to do this work to enable clear decision making and prevent it from straying too far from its core. But a company led by Jeffrey Hollender or any other highly creative entrepreneur particularly needs to be explicit about essence as a means to focus and channel the continual flow of ideas. Without this focus, too many exciting directions, options, and opportunities present themselves and the organization becomes dispersed and even exhausted.

In addition, clarity about essence helps a company become nondisplaceable in its market. A company that operates from essence creates offerings and ways of working that cannot be duplicated because no one else shares that essence. As we talked about creating this clarity, Jeffrey acknowledged that it was something he needed to do. He was excited by it but also terrified because he loved being able to manage the business organically. Still, he knew he couldn't continue to grow the company without introducing this higher level of focus.

I loved supporting Jeffrey in his dedicated efforts to grow the next generation of strategic leaders in a strategically focused company. Early on, Jeffrey shared with his management group the story of Seventh Generation's founding and his reason for choosing this path. (That story can be found in Jeffrey's book with Bill Breen, *The Responsibility Revolution.*[4]) From the company's earliest days, he was able to articulate its essence in terms of three distinctive pursuits:

- Being committed to calling out dissonance in the system
- Being fully transparent in actions and results
- Enabling others to live and operate authentically

When the management group shared these thoughts with others in the company, their colleagues reacted with astonished delight: "That's why I came to work here!" "I couldn't have said it in words but that's what I saw in the way you hired me." "It makes me proud to know that I can live my values completely where I work." Jeffrey and his team learned that people are attracted to a company and come to work for it because of who it is.

The group went on to define in precise and compelling language the company's unique work, differentiating it clearly from its competitors. This gave Jeffrey the lens he needed to be more discriminating about which ideas to pursue. Many of his colleagues reported that for the first time he began to relax around his role as "idea generator." They also had a rational basis for pushing back on ideas so that creativity could be enhanced rather than stifled. All of this gave Seventh Generation the platform it needed to take on a really deep investigation of its customers and how to better serve them.

This description of Seventh Generation's essence resonated deeply with Jeffrey, who has always diligently pursued his own personal growth and development. He tends to examine every aspect of his behavior and its effects and endeavors to be completely transparent to those around him, traits that have made him a much-loved and respected leader. The company's essence mirrored the essence of its founder, which gave it a solid basis for moving forward.

Know Your Buyer Classes

A company needs to understand its essence to remain authentic and on track. To operate strategically, it also really needs to understand its customers. This means being able to distinguish them based on essence characteristics rather than nonessential demographics. I call groups that have been distinguished this way *buyer classes*.

When I first asked Jeffrey how his company made decisions about what products to make and how to go to market with them, he spent a good five minutes apologizing for the inadequacy of Seventh Generation's market research and explaining how it was being upgraded. I let him continue in this vein for a while because I knew from thirty years of experience that dependency on market research is one of the hardest bad habits to break and I wanted to interrupt him in a way that would be deeply disconcerting.

"I invite you to put less emphasis on market research, not more!" I offered. "Consider the power of relying a lot less on abstract surveys and a lot more on putting yourself into the shoes of your buyer classes. You would get a living, visceral experience of them and a deeper caring about them, not more data."

Jeffrey seriously contemplated the idea, although it was outside his prior experience. He opted for prudence and allowed the research effort already underway to be completed. In the meantime, the leadership team went to work, seeking to describe the essence and desired effects for distinct groups of buyers through imaging what it was like to be in their shoes. The first customer group they committed to understand was natural groceries, stores already dedicated to educating and serving the health of conscious consumers. By working on the education of their shared customers, Seventh Generation could evolve a whole new order of relationship with this key group of buyers because they had a natural synergy with Seventh Generation's own educational mission. This insight led to joint merchandizing as a sincere educational process, a rarity in the world of consumer products.

Seventh Generation's exemplary work with Whole Foods Market was a result of its efforts to see the world through the eyes of a member of this natural grocery buyer class. At the time, Whole Foods Market was the company's largest distribution channel. By thinking first about the buyer class that Whole Foods Market is a part of, and then about the essence of Whole Foods Market itself, the team was able to see the natural foods retailer in an entirely new way. Beyond sales data and feedback forms, they came to recognize an important and visionary ally in their mission of creating a better world. This launched an extended creative partnership between the two companies, one that fed the success of each while furthering their shared values.

It's important to note that a process to understand a buyer class frequently starts off on the wrong foot. When there has been a history of rough relationships with a customer, there is a strong tendency to stereotype, focusing on all the things that are "wrong with them." By contrast, essence always represents the highest nature of a person or entity, what they are continually trying to become or realize. Everyone, including businesses, has behaviors and personality traits that stand in the way of this realization.

Articulating the higher essence establishes a reference point, a reminder that all people in all organizations have a meaningful and important contribution to make. The job of a Responsible Business is to help them do that better and more often.

Another buyer class that Seventh Generation discovered was people that clean houses for other people. In general, these low-income workers faced two distinct challenges. First, their work offered very little opportunity to improve their income. Second, most housecleaning products are toxic, making workers ill and causing them to miss work.

Based on this insight, Seventh Generation developed a vibrant partnership with WAGES, a Bay Area worker cooperative primarily made up of Hispanic women housecleaners. Through selling its products to this group, Seventh Generation helped these women distinguish themselves by offering nontoxic cleaning services. The company has continued to work with the women of WAGES over time, helping them provide better services, grow their businesses, improve their income, and, as a result, create a new outlet for Seventh Generation products.

In that relationship, everybody has benefited. It has opened an entirely new channel of direct sales and created word-of-mouth marketing; one could never afford to pay for the kind of marketing that these enthusiastic women are creating spontaneously. Now the company is working on a program to enable the women to sell products directly, creating a new revenue stream for the women and for Seventh Generation.

Articulate Global Imperatives

The third and at times most challenging phase of the early strategy planning was to state Seventh Generation's global imperatives. Global imperatives emerge from social and ecological necessities forming the non-negotiable requirements that Earth and society would make if they could speak. They provide the basis for the ethical direction that a company is committed to pursue. One would expect a company as values-driven as Seventh Generation to have an easy time with this task, but the group was so accustomed to swimming in those waters that they had a hard time creating enough perspective to be reflective about them.

Since its founding, Seventh Generation has had a strong commitment to social justice and the environment. But this doesn't mean that it has always been strategic about working in ways that really make a difference. There were many conversations, first with Jeffrey and then with his team, about the difference between doing less harm in the world and proactively making it better.

Improving the world, I offered for consideration, would require asking how every transaction, every product offered, and every use of that product would evolve ecological and social systems to a more vital and viable state. Could laundry detergent and its manufacturing processes not only be nontoxic but also actually purify water and contribute to the health of watersheds? Could the way Seventh Generation sold products make low-income workers more independent and self-sustaining? Could a national brand help local communities strengthen their own identities and cultures? It is a testament to Jeffrey's authenticity that these questions caused him to become even more rigorous. "Global imperatives is one of the most exciting ideas I've heard about how to use business to make a better world!" he observed.

The core team worked on the question of global imperatives iteratively and in depth for nearly four years until they felt they knew where their commitments would really have to lie. This work is still in progress and will probably continue for as long as the company remains in contact with its essence, but here briefly are some of the commitments that guide them now:

- Systemically educate consumers
- Create a public that understands the total effects of its buying choices, not just in homes but in the lives of farmers, workers, rivers, and soils throughout the world
- Include our consumers—and their customers—in our effort to see beyond harm reduction to ecosystem and community regeneration

CO-CREATE INNOVATION

Over time, the Seventh Generation leadership team got better and better at engaging the rest of the organization in business development—sometimes at the insistence of folks who weren't involved but were intensely interested. By the third year, Seventh Generation was holding companywide events one day a month. These business meetings were designed to develop personal capability and reflection while advancing projects and strategic initiatives.

Seventh Generation's efforts to engage co-creators extended beyond employees to include the many organizations with whom they partnered. The company came to understand that offering superior products required working with contractors and growers familiar with the effects it was trying to produce for customers— healthy babies, healthy homes, healthy ecosystems. It brought together all of its manufacturers for a three-day event. Together they worked on understanding the essence of shared customers as well as the unique essence-offering match that Seventh Generation was endeavoring to create through its product offerings. This made it possible for each contract manufacturer to assess its own success based on criteria other than merely cutting costs and meeting standards and to become creative contributors to the beneficial effect Seventh Generation was committed to delivering into the lives of its customers.

But it didn't stop there. Seventh Generation then engaged its contractors in exploring their own essence and what they felt their unique contribution to this value-adding process could be. Contractors were encouraged to find their own creative ways to bring the uniqueness of their companies into the relationship so that together they could design and manufacture increasingly beneficial products.

These contractors reported that they had never been invited into the creative process at this level. It is hard to describe the gratitude, connection, and loyalty this work generated. The efficiency and effectiveness of the working relationships improved. But far more important, they all reported how much more meaning and significance they derived from their work once it had been connected to the life of the end user.

In another co-creator innovation, Seventh Generation integrated an education function into its sales department. Susan Johnson, the company's most experienced and successful salesperson, had made a promise-beyond-ableness. She wanted to enable the company's entire sales force along with salespeople inside key distributors to help consumers understand the global imperatives Seventh Generation's products were designed to address. One of her most successful efforts was with Babies"R"Us. Susan helped train its salespeople to be able to help shoppers meet their environmental objectives. She also built into this program the development of critical thinking and reflective capabilities—skills that had strengthened her as a salesperson and could now strengthen the salespeople of a key distributor.

SETTING THE STAGE FOR TRANSITIONS

In our fourth year of working together, Jeffrey implemented a process to become a co-chairman of the board and hand over leadership of the company to the next generation. He found a new CEO, Chuck Maniscalco, who resonated with Seventh Generation's essence and would continue to pursue its global imperatives. The strategy work we had done helped focus and grow the company based on who it was and the values it held. In the process, it had developed a deep organizational capability for reflection, critical thinking, and value-adding perspective. Jeffrey provides a clear explication of his process for replacing himself in "How I Did It: Giving Up the CEO Seat" in the March 2010 issue of the *Harvard Business Review*.[5] These days, Seventh Generation has begun to extend its environmental agenda into more regenerative goals, including sourcing materials that support healthy farming and families in countries around the world. It is working to encourage sustainable production of Southeast Asian palm oil, a key ingredient in its soap products. It continues to look for more regenerative ways to contribute to healthy communities.

As for investors, Seventh Generation is a private equity company. Beginning in 1993, it went public for six years, only to discover that this approach to growth felt like it was making a bargain with the devil. It simply didn't have the capability at that time to reconcile the required quarterly reporting and emphasis on share value with its purpose and mission. So Jeffrey and a close-knit group of investors took the company private again. They learned the critical importance of inviting future investors based on shared commitment to the strategic direction and global imperatives that they held dear. This has led to a more interactive process at board meetings, where investors are educated about the company's evolving approach to the management of its people, its strategies, and its pursuit of global imperatives.

Change the World by Changing the Business: Colgate, South Africa

When I supported Stelios Tsezos in his work in South Africa, we knew we were up against one of the biggest and most compelling challenges of our respective professional lives. Nelson Mandela's South Africa held enormous symbolic importance for the world at that time and nobody knew if it would successfully make the transition to a modern, racially integrated society or collapse into civil war.

It would have been a fatal mistake to think that this change process would be like the one we had worked on together in Europe. We needed to start at the beginning, understanding what was unfolding in real time and what potential it held. Though Stelios was accustomed to big challenges and even thrives on them, this was a hundred times more challenging than anything either of us had ever taken on. But we said to each other repeatedly, "We have no choice."

I enthusiastically shared Stelios's aim, which was to help a nation rebirth itself by regenerating a company. In a series of phone conferences, we thoroughly examined the forces at work. We organized our thinking around a systemic framework that enabled us to look in detail at the restraints we were facing, the highest purpose that we could imagine pursuing, and leverage points where we could create early success. Through this careful and deliberative process we built an inner strength, an inner gyroscope or compass, which anchored and balanced us when things got overwhelming.

In Europe, we had had the luxury of several months to prepare the Colgate leadership before bringing the operators into the process. The Europeans shared a common mind-set that all participants were more or less equal. South Africa, by contrast, was neck deep in apartheid. The white leadership believed that the black workforce was both ignorant and incorrigible. Many blacks were unable to read and write and were confined to the townships by travel restrictions. All the factories within a hundred-mile radius of the Colgate business site had experienced violent strikes. The country was close to the boiling point. We needed to change the cultural assumptions from day one.

I joined Stelios in Johannesburg two weeks after he arrived to become general manager for Colgate in southeastern Africa. The airport was overrun with very young uniformed men with AK-47s. Accidentally stepping out of line could land one in an interrogation room. After security my first image was of barbed wire and military vehicles. A limousine took me to a hotel with steel gates at the entrance and a thick perimeter wall crowned with broken glass. As I entered the hotel, I stepped into a four-star world of jacaranda trees and elegant service. The contrast between the luxury and prestige inside those gates and the angry chaos outside was shocking. I had a visceral experience of the effects of apartheid—there were places people could go and places they couldn't. For me, the contrast between freedom and constraint had never been starker.

Although Stelios had advised his mostly white leadership team of his intentions, the first meetings destabilized everyone involved. For the most part, the whites on the team had never been asked to regard black workers as intellectual peers in a strategic planning process. Many of these poor black workers were living without electricity or running water in townships that were little more than slums. The expectation that they were to step forward as equal participants must have felt both liberating and terrifying to them. Stelios completely disregarded all protocols regarding hierarchy and racial position. He never even mentioned them. Instead, he held a business meeting, a true business meeting. He included black line operators and other workers who had served as an informal and largely unrecognized leadership within the workforce. He made it clear that this was to be a collaborative effort, cross-functional, cross-ethnic, and cross-racial.

IN TIMES OF CRISIS, GREAT OPPORTUNITY

As he began that first business planning meeting, Stelios shared his personal aim of actively participating in rebirthing South

Africa. He reminded his team of the need to regenerate the company so that it could survive and prosper through a tumultuous and potentially violent time. In a context poisoned by apartheid, he stated his belief that every human being was intelligent and could contribute to this work of creating a new company and a new nation. He said he would accept nothing less than for every leader in that room to work from those aims and beliefs. His vision was more than ambitious, and they were clearly skeptical.

Stelios announced the immediate initiation of cross-functional and multilevel meetings that would redesign the business—from how it operated to how people were involved to how it engaged the stakeholders outside its walls. The opening session teams had been organized around various Colgate offerings, including toothpaste, laundry powder, and bath soap. We began by shifting how people thought about the business, moving them from a functional to a value-adding process perspective. We invited participants to bring the materials to life and to see the special contributions they could make to the people of South Africa. They did this in a joyfully African way, acting out the parts of minerals, animals, children, and mothers. Because they could so immediately internalize the living processes they intended to serve, they could quickly jump to the business and social opportunities that they had previously failed to recognize. In a matter of hours, they were able to generate a whole set of ideas for changing the business.

Those ideas were immediately tested for validity by the rest of the organization and enriched and made more concrete in the process. Then they were put into practice with management support but without management oversight, with each group doing its part of the work and reaching out as needed to resolve conflicts they could not address on their own. Within six weeks, almost every business improvement idea was either completed or significantly advanced and people were beginning to extend what they had learned into new arenas.

This amazed me. In my years consulting with businesses throughout the Americas, Asia, and Europe, I had never encountered anything like it. In the United States, for example, people generate more excuses than successes when they take on something new. The South Africans, however, had created more results in six weeks than most companies accomplish in a year. On my next visit, they complained loudly that they needed me to give them a lot more to work with. I must say that this has never happened to me anywhere outside of Africa, but it was a consistent pattern as we moved into Kenya, Zimbabwe, and Zambia. I think a combination of factors, including the hunger and aspiration held back for almost a century, and Mandela's promise to obliterate apartheid, awakened something rare and alchemical.

The extraordinary results of those first six weeks continued to evolve and spread. The initial cross-functional business teams began meeting every morning for half an hour with groups of workers. Their purpose was to transfer information and capability to others, bringing them into the creative process. The various business teams also continued to meet together weekly so that they could share and test ideas, moving them rapidly through the whole organization.

During the second trip we formed a core team drawn from the initial group, and they also continued to meet weekly. Core team members brought to the leadership of the company their understanding of what was going on in the various businesses and operating teams. They learned to provide more strategic thinking and to open channels into government and other stakeholder groups. One of their most important roles was to keep Colgate headquarters informed of the rapid progress being made in the business. This bought them the precious time and resources they needed to accomplish their collective aim.

During the following two years we continued to meet for a week every other month. The business teams continued to move major business and social initiatives forward in parallel. In every case they were improving their critical thinking skills and learning to take on bigger and bigger business system changes. This changed the atmosphere so significantly that the intertribal conflicts that had been festering within the company evaporated. Workers no longer threatened to walk off the job because of mistreatment by management. The perspective of top managers changed so radically that they became champions for building the capability of the black workforce and made rapid promotions that further raised spirit and improved the ability to deliver business results.

One Afrikaans manager had come to Colgate after running gold-mining operations, an industry where one in three black workers were dying or being injured as a result of core management practices. At the end of the third month he pulled me aside to say, "If you had asked me when we started about dismantling apartheid in this plant, I would have told you it was immoral. Now I believe that this is the most moral work I've ever done."

The powerful impact of this work was not confined to Colgate alone. Various teams reached out to other allied businesses to help them negotiate the difficulties of this unstable political climate. For example, one of the teams built a relationship with Consol, a bottle and packaging supplier. One of the largest companies in South Africa, Consol was being challenged by racial unrest. The Colgate team spent some time educating Consol's leadership about how to work more collaboratively. As a result, Consol was able to stem the tide of violence, ensure employment for hundreds of workers, and increase the safety of its workplaces. Similar to Colgate, these improvements spilled over into township councils, and Consol workers were tapped to help with community efforts.

Colgate's cross-functional teams built leadership and profound capability, creating the conditions for rapid promotion of black employees. In half the time required by government mandate, Colgate had achieved a mix in management that reflected the racial makeup of the nation, an accomplishment that most other companies believed was impossible. Colgate's success was often cited by South African leaders as proof that Mandela's vision and the conditions of the new constitution could be realized, and the company became a standard bearer for the transition to fully integrated democracy. It helped give the new constitution legitimacy and force. Other companies turned to Colgate for help with their own transitional processes.

When the company extended its work to other African countries, the South African teams provided support. In some cases team members who had never flown (or for that matter slept in a bed) served as mentors to business leaders thousand of kilometers from where they lived. They spent many hours on the phone answering questions and giving advice, mentoring people who wanted to play similar roles and take on similar challenges in their respective countries.

Needless to say, Colgate headquarters in New York was incredulous. They asked Stelios to come to New York to report. He took a couple of operators with him and let them tell the story themselves. Afterward Colgate's president told Stelios that he wished they had taped the story to show shareholders. And he said, "Not only has this effort ensured Colgate's presence in South Africa, but all the jobs and community benefits that flow from it. It provided good returns for investors, while simultaneously improving their image in the world" (personal communication).

PROUD TO SHARE THEIR NEW SMILES

With all the inherent drama of the Colgate, South Africa, story, it is easy to overlook one of its loveliest and most humane dimensions. The African people we worked with had a vibrant and celebratory storytelling culture. By inviting them to think of their work as a living process, it became accessible as a story for them. This tapped into a core aspect of their essence and unleashed powerful energies for change. The work of the toothpaste team gives a good illustration of this.

The team was asked to image diatomaceous earth, the cleaning agent in toothpaste, through all the transformations from mining to toothbrushing. We proposed they do this in the context of improving oral health for children. Because they could readily see Earth as a living being, they quickly grasped the concept. Through this one exercise, they were able to link customers, cocreators, raw materials, and communities. They told their story from the point of view of diatomaceous earth, immersing themselves in its experience as it changed and moved. Then they became the child and parent using the finished product. This brought meaning and life to what had been only abstractions—formulas, standards, and production goals. I cried as I listened to these storytellers bring to life a principle that I had tried to help people in so many other places around the world understand: *design from living process*. They did it spontaneously, without coaching or cajoling. In that moment I fell in love with a nation.

Their story clearly revealed to them a host of costly activities that added no value to the oral health of a child. They also became painfully aware of how little access children in the townships had to the means to improve their own oral health. By the end of the first day, they had reduced the cost of creating a finished product and freed up funds to take on projects to bring toothpaste into the townships.

On the second day, the experience of the toothpaste team was conveyed to the others, who immediately recognized the business and social opportunities. By that point, an observer would have been unable to distinguish contributors to the conversation based on level in hierarchy or ethnicity or tribe. They were all equally and fully engaged with the challenges Stelios had given them. In fact, during the reflections at the end of the day it became obvious that the participants had observed the same thing. In two days they had started to live from the belief that all were equally intelligent and able to contribute.

In order to concurrently stimulate interest in using Colgate products and improve oral health for children, one member of the toothpaste team, Isaac Mashile, worked on setting up a collaboration with the South African Dental Association to bring teeth-cleaning services into the townships. He and his co-workers began to tell the oral hygiene story to poor families in their neighborhoods. Together, they designed a system to measure the improvement of oral health in Alexandria and Soweto.

In an unexpected development, by the end of the first year every production worker considered himself a member of the R&D team in his township and a member of the sales force in his neighborhood. The toothpaste team realized that township residents simply couldn't afford to buy a tube of toothpaste all at once, so they organized small-lot sales that could never have been taken on by a traditional store. Selling toothpaste by the capful, they doubled the company's local sales in less than six months at a time when most white salespeople could not safely or practically make all of their sales calls.

This meant that for the first time, toothpaste was affordable for township residents. Families learned about the importance of and correct practices for oral hygiene and created a rapidly growing demand for Colgate products. As their educated use spread with the help of dentists and hygienists, the number of lost teeth, cavities, and gum disease dropped steadily. Children began to feel cared for and were proud to share their new smiles.

The Alexandria Township Council, one among township councils founded by Nelson Mandela to increase community stability, acknowledged Isaac and his business team for the contribution they made to township health and welfare. The team's greatest pride was in the difference they made with their neighbors, fellow tribesmen, and most especially, the children.

I think the most profound lesson I learned from this experience was to never underestimate the power of the human spirit. It's often in the most extreme, chaotic, and violent situations that the will and aliveness of people are most strongly present. When workers are empowered to engage creatively with the problems of their own communities, they are able to draw on a deep and invaluable well of experience and understanding. I believe it will be important to remember this as the world faces challenges of increasing scale, complexity, and urgency. I know for certain that inspired people can transform almost anything.

CONCLUSIONS

The biggest challenge for a company that aspires to be a Responsible Business is to stop working on parts and start recognizing and working on whole systems. Red Hat could see that its customers were its co-creators, its community, and its investors. It wasn't trapped by traditional categories. Colgate, South Africa, knew that its co-creators lived in its communities and that these communities were an important emerging source of customers. So fared the community, so fared the business and its workers. Developing the potential of workers was the best way to help both business and communities to thrive.

Any company that begins to understand how stakeholders work as a system will certainly increase its efficiencies and simplify its priorities. But when a business fully accepts

(Continued)

its responsibilities to its stakeholders, investors will gain. Businesses that fail to live up to their responsibilities cause decay, decline, and diminishment of returns for every stakeholder in the system. Responsibility is a no-brainer, though it takes brains to pull it off.

 Free download: If you would like to remind yourself and engage others with ideas, aphorisms, and sayings in this chapter, go to the free downloads section at www.The-Responsible-Business.com.

PART TWO

MAKING IT WORK: THE MAP TO THE TERRITORY

The pentad is a framework that enables a business to make decisions in a complete, systemic, and disciplined way. It provides a common language for a deeper dialogue within the business and among its stakeholders. It offers an intelligible and inspiring path for people entering businesses to develop their own thinking discipline. Decision making changes radically when the stakeholder pentad becomes an integrated part of operations and a business becomes more jazz ensemble—improvising around a guiding structure and strategy—than marching band.

The chapters in Part Two introduce characteristics and ways of working that enable a business to use the pentad effectively. Chapter Six describes four phases in the evolution of an existing company into the Responsible Business as it transforms its culture and strategic processes, builds capability in co-creators, educates its investors, and redesigns its work systems. For the start-up of a new business, the process works by reversing the phases.

Chapter Seven focuses on the development of nonhierarchical decision making and four self-organizing capabilities essential for responsibility, including living-systems thinking, pattern generation, internal locus of control and external considering, and intrinsic motivation. A commitment to developing these capabilities is essential to the Responsible Business.

CHAPTER SIX

TEACHING AN ORGANIZATION TO STAR

All that is valuable in human society depends upon the opportunity for development accorded the individual.
ALBERT EINSTEIN

When I first told the stories in this book to Rebecca Henderson, the John Heinz Professor of Environmental Management at Harvard Business School, she said, "You're describing the businesses of the future!" I expect that she'll turn out to be right and that within a few decades Responsible Businesses will be the norm. Already some high-profile companies have discovered how to bring dimensions of what's described here into their ways of working, often as the result of a strongly held principle on the part of the founder. Google has rocked the world by creating a culture in which engineers have real freedom and dedicated time to innovate. W. L. Gore, of Gore-Tex fame, has been widely studied for its self-organizing work design (although I suspect it does not fully understand what it has and why it works). Software developer SAS was recently named the "best company to work for in America," primarily because it offers generous benefits and has created a culture based on trust. Still, these examples are notable mostly for their rarity and the fact that they were unconventional from the beginning. There is plenty of fun, challenging, and very rewarding work to be done retrofitting the world's existing businesses (not to mention its next generation of start-ups) into Responsible Businesses.

To operate as a Responsible Business and to work with stakeholders in the way the pentad framework reflects, a company must face up to the limitations presented by its current culture, approaches to markets, strategic planning, workforce capability, and the way work is designed and carried out altogether. A value-adding perspective of stakeholders suggests a shift in many of the foundations of a business. But the good news is that others have made this shift successfully and their examples provide great maps for how they got to where they are. Although they will be approached differently in every business, the following four phases provide a path to follow.

RETROFIT AN EXISTING BUSINESS

Often companies that are recognized for their innovation are founded with an approach that is based on their founders' visions. Google, Apple, Facebook, W. L. Gore, and others we have looked in this book are all fairly young companies with founders who put their style into the company. As we admire them, it is important to remember that we are talking about changing a company, not setting one up. The approach must be very different. Understanding the difference will make it possible to create a truly innovative and responsible company even if it did not start out that way. Once this concept is absorbed, it becomes easier to see how any company can be extraordinary in many of the same ways that our exemplar companies are without losing the essence of what makes them unique.

The process for transforming an existing company to working with stakeholders in a value-adding system begins with transforming its culture. From there it becomes possible to set a new strategic direction, develop capability to deliver strategy, and redesign how work is organized and conducted. The problem with so many corporate responsibility programs is that they try to do the last step—reorganizing work—without the first three, a bit like changing the ingredients in the cake after it is baked. What follows is a thorough description of a four-phase process for growing a Responsible Business. (The process for creating a start-up company looks a little different. More on that at the end of the chapter.)

This process works and it has worked in many different types and sizes of companies in many different nations and cultures over many decades. That doesn't mean it's easy. The key for an executive who wishes to lead this kind of change effort is to remember that it is fundamentally developmental—it builds capacity of people and teams. It requires reflection and a willingness to adapt. It requires transparency about shortfalls and successes so that everyone can learn together. And it requires iterative work. When I use the word *phases,* I mean something like phases of the moon. Waxing always comes before full, which is always followed by waning, and the cycle repeats again and again. Opportunities to improve and grow don't end just because a company has gone through the cycle once. A Responsible Business keeps on learning and evolving forever.

Phase One: Cultural Evolution

To begin, an organization must undertake a deep reflection on its culture, ideally going all the way back to its founding. This reflection is divided into four lines of inquiry.

Status

All organizations convey status through a variety of actions and structures, marking in ways that are subtle or overt who is the top dog and who's on the bottom. Status can be indicated through elaborate reward and recognition programs (the semi-mythical corner office and key to the executive restroom). Or it can be signaled by who's notified first of important happenings, who's invited to particular kinds of meetings, and whose ideas are advanced. The questions, "How do we convey status and how does that limit or advance us? What does it produce?" should be explored in a neutral way, without making anyone or any practice right or wrong. This can become a rich source of insight about which activities and behaviors need to change.

At Colgate, South Africa, whites were managers and blacks were not, with very few exceptions. At the Kingsford company, having a PhD meant you were intelligent enough to redesign formulas, while having a fourth- to fifth-grade education meant you took orders from someone else. It was apparent to Stelios

Tsezos from the beginning that this had to change immediately if he was to have any hope of improving things at Colgate. And Will Lynn said he felt a huge sense of loss when he saw how much potential the company was losing because of these unexamined cultural assumptions. Both of them experienced a strong inner drive to dislodge these status indicators as quickly as possible.

Symbol

Symbols are used in all cultures to evoke loyalty, belonging, and spirit. The questions a company needs to ask are, "What is repeatedly held up to evoke an emotional response to a corporate ideal? What effect does that repeated evocation actually produce?" Modern culture is so awash in symbols designed to manipulate the emotions that people have become skeptical and even cynical about corporate symbolism. Given how important a symbol is to creating a sense of unified purpose, it is critical that all the symbols a company uses be authentic and meaningful. This is one of the worst possible places to rely on auto-pilot.

Prior to Stelios's arrival, Colgate, South Africa, made job security a central symbol and constantly reminded people how lucky they were to be employed. This was intended to promote showing up on time and working hard. When Stelios substituted the idea of birthing a new South Africa for the much less potent one of personal security, it resonated across the company and beyond, becoming a rallying cry that unified the workforce. In DuPont, where the founders' vision included safety for all, the constant refrain of "How safe was our work today (or overnight)?" was used to evoke pride and connection to the company's traditions and make conscious everyone's shared responsibilities to the world and to one another.

Ritual

Next, a company asks itself, "What do we do over and over (probably unconsciously) to try to maintain form and uniformity? How do we need to transform our rituals so that they help people become independently creative in pursuing the path we are on?" Two forms of ritual show up very commonly in modern companies. In the first, meetings are structured with agendas that systematically exclude creativity. In the second, motivational sessions—such as "all hands" meetings that all employees are expected to attend—use media presentations and inspiring speeches to create a bubble of energy. Herban Feast transformed its rituals with regard to preparing for an event. At one time salespeople handed off a form with the requirements specified. Now the hand-off has become a storytelling ritual, with a salesperson bringing to life for the staff the aspiration of the client. This enables the people responsible for execution to bring their own creative ideas to the story.

Taboo

The fourth line of inquiry concerns taboos. "What taboos do we currently have that limit change and creativity? What taboos need to be put in place to unleash change and creativity?" Every culture has taboos, which are usually a way to avoid repeating a negative event from the past. Business taboos can grow up around a significant market failure, a disappointing or alienating human resource program, or certain kinds of damaging behavior, such as avoiding risks and creating excuses ("We tried that and it didn't work").

When taboos become unconscious they can be counterproductive, even toxic, especially if they limit rigorous examination and discovery (for example, a taboo against questioning supervisors' decisions). However, some things need to be taboo, such as advancing an idea without rigorously examining it. The strategy team at Seventh Generation eventually made it taboo for Jeffrey to bring them an idea without having first validated it with regard to their aligned corporate direction. This was particularly difficult because Jeffrey tended to have very good, appealing ideas in terms of business and corporate responsibility. But because they didn't all fall within the direction the team had developed for the company, establishing this taboo early on was necessary for the intentional and well-ordered evolution of the corporate culture.

Having engaged in these four lines of inquiry to generate insight, a company needs to ask itself, "Which of these discoveries must we act on as we begin? Which can we work on over time because we don't believe they pose an immediate threat to our progress?" It can then begin to focus on specifics by asking, "What particular new ideas do we have for conferring status? How do we either change our symbols or bring meaning back into the traditional ones? How can we revise or eliminate rituals that have become routine and institute rituals that bring new spirit to people and to the business? How do we eradicate inappropriate and outworn taboos and articulate healthy new ones?" Companies only need to make this kind of inquiry pervasive to see significant reductions in inertia and friction. Core teams often take on long-term responsibility for this intentional evolution of business culture.

Dick Stewart, site manager at DuPont's Chambers Works site, described two profound effects this work had on his organization. Cultural patterns had been wielded as political weapons and could no longer escape scrutiny. For example, in the past a senior scientist or manager could advance an idea knowing that it wouldn't be challenged for its environmental effects. This was because there was a taboo against revealing environmental concerns that, if leaked to the media, could affect stock prices. Dick and his team were appalled when this pattern came to light— it was so very self-defeating. They immediately put in place a new process for rigorously examining ideas with regard to their effect on all stakeholders, including the environment. This set the stage for the revolutionary work they were able to do on refrigerants.

Dick's team also observed that members of the organization had tended to be excluded because of questions of status and taboo. As this began to shift, people who had held back because of perceived lower status began to participate fully. Their input helped solve customer relations problems that were decades old. "We tried that and it didn't work" was no longer tolerated as an excuse to avoid change. Eventually, the Chambers Works leadership team adopted a ritual of periodic reflection on company culture that set the stage for them to move into the second phase of work.

PHASE TWO: STRATEGIC DIRECTION

During this phase, a company directs the energy it has unleashed in phase one toward setting a systemic and compelling strategic direction. To be effective, this work requires an authentic shift in corporate culture. For example, Stelios realized almost immediately that Colgate, South Africa's, culture had a strong taboo against including black workers in planning and decision making. In the very first meeting he broke that taboo by inviting a diversity of workers—black and white, multiple tribes and ethnicities. By connecting them together, he drove the lesson home during the entire week of meetings. In the new culture it became taboo to engage in any strategic thinking and decision making without reflecting on the perspectives of all constituencies in the business. Had Stelios not made this bold move, the systemic strategic planning process might never have gotten off the ground.

There are three dimensions to setting direction strategically. First, one must understand how the company's markets work to produce success, especially with regard to targeted customers. This includes understanding the effects of global and supply dynamics on the business. Second, one must consider what is unique about the business and how this uniqueness can be employed to create a nondisplaceable position in the market. This includes thinking about what nature of tangible and intangible differentiation the business aspires to offer. Third, one must determine what managing philosophy the business will use with regard to governance and engaging its people to enable them to work effectively with one another.

Connect to the Lives of Customers

The stories about Herban Feast, Colgate, and Red Hat illustrate how connecting people to the lives of their customers can bring a whole new order of meaning to their work. In general, the key is to shift the point of view from one's own vantage point to the homes, warehouses, and offices of customers. This goes beyond data and reports; everyone in the business needs to develop the capacity to imagine the lives of those they aim to serve. This clarifies and vivifies the values, purposes, and philosophies that drive customer aspirations. Besides helping companies create better product offerings, this work focuses market strategy.

As the team at Seventh Generation mentally walked through the homes of their customers, they could see four or five distinct clusters of buyers based on sets of shared values and motivations. Market research, which is generally based on demographic differences, had never enabled them to distinguish among these value-driven buyer classes.

The insights they generated about customers became central to their planning. For example, they could see that new parents are extraordinarily protective toward their babies and they choose products that support a healthy baby, not just soap for washing diapers. The intensity and focus they bring to their decisions are completely different from those of a customer who is seeking to protect the environment. Different motivations and purposes generate different screens and filters. Yet Seventh Generation found that it could create product characteristics at the boundary between the two, making it possible to serve both customer classes—and other customers as well—at the places where their values overlapped. It had also become possible to relate personally to these customer groups, which evoked caring and matched the emerging culture at Seventh Generation. Customers were understood precisely and vividly and everyone in the organization could apply the understanding to his or her own work. As a result, work became increasingly meaningful.

Reveal Essence to Ensure Nondisplaceability

The second dimension—understanding a company's uniqueness—introduces excitement and focus. Far too much strategic thinking starts with competitive analysis or environmental scans, which can only provide information about what exists in the world. The true genius of business is to discover what hasn't been done, what wants to be brought into existence. When a company really knows itself, it can provide distinctive or differentiated offerings in undiscovered arenas. It can't be copied because nobody else has the same essence and nature.

Sometimes a company will live its essence in some domains and not in others. BJ lived out his passion for authenticity in his personal life and his engagement with clients but it didn't always show up in Herban Feast's events. Making authenticity an explicit and essence-based focus channeled the energies that were being created through the company's shift in culture. Authenticity became a reference point for decisions about buying, hiring, menu planning, and repurposing the building that became their new home.

Articulate Management Philosophy

Management philosophy requires that an organization come to grips with its beliefs about people, their management, and development. A company's philosophical stance with regard to people plays a significant role in defining who it is. In their book *The Future of Management,* Gary Hamel and Bill Breen state that management philosophy is the best predictor of an organization's long-term viability and status.[1] It is interesting to note that by examining their own cultures, the companies whose stories I have shared became aware of the social and business imperatives for shifting to a more organic, self-organizing team approach, one that encouraged individual initiative ungoverned by organizational hierarchy.

Company leadership must first lay out its beliefs about people and their roles in business. It must go beyond platitudes such as "People are our most important asset," the kind of phony symbol that elicits groans from employees, and ask some really hard questions. When Stelios told his management team, "I believe every individual has a significant and meaningful contribution to make and an intelligence that can be engaged and developed," he redefined for them the beliefs that would guide their operations. Ordinarily, an organization would create dialogue rather than a dictum around such a redefinition, but the culture was so toxic in South Africa that Stelios had to make its acceptance a non-negotiable condition. Only after six months of living with this new belief could the team engage in reflection and dialogue about it.

Once an organization is aligned around its beliefs, it needs to establish new principles to guide its management of people. These, too, require dialogue as well as a ritual for periodic reflection on how well the organization is living up to its principles and how they should be improved. Colgate, South Africa, adopted the principles, "Each person will be developed to the full potential that he or she sees possible," and "Level of contribution will not be limited by role or position." These were such new ideas that the teams reflected on them daily as a way to raise the level of consciousness. This not only allowed but also encouraged them to work outside their job descriptions to contribute to the new direction.

Although I have described these dimensions sequentially in order to distinguish them, work on them generally occurs simultaneously. In other words, defining strategic direction requires looking at the relationships between what a business wishes to become relative to its newly understood market and how it will evolve its managing processes in order to play that new role.

PHASE THREE: CAPABILITY BUILDING

I get a lot of questions about the management transformation this process seems to require:

- Is it even possible for people to step up to this level or nature of business?
- What do you do with people who don't care?
- What about the overly ambitious ones, those who need to stand out above others?
- How can I risk allowing a person with no sales or marketing background to define a customer relationship?
- Because it's not possible to understand a business from the bottom in the way you can from the top, how can you ever let go of the hierarchy?

I answer all of these questions the same way: the issues being raised have nothing to do with structure, intelligence, or motivation; they have to do with capability. For this reason, the most exciting and rewarding part of this work has always come to full fruition in phase three, which centers on capability development throughout the organization.

Capability development is not training. Training is "cold storage"—it's intended to be used at some point in the future, it has no direct bearing on decision making, and it gets plugged in as schedules allow. By contrast, capability building is always accomplished in the context of real and necessary work, by existing teams or by cross-functional teams that have been formed to develop new thinking in critical arenas. It generates capabilities needed for a strategically defined future state. Research indicates that learning through doing meaningful work is faster, more lasting, and more to the point for both the learner and the business.

A Responsible Business uses regular and ongoing meetings that combine both business and education to build three types of capability: business acumen, technological competence, and critical systemic thinking skills in conjunction with personal development. The work focus can include any number of business endeavors, including projects, strategic thinking, new product offerings or businesses, and market development. As new capabilities develop, they are put to work in service to these endeavors.

Business Acumen

When people develop business acumen, they begin to think like owners, and people who think like owners make better decisions than people who think like job descriptions. They learn to understand financial effectiveness, that is, how their actions affect earnings, margins, and cash flow, and they learn to build business plans for their expenditure requests. Working through cross-functional and multilevel meetings, they come to understand the systemic complexities of serving all their stakeholders. Development of business acumen enables an organization's members to understand and address increasingly complex and sophisticated issues, such as market dynamics, competitive effectiveness, and business acquisition and divestiture.

At both Kingsford and Colgate, capability development was driven by promises-beyond-ableness. People designed their own performance plans and evaluations based on their contributions to earnings, margins, and cash flow in the lines of business they targeted. This meant that every individual had to develop some level of mastery over what had hitherto been an obscure aspect of accounting. For example, they learned that cash flow relates to the qualitative characteristics that a customer expects, for example, the steadiness of burn on a charcoal briquette. If they were working on improving those qualitative characteristics, they should be able to measure their effects in terms of cash flow within a specific period of time. Although most people believed that improving a product was an inherently good thing, they came to understand that it also meant the creation of a sustaining source of revenue.

Technological Competence

Developing technological capability is another rich and nearly limitless source of improvement for a company. Technology is the translation of science into practical application. For example, operators who move beyond carrying out procedures to engaging the science that informs the work they do can become inventors, and salespeople who understand sociology and psychology can go from counting volume or revenues to coaching their customers on how to improve their own businesses.

At Kingsford, a pair of operators led the charcoal reformulation effort—a promise beyond their current ableness. At DuPont, the airbag sales group learned the foundations of electrical engineering so they could better integrate with auto manufacturers. DuPont's peroxide marketing team became expert in forestry as part of their initiative to help paper manufacturers improve the quality of their products, and in the process they made both forestry and paper bleaching more sustainable. In South Africa, Colgate workers became so expert at understanding the biochemical role of all the materials in toothpaste that they became powerful spokespeople for oral health in their communities.

In these examples, individuals and teams saw for themselves the clear business need for the technological capabilities they pursued. They weren't following assignments or trying to get themselves promoted; they were looking for ways to serve their customers better. In many cases, one or more people went on to pursue degrees in the fields that they had become interested in through their work on developing technological capability.

Critical Systemic Thinking

Development of critical systemic thinking and the personal development that goes with it is so important that Chapter Seven is dedicated entirely to the subject. Business and technological capability are incomplete without the ability to recognize and develop the relationship between quality of thinking and quality of result. When people develop a systemic understanding of dynamic and complex phenomena, and when they learn to manage their own state with regard to those phenomena, then excellent decision making becomes not only possible but also almost inevitable.

PHASE FOUR: WORK REDESIGN

Most businesses start change processes by trying to change the way they design and govern their work, usually by reorganizing or altering procedures. That's why so many change processes fail; they view change as a strictly functional phenomenon. The extraordinary energies delivered by a process that includes personal growth, opportunity and motivation to contribute, and a drive to be part of something that makes a difference go beyond the purely functional aspects of work. Without them, it is very difficult to overcome organizational inertia, much less evoke creativity and will to change.

Work redesign brings an organization's governing processes into alignment with its cultural aspirations, corporate direction, and developing capabilities. It can take years to accomplish, and it addresses three key aspects of organizational governance: structures, systems, and processes.

Structures

Structures create patterns in how an organization functions. They're intended to align behavior by design but they also tend to "fix" patterns, which makes them rigid and inflexible. For example, the authority a particular department has over certain kinds of decisions can become entrenched. Job titles and job descriptions are examples of structures, as are procedures that lay out precisely how certain tasks are to be done. Pay and progression structures guide patterns of performance and are usually linked to seniority and annual reviews. Taken together, these structures define acceptable ways of working, particularly with regard to decision making and allocation of resources.

Systems

Systems tend to be developed for recurring or complex tasks that need to be aligned across an organization. Personnel systems are designed to manage performance of people. Planning systems, such as those developed around budgeting, maintain direction and clarify evaluation processes. Managing systems allow teams to deploy resources consistent with a unified aim. All of these systems are intended to help an organization follow a similar path every time it carries out a complex task and avoid variances in approach and outcome.

Processes

Processes are specific to a situation, time, and place and cannot be systematized or proceduralized. For example, mentoring new employees will be most effective when it is specific to the capabilities and temperament of mentor and protégé. Questions asked in a hiring interview will depend on how the conversation unfolds, although an interviewer may hold a structure in mind to be sure that essential topics are covered. A sales call may be guided by principles, but the conversation with each customer will be distinctive and relevant to the relationship. Process requires presence. People have to identify and create the right thing to say and do in each event. Processes are often confused with procedures, which are actually a form of structure, because they define an unchanging expectation about behavior.

I have described structures, systems, and processes in the sequence that makes them easiest to distinguish and understand. However, when using them to retrofit an existing organization, one works in the opposite direction, beginning with processes then moving to systems and then to structures. This overcomes the common resistance to change and allows the organization's members to build their own rationale for why the retrofit is necessary and make informed contributions to how best to accomplish it.

Many approaches suggest finding significant players from across the organization to serve as champions for a change effort. Unfortunately, these leaders are almost always asked to implement changes in system and structure design without any significant change in processes. For example, involvement, quality, and reengineering programs are introduced as procedures to be followed, usually coupled with some systems redesign to create uniformity in application. But without a fundamental change in day-to-day processes of human interaction and thinking, people either work around the new procedures, call what they're currently doing by the new program's language, or change their actions without much change in heart.

Usually when a program attempts to institute new processes, it will fail to engage in systems and structure redesign. Two cases in point are 360-degree feedback, which aims to make people more reflective, and Steven Covey's method, which engages organizations in managing from principles. Other programs emphasize emotional intelligence or building trust. All of these approaches understand how important process is to performance and culture, but they cannot stand alone. To have any staying power, a shift in process must not only become ubiquitous, it must also be sustained for at least three to five years, backed up by redesign of systems and structures.

Failure to integrate all three phases—systems, structures, and processes—accounts for the prevalence of "programs-of-the-month." Companies trying to find ways to change often pursue one incomplete program after another with predictably unsatisfying results.

In Responsible Businesses, processes are systemic in nature; they take into account what goes on both inside and outside of people and they overtly disrupt mechanical thinking. Disruption shakes people out of their comfort zone and is an effective motivator. It should be neither erratic nor random but tied to specific work practices that are relevant to business direction. For example, one can shake people up by using appropriate reflective processes to challenge current assumptions and ways of behaving.

A systemic process comes from using regenerative and systemic frameworks rather than depending on mechanical procedures such as agendas. For example, designing all meetings around a customer-centric or strategic purpose connects the mind to systems beyond the one represented by the people in the room. At Kingsford this idea of connecting to the purpose of markets and customers became so pervasive in all meetings that leaders who later went on to work for other companies took it with them. For example, at Hunt Wesson, where many Kingsford managers moved, the first question at meetings is, "What do we know about our customers that we didn't know before?" When operational changes are under consideration, they ask, "How will this affect our customers and distribution to them?"

When intentional thinking processes rather than procedures are ubiquitous and practiced without coercion and with discipline, they will make an organization more flexible, relevant, and creative. Eventually, it becomes obvious to everyone that some old systems are impeding movement in new creative directions that matter to everyone. Thus the demand for change will be generated from within the organization rather than imposed by an outside executive or program. As the Responsible Business engages in system redesign, it demands that upgrades, improvements, and evolution occur every time a system is engaged or used.

At P&G, Lima, technicians qualified in maintenance crafts became the best in the world at improving machines and the fastest in the world at changing out a machine. Their speed and determination came about because they sought to find ways to improve a machine's operations and longevity every time they maintained it. They met routinely to evolve their electronic, mechanical, and human systems and any procedures within them. Even as a machine was being maintained, they upgraded it and the systems supporting it. Systems were the means to ensure that something got better every time it was used, as long as the teams took time to reflect as they worked. A process like P&G's prevents systems from becoming so routine that they put people to sleep.

Julie Atwood, executive vice president of Finance and Administration at Seventh Generation, led a fundamental change in the company's budgeting system. She wanted everyone in the organization, including her accountants, to see the systemic significance of what appeared to be "just numbers" on a spreadsheet. She made budgeting more interactive with dialogue around strategic options to make resource allocation living and systemically rationalized work. She invited people from all departments to talk with one another in order to understand and support trade-offs that benefited the business as a whole. She insisted that for every number they proposed people needed to reflect on the effect on customers.

At different stages in different companies, changes in processes and systems will make it obvious that some existing structures are no longer useful. Once they become inconsistent with new and superior processes, obsolescent structures will be ignored or lose their rigidity and become soft guidelines. People will demand more relevant, meaningful, and effective structures that reflect how they are actually working. Failure to evolve these structures will erode the authority and integrity of a business.

Structuring is the last stage of work redesign because it is often the hardest change for existing leadership to make. Starting with redesign of processes and systems softens the impact by demonstrating that change isn't going to destroy the business and pointing to the evolved role that leaders can play. It enables leaders to detach from a feudal or hierarchical model, which may have seemed to be the only plausible option for people who have climbed their way to the top. Once the rewards become self-evident, so does the need for structural change.

Most organizations are structured to assign tasks and make sure they get done. Responsible Businesses redesign structure to inspire individual initiative, innovation, and improvement. In most evolving organizations, almost every aspect of decision making and evaluation will shift from current practices. Herban Feast originally structured work around the delegation of tasks by supervisors. Now teams build shared understandings of their customers' stories, which allows them to structure their own work with the aim of expressing those stories through memorable events. Delegation by supervisors meant that people followed the rules. Herban Feast's new approach inspires everyone to design *live* and in the moment, improvising and solving problems as they appear.

Redesigned structures start to show up in a variety of forms. Self-organizing teams make decisions guided by intended effects rather than supervisors. Individuals become champions for strategies or customers to whom they previously had no connection and build teams around the new work. Workers, including nonemployee contributors around the world, become co-creators organized around buyer groups rather than departments and roles. Cross-functional, multilevel core teams take on decision making that was previously the province of top management. Pretty much all of what is thought of as traditional organizational structure evaporates, replaced by something more like Duke Ellington's orchestra. Everyone in the business is simultaneously composer, improviser, soloist, and collaborator.

REVERSE PHASES FOR A START-UP RESPONSIBLE BUSINESS

Start-ups work through this same four-phase process but in the opposite direction. Phase one for a start-up begins with designing ways to hire, pay, and assign roles to people. Developing co-creator capabilities becomes the focus, especially the unique capabilities required for this particular business. As the company grows and more people are brought in, new business opportunities will call for setting strategic direction. Finally, a culture will emerge from the way the other phases have unfolded.

Consolidated Diesel Corporation (CDC), founded in 1979 to produce small engines for lawn mowers, motorcycles, and some farm and construction machinery, is a particularly good example of working the process from the point of start-up. Because it was a joint venture between Cummins and Case Engines, it had the freedom to break all the traditional rules for starting a business. Its founders began with a clean slate and involved everyone available in both parent companies to help think the business through. I was part of a business design team that included my colleague Ken Wessel, who had played a key role in the P&G start-ups in Lima and Ivorydale. We worked with Ron Gratz, CDC general manager, as the business was being formed.

We started with structuring—finding a site and laying out the architecture of the building and production process. We wanted to connect everyone in the operation to two key streams: the actual production and the users of the products. Beginning with the original design, administrative offices were placed so that they would look down into the production lines, and every nonproduction person was a member of a production team. In addition, everyone in the organization was to be connected directly to one of the outside businesses that would be integrating CDC engines into their products or to one of the distributors that would be selling CDC's finished products. Structural decisions were guided by a principle—*no one is isolated; everyone is a strategic contributor*—which showed up in both the design of the physical plant and the working relationships across teams. There were no supervisors, only team leaders who were rotated as the teams decided it made sense.

CDC saw itself as part of a continuous flow that began with nuts and bolts purchased from upstream co-creators and extended all the way to tractors and construction equipment as they were put to use plowing fields and building roads. This view of the value-adding stream structured how teams were organized and the way facilities were built. Because of it, CDC set out to structure co-creator relationships with suppliers, recruiting and supporting them to construct key component facilities adjacent to its own site.

Next, CDC designed systems to be consistent with its operations. Whereas budgeting systems are usually departmentally based, CDC's were customer-strategy based. The team that developed the budget was intimately familiar with customer strategy and budgeted accordingly. Members of the budget team participated at the core-team level to ensure that the budget enabled fulfillment of obligations to customers. Teams responsible for planning, control, and evaluation were engaged in the same way.

The company also committed to developing, engaging, and honoring the uniqueness of individuals as a source of creativity in the design and execution of systems. CDC's systems allowed individuals to define unique and distinctive roles and evaluation processes, connected to and consistent with the principles of the organization.

The third step in CDC's work design was to establish principles that would ensure that its core processes were developmental. For example, when hiring, the company interviewed applicants in groups of three or four, who then were asked to collaborate on the development and execution of a part of the interview process. They were each asked to ensure that the design included something that represented each of them and to figure out together how to incorporate that into the interview. The majority of these applicants came from farms and rural areas where many of them had been owners of family operations (one of the reasons CDC had selected this site). They were used to collaborating and exercising initiative. Although the interview process was a bit intimidating, it revealed highly creative individuals who were skilled cooperators and innovators.

Once structures, systems, and processes were designed, it became clear what capabilities would be needed to execute CDC's work. The first workers who were hired became core to the creation of capability building processes. Not only was the program designed to support their own development but they also went on to serve as resources for the hirees who followed.

Our focus at this stage became one of building internal resources needed in a nonhierarchical organization, where systems were constantly being upgraded and everyone was engaged in developmental work. Although some strategic work had been completed before the business was launched, ongoing strategy became the responsibility of the core team and many of the customer field teams. In the course of several start-up years, a culture evolved: status was assigned, symbols were developed, and supportive rituals and taboos were adopted.

The start-up philosophy practiced at CDC led to a launch that was below budget and ahead of time. The company met its return on investment targets in one-third of the time projected. And it developed an enduring culture that has sustained itself in up-and-down markets and changing technology in the machine industry. For these reasons, *Fast Company* magazine featured it as a stellar, high-performance business.[2]

CONCLUSIONS

I believe that the most fundamental change needed for the emergence of Responsible Businesses is the evolution of nonhierarchical organizations, what authors Ori Brafman and Rod A. Beckstrom call *leaderless corporations*.[3]

In their book *The Starfish and the Spider,* Brafman and Beckstrom use a compelling story to illustrate this theme. While so many other tribes were being defeated, the Apache successfully outmaneuvered European invaders for decades. The key to their success was a decentralized organizational structure, one where no single person made decisions for all the others, and that allowed new leadership to emerge effortlessly. The leadership, called *Nant'un,* was vested in people who carried the tribe's spiritual and cultural traditions, people who set an example rather than exercising coercive power. New Nant'un could and did arise as needed, when one was lost or bands were scattered.

The starfish of the book's title represents a creature that is resilient in the face of attack. A starfish can regrow an arm after it has been cut off, while a spider has a centralized design and no fallback position. Like a starfish, a business will be more resilient in the face of competition and environmental challenges when a self-organizing design enables it to reform itself as needed. At W. L. Gore, for example, intelligence is spread throughout the system and members are flexible enough to step in to replace one another—always getting the job done in their own ways based on their unique capacities and capabilities. In the Responsible Business, every person is a businessperson working without regard to isolated functions or department boundaries. Each carries responsibility for the success of the whole and is not limited by narrow consideration for team or department goals.

Starfish mutate readily and have a strong influence on their environments. Starfish companies such as Google, Facebook, Amazon, or Apple have restructured entire industries as a result of their ability to predict and evolve markets. They have caused these industries to recalibrate their business models and performance indexes. All of them operated more or less according to the principles I have described here, although sometimes with significant variations that hamper them on occasion. When they don't make the principles explicit, they are hindered in efforts to extend them fully and act with consciousness.

Free download: A one-page graphic of the four phases of the business redesign process can be found in the free downloads section at www.The-Responsible-Business .com.

CHAPTER SEVEN

NONHIERARCHICAL DECISION MAKING

In mature natural systems there are no authoritarian governments. What species is in charge in a rainforest? What part is in charge of your body? Imagine doing world politics in our bodies. Imagine the brain deciding not to allocate resources to certain organs, but keeping them to itself. You can't have some organs exploiting the others. You would die.
ELIZABET SAHTOURIS, BIOLOGIST

HIERARCHICAL MANAGEMENT IS IRRESPONSIBLE

Pravin Jain has been involved with several companies with distinctive products and business models. He is currently the founder and CEO of Synergen, a high-tech solar technology innovator. Recently he reflected with me on how much his thinking has changed in the more than thirty years that we have worked together. Pravin grew up in India, then moved to the United States to study engineering at Oregon State University. After graduating at the top of his class, he went straight into Tektronix, Inc., where his gifts as an engineer and designer earned him rapid promotion. He was managing a large team of engineers when the team who built the detergent business at P&G, Lima, brought the developmental approach described in this book into Tektronix.

Pravin was surprised (annoyed, actually, is the word he used) by our insistence that he reflect on how he was thinking about what he was thinking about. But the lesson stuck, and for the next thirty years he worked to improve the quality of his thinking and self-management as a leader and family man.

Since he worked with us at Tektronix, Pravin has taken on leadership roles in a number of companies. At one point, he agreed to manage a new business called Greeting Seeds. Stepping outside of his professional engineering world into the role of general manager required flexibility and creativity. For the first time, he was dependent on a cross-functional team to ensure success.

One day he found himself confronted by questions from a young woman who was part of the team. He wondered if what she was asking about was any of her business, given her role in the company. He caught himself and started to laugh. He had been thinking about people as though they were their job titles. He confessed this to the young woman, promptly answered her question, and invited her to explain what made her interested in issues outside of her job description.

This dialogue generated a suggestion that the entire team adopted, a new distribution approach that launched the company's success. Later, Pravin told me that the experience taught him that there was a caste system in his mind, and if he didn't watch it, his mind would always operate from that point of view.

Some years later, Pravin founded a company that was eventually purchased by Enron. He agreed to work for Enron during the year of transition on the condition that they give him a challenging assignment. He was made responsible for Enron's South American telecommunications business, and he reported to Jeffrey Skilling, the now infamous former head of Enron Energy. He was in an elevator with Skilling on the day that he resigned from Enron, just a few weeks before the company's total collapse. Skilling's last words to him were, "Pravin, I think the most important thing I learned from you was to think about my thinking. How should I be thinking right now?"

They never got a chance to discuss that question. As the elevator door opened and a crowd of reporters pressed forward, Pravin had a useful insight: Enron had been brought down by its inability to think about its own thinking and the effect it had on the world around it. He silently reminded himself how grateful he was to have built that capability in his own life.

Currently, Pravin finds himself again in the role of entrepreneur. In a recent interaction with his venture capitalist, he found himself angered by what he perceived to be unnecessary anxiety and suggestions as to how he should change his management team. He drew on his years of experience observing his thinking and asked himself how to shift it to gain a new perspective. He decided that the best way to get that perspective was to put himself in the other guy's shoes. He could see that his venture capitalist was understandably influenced by market conditions in the solar industry, disruptions in the world of venture capital, and a personal sense of responsibility to those who had invested in the fund.

Stepping back to reflect enabled Pravin to appreciate the man and his situation. Pravin began to talk about ways to see the current situation as an opportunity for this investor to achieve personal and organizational goals and to build capability in engaging other investors. Pravin told me that his shift into caring mode was personally exhilarating. He identified with this man as a human being with struggles of his own in life and business. The agreements that came out of that conversation were different from what either of them went in expecting. Both reported that they felt a real shift somewhere in their conversation and knew that they had come to a better plan about how to manage the company than either had thought possible.

SELF-ORGANIZING DECISION MAKING IS RESPONSIBLE

Because a Responsible Business is an open, living system, it evolves toward a condition in which self-organizing people and teams work in highly autonomous and independent ways. The co-creators inside and outside a Responsible Business are called on to make small and large decisions all the time—live and in the moment—decisions that will affect all of the company's stakeholders. This has always been true for organizations of all kinds, but very few have really understood it and worked with it to strategic advantage. Thinking about the effectiveness of a given mode of thinking for a particular task is key to developing excellent decision making across an organization and key to working with the stakeholder pentad. Like any other skill, thinking can be significantly improved over time and through experience and it needs to be adapted to different tasks and objectives. Developing the workforce capacity to consciously choose appropriate modes of thinking is part of a Responsible Business and garners a significant return for the investment.

A Responsible Business evolves by enabling people to consciously pursue greater effectiveness, building their desire and motivation to become better decision makers. This is not accomplished with programs or projects, or by restructuring the organization, and certainly not by scaring people with threats. It is built by cultivating in all stakeholders a vivid awareness and sense of responsibility for the implications and effect of their decisions.

Decision making becomes conscious and leads to innovation when people learn *to see and manage* what *they are thinking about and* how *they are thinking about it.* For the most part, thinking is governed by ingrained patterns—unexamined assumptions, filters, and approaches—that may not be appropriately matched to subjects. The skill to break those patterns and choose one's thinking process is the first step to conscious decision making and ultimately innovation. This chapter describes the four fundamental capabilities required for conscious decision making.

FOUR SELF-ORGANIZING CAPABILITIES

The first of these capabilities is regenerative systems thinking, derived from the way living systems work. The second capability is to generate patterns rather than just follow them, overcoming the strong human tendency toward mechanical routine. The third capability pairs internal locus of control with external considering, which means that one should become profoundly responsible for oneself while engaging in deep caring for others. The fourth capability is the integration and simultaneous engagement of function, being, and will to create intrinsic motivation.

LIVING SYSTEMS THINKING

Experience has taught many businesses that attempting to work on problems by addressing a single, urgent, and immediate cause can lead to a cascading series of unintended consequences. For example, narrowly focusing on improving on-time delivery to customers may result in delivering the wrong things. Professor Peter Senge, author of *The Fifth Discipline,* and his colleagues at MIT have created an industry around the application of systems thinking to organizational practice, and as a result *systems dynamics* is now a fairly pervasive concept in the business world. In this model, the connections and dynamic interactions among different parts of a system are identified and analyzed. For example, a practitioner might evaluate the relationship between changing consumption patterns and production forecasting.

Feedback loops are often used by systems dynamics to explain how businesses work. Feedback loops are created by downstream actions that affect upstream decisions. Senge's *The Fifth Discipline* introduces a "beer game" to illustrate the feedback loop phenomenon as it manifests in the distribution system for a perishable product, beer.[1]

The system works well until a sudden spike in demand creates difficulty maintaining adequate inventories at the retail, wholesale, and production levels. The feedback loop comes into play when each part of the system increases its orders to try to rebuild inventory. However, there is a lag time between when the order is made and when the beer is produced. By the time production can catch up with the accumulated orders, the wholesalers and retailers have ordered too much inventory of a perishable product, which arrives all at once. Because they are unable to see the systems dynamics at work, wholesalers, retailers, and producers blame each other for spoiled product.

In this instance, feedback moves upstream as an overreaction to inadequate supply. Later it will move back downstream again as the producer cuts production because of the perceived "collapse" in the market, setting the stage for yet another cycle. The accepted remedy for a feedback loop of this nature is to move upstream to try to understand the cause, that is, the spike in demand.

Feedback loops are an example of the "cybernetic" approach to systems thinking, which uses machines as models. A controller on a machine is an example of a simple feedback loop. It registers that the machine is overheating and shuts it down so that it can cool. A mechanical model of systems looks at parts and works to improve each part and its relationships.

But this mechanical model is problematic in all but the simplest cases. In complex living systems, there are no simple cause-and-effect relationships. Nothing in nature is actually organized around a feedback loop. Our habit of thinking in machine-based metaphors causes us to oversimplify what's actually happening. For example, the current debate on global warming is largely framed in terms of feedback, as though the planet were itself a machine that is overheating.

Recent writing in the field of science and economics is helping illuminate the limits of mechanical models as the bases for understanding life. Brian Arthur, cited by Joshua Ramo in *The Age of the Unthinkable*, notes that the intellectual lineage of the Renaissance is outdated and limits the reliability of observations. "Our standard view of an economy goes back to the enlightenment where everything was mechanistic. When something was complicated in an attempt to understand, it was viewed as a series of objects with linkages between them. Subjects and objects are neatly separated. But in a living complex order, subject and object cannot be separated so neatly. The economy reflects behavior that can best be described as organic, rather than a well-ordered, gigantic machine."[2]

This kind of oversimplification has consequences. It can cause a business to work long and hard on a problem only to discover that its solution wasn't really relevant to the business's overall direction. Such a process is slow, partial, and inappropriate in the rapidly changing circumstances a business currently faces.

At the same time, working to identify causes for problems frequently leads to blaming rather than understanding what's happening systemically. It creates cultures that scapegoat and results in dangerous blind spots for business leaders. One can work backward up a chain of causality forever without ever being prompted to look at the system itself. Clearly, a fundamental shift is needed to overcome the pervasive training that leads people to look at things in isolation. Businesses need to learn literally to look at everything at once.

Unfortunately, this isn't going to be easy. Western culture is disabled by a deeply engrained bias. Westerners focus first on what they believe to be the most important object in a mental or physical landscape. They don't naturally see integrated wholes. This is demonstrated by startling research conducted by Richard Nisbett at the University of Michigan.

Nisbett, an experimental psychologist, has devoted himself to understanding how culture affects the way people think. Until the early 1990s he believed that all humans from all cultures thought and reasoned the same way. He recruited fifty graduate students, half raised and educated in the United States and half raised in China, and all currently enrolled at the University of Michigan. On computer screens that could track their eye movements, the research subjects were shown thirty-six images for about three seconds each. All of the images had a similar visual motif, an image of a large object in a realistic, complex background (a tiger in a forest, a horse in a field of flowers, and so on). After each image, the screen returned to a white background with a cross, and the students were asked to refocus on the cross. When a new image appeared in a few seconds, the eye-tracker silently recorded where the students looked and for how long. Then the process repeated.

The research revealed a pattern so clear that at first Nisbett assumed he had made a mistake. Students raised in America immediately looked at the foreground object—the horse or the tiger. Once they spotted it, they spent most of their time looking directly at the object. The Chinese students, by contrast, usually looked first at the environment around the main object, probing its complexities. Though they did eventually look at the focal object, it was for far less time than the Americans. "There was no point in time where the Chinese were fixating on the object significantly more than the background," Nisbett reported.[3]

The pattern held true when each group was tested later on what it had recalled. The Americans recalled the object and the Chinese recalled the background in detail. In fact, by changing the background only, the research team could trick the Chinese participants into believing that they had not seen the object in the foreground before.

What does this pattern mean? Nisbett theorized that in Asia, complex social networks carry a highly prescribed role structure that emphasizes context. In the West, societies are far less constraining and independence is stressed, allowing people to pay less attention to context. Westerners tend to see the world as something to be understood and dominated, while Asians tend to see it as something into which to integrate themselves.

This bias causes Westerners to have trouble seeing larger systems—it makes them "change blind," to borrow Ramo's phrase. In a rapidly changing world, this places business practices rooted in Western culture at a disadvantage. They need to learn to see contextually. The same set of skills is needed for social and planetary evolution. Learning to use living systems thinking—seeing both object and field in detailed and dynamic ways—allows businesses to integrate themselves successfully into an always-emergent future.

In contrast to a view that focuses on objects and ignores context, a living systems approach views the working of a system through the metaphors of life. It enables seeing the whole all at once. This is the foundation for effective use of the stakeholder pentad. It brings the pentad to life.

A living systems framework allows a business to grapple with complexity in ways that are workable and intelligible without oversimplifying what is inherently complex. Though people are learning to apply this approach to the ecological sciences, it hasn't yet penetrated the world of organizations and businesses, although the businesses described in this book have been pioneering its application. As a rule, when systems thinking is discussed in business, cybernetic models based on the functioning of machines still reign.

Regenerative systems thinking depends on being able to understand and work with five key living systems concepts.

Living Systems Are Nested

For example, a circulatory system is nested within a human being, which operates within a family system, which is part of a community, a culture, a species. Energies are exchanged up and down levels of scale. Generally, a system is dependent for its survival on the larger system within which it is nested—the circulatory system requires the body—and the larger system requires the smaller system for its well-being.

Scale is not the only way to think about nested systems. Some systems are nested inside of one another through levels or orders of conceptualization. Ideas or concepts can be nested inside one another and influence one another reciprocally. For example, the American legal system is nested inside of a set of principles embedded in the Constitution, which in turn is nested within the historical and cultural context of the enlightenment ideal of individual freedom.

Living Systems Are Characterized by Dynamic Relationships

Dynamic interrelatedness occurs within and among levels of systems. For example, any one member of a family affects the other members and the family as a whole. As an individual changes, so does the family. This book depicts a system of business stakeholders who are related in intimate, inextricable, and continuously changing ways. A healthy business manages these changing relationships to maintain balance as well as to take advantage of opportunities that become available. For an organization to stay healthy, it must be able to extend beyond a narrow focus to see links and connections. Understanding systems in terms of dynamism and relationships enables single actions to yield multiple results.

Every Living System Is Distinguished by a Unique Essence

Understanding the uniqueness of a living entity is a critical prerequisite to working with its potential. It is easy to see this with a musical child or a herding dog, who will always try to express its nature and will be unhappy or diminished if that nature is thwarted. The same is true of a production line or a watershed. Qualitative distinctiveness is the basis for evolution, allowing a product or species to move into a new niche.

Living Systems Are Intelligible Through Their Working

Living systems can be imaged. Imaging *live* enables the human mind (specifically the right brain) to look beyond the evidence of the senses to see the patterns of wholeness that operate within living systems. Imaging, creating a vivid mental picture, allows one to understand something in terms of its aliveness, its relatedness, and its uniqueness.

Here's a story that illustrates what I mean. A professor who had been a Peace Corps volunteer spoke at my daughter's Phi Beta Kappa induction ceremony. He had gone to Zimbabwe to teach English and biology to primary schoolchildren. One morning he asked each of his student to catch a frog—an assignment they loved! He then told them to kill the frogs in preparation for dissection. The children scattered, wailing, and the adults came running to see who'd been hurt. The village shaman strode up with a stern face. "Why do you wantonly destroy our brothers and sisters?" he demanded.

The confused young man tried to explain dissection as a way to understand the frog's circulatory and digestive systems. The shaman fell to the ground laughing. He pulled the young teacher down and guided him into a crouch. Then he began to hop and croak. The children released their frogs and hopped alongside. They searched together for frog food and frog places to hide. After a while the shaman gathered the children around him saying, "That's how you understand how a frog works." He turned to the young man and said, "It cannot be understood using your methods," and walked away. The shaman had given that aspiring young professor a remedial lesson in imaging that he never forgot. In time he would be able to do the same work in his mind—seeing the frog live and whole, as part of a context, rather than dead and in parts.

The mechanistic mind assumes you cannot understand a thing until you have dissected it, but this is not true. Dissection provides knowledge but no understanding. What matters more than knowledge is improving how people and things work within larger systems—and only understanding makes this possible. For example, naming all the parts of a drawing pen doesn't tell you how to improve it. Only watching a pen at work in an artist's hand on a variety of writing surfaces can provide the necessary understanding to change the pen for the better. This is why 80 percent of new product offerings fail in the market within six months.[4] They are improvements to parts but they are not improvements to the ways previous offerings work in their environments.

Every Living System Has a Unique Purpose Toward Which It Evolves

Purposeful evolution refers to the way living systems change through time and the direction toward which that change is moving. Living entities secure an enduring place for themselves by playing a contributing role within a larger system. They evolve by becoming better at playing that role or by discovering new roles.

Within its ecosystem, a bee's purpose is to pollinate. People work with bees to ensure pollination of introduced crops. At best, this process creates an agro-ecological system in which humans enjoy a dramatically increased portfolio of useful plants and bees enjoy enriched nectar opportunities.

To give an example from business, the purpose of a purchasing department could easily (and mistakenly) be viewed as buying things in a way that makes the most effective use of financial resources. Its real purpose is to support creative work by providing appropriate materials and services when they are needed. A purposeful purchasing—one that takes a systems view of its customers rather than only a transactional one—department enables the elegant realization of an organization's unique offering, and if it is consciously engaged in that purpose it will seek to become better and better at it over time. Operating from this perspective allows a Responsible Business to notice how clients and customers can be helped to improve through time, thereby evolving their own relative competitive position through unique offerings.

PATTERN GENERATION

Human beings tend to become attached to their ideas and even more attached to the way they generate ideas. They rely on familiar patterns of thinking that have worked well in the past. This is called *pattern-following*. It manifests itself in the predictability of an individual's response or approach to challenges. Pattern-following is also related to the ability to learn from and understand the environment and is necessary for survival. Without it, one would be continually faced with an overwhelming level of complexity. Pattern-following facilitates fitting in with family and community.

Pattern-following allows one to identify consistently successful methods for accomplishing particular tasks. Mastering certain kinds of patterns frees the mind to pursue higher-order accomplishments. For example, learning arithmetic and algebra opens the way to becoming proficient at calculus and symbolic logic. Learning to play the saxophone well opens the way to creating beauty in performance and improvisation. The complex, creative activities described in these examples require pattern-generating, which depends on prior mastery of pattern-following.

Human beings are capable of engaging in many kinds of thinking, all of which are useful and appropriate in the right circumstances. But without the development of reflective capacity, people are not always able to choose the kind of thinking that is most appropriate in a given situation. Deeply entrenched patterns, such as eating habits or even a career path, can be difficult to change because they are embedded in thinking as well as in behavior.

A key element of creativity is related to seeking a goal, something that demands a new perspective. Creativity calls for something different from traditional pattern-following. It requires letting go of current patterns and conceiving entirely new outcomes and new ways of getting to them.

Pattern-following gives comfort, while pattern-generating is inherently destabilizing. Creative individuals, organizations, and even nations have embraced the value of being destabilized in order to exercise this uniquely human capacity for pattern generation. They are able to access the evolutionary capacities that systems thinking makes possible. To give an example, thinking of something as an opportunity rather than as a problem shifts the context and invites creativity into play. Better governance, better relationships, better ways of living, the solutions to seemingly intractable problems—all become possible when creative people let go of the tendency to follow patterns that are outdated or irrelevant to current conditions.

On a larger scale, most organizations have particular ways of working on strategy, sales, or product development. Following those patterns is almost certainly inhibiting innovation and will continue to do so until organizations alter the way they work to transform their offerings to truly serve their stakeholders. In other words, they need to generate a new pattern of thinking. Even industrywide or cultural patterns limit decision-making capacity and should periodically be examined through dialogue.

A Responsible Business cultivates autonomy, self-organized pursuit of higher-order goals, and self-motivation with regard to personal development by evolving a culture that includes rituals for disrupting entrenched ways of thinking, fostering the reexamination of existing patterns, and inviting the generation of new opportunities. Such a culture asks first *how* to think about something—"What new pattern can we generate?"—rather than simply reverting to old patterns. The businesses whose transformations are described in this book all work from a principle of never doing anything twice in the same way. It's a good place to start.

I'm not recommending throwing away traditional ways of working and thinking; they are often useful but only when careful, creative reflection has revealed them to be the most appropriate response to a new situation. Conscious engagement with even the most familiar patterns will make them new and allow them to be evolved and extended.

Internal Locus of Control and External Considering

Locus of control is a psychological term that describes how one assigns responsibility for one's experience. A great deal of research reports that when individuals or groups feel responsible for outcomes, whether they are good or bad, they tend to be happier, healthier, more successful, more engaged, and more innovative. Conversely, when individuals or organizations blame forces other than themselves for outcomes, including crediting luck for their achievements, they are far less successful and more reticent to take on anything new and they experience poorer quality of health and lower levels of happiness.

Locus of control is not a neutral factor in business success or the value people have for their work. It can be hired—one should seek people with strong internal locus of control who source their own sense of responsibility—but it can also be developed. Only when people are accountable for their own decisions can they develop the rigor and the discipline called for in high-quality decision making. When a person is asked, "Who's in charge here?" the answer should be, "I am!"

In order to become capable of self-organization, an internal locus of control must be coupled with something called *external considering*. The concept, *locus of consideration*, was developed by several philosophers, including Socrates and George Ivanovich Gurdjieff. It offers a perspective on the question, "Are humans by nature selfish or altruistic?" Do they characteristically ask, "What's in it for me?" or wonder, "How do we make the world a better place?"

People are both self-interested *and* altruistic. They have a choice in any situation. But self-interest is the default for most people. Altruism requires development. Many religious traditions emphasize the importance of external considering and strongly promote giving to the poor and loving one's neighbor. Decision making suffers when consideration of self and other are polarized and it benefits when they are seen as nested, one within the other, reflecting the fact that they live within natural and social communities.

Organizations that seek to motivate with threats or rewards unwittingly tilt people toward engaging in internal considering, taking only their own well-being into account. This is counterproductive because organizations depend on the cooperative efforts of many individuals. By making people selfish, fear-based management undermines the quality of their decisions. In Responsible Businesses, decision making always takes into account the larger circle of stakeholders.

Many conventional work systems—including incentive plans, reward and recognition, performance reviews, and goals and objectives setting—evoke internal considering, blinding individuals to the collective nature of work and to the effect of all actions and decisions on stakeholders. These motivational devices are based on psychological theories that exclude systemic effects. Not only do they promote internal considering but they also tend to support external locus of control, guiding behavior by what it takes to please and satisfy others. This is diametrically opposed to an organization's best interest, which lies in fostering independence of thought and self-accountability.

However, work systems can be designed to create cultures oriented toward internal locus of control and external considering, cultures that grow the quality of decision making. In Responsible Businesses, the heart of every decision is the well-being of stakeholders.

One of my all-time favorite authors is Daniel Pink. I depend on him to push me and help me coalesce ideas that are churning in my mind. He has so often confirmed through exhaustive research what I have observed from my own experience and presented in my published work.[5]

One of these confirmed observations is that systems based on external locus of control make things worse. In his book, *Drive*, Pink reports that systems based on awakening intrinsic motivation (internal locus of control) have results that far exceed the carrot-and-stick model. Thus, there is a direct correlation between the locus of control and motivation. Extrinsic motivation (rewards, incentives, public recognition) diminishes the internal sense of personal agency. This promotes a loss of agency and invokes external locus of control.[6]

The exemplary companies in this book have demonstrated through years of practice that intrinsic motivation is the fastest and probably only route to internal locus of control. Innovation is fueled and nourished when intrinsic motivation is enabled and internal locus is discovered. This is the lifeblood of market non-displaceability. In the Responsible Business people believe they can do anything and overcome all odds. They know that they can choose to be the source of success.

INTRINSIC MOTIVATION

Business organizations almost always separate three aspects or levels of work: *function, being,* and motivation or *will*. If an organization is to be whole, these three levels must be integrated. Unless an organization is whole, it cannot be responsible.

When organizations are designed or redesigned, the focus is usually on function, what is needed to deliver products and services. Projects, whether aimed at improving internal working or changing relationships with external stakeholders, are almost always organized around functional tasks and the roles needed to carry them out, and training usually improves skills needed to carry out functional roles.

The second level, being, is the development of character and inner self-management. When it is considered at all, it is generally treated as an entirely separate piece of work tied to the development of leadership. Capability is built in one group of people, leaders, or managers who are held responsible for ensuring that the quality of energy and morale in the organization is maintained and that individuals feel inspired by their work.

A third level of work has to do with the motivation of co-creators. Most businesses adopt models from behavioral psychology, rewarding behaviors they want others to mimic. A few high-performing organizations have made motivation an art. They make food available around the clock, build on-site gyms, offer benefits that ensure families are taken into consideration, create environments of trust and openness, and provide opportunities for individuals to exercise personal choice. These efforts attempt to manage what people have will toward, but this is a losing proposition. Responsible Businesses develop systemic thinking, excellent decision making, and self-accountability in their co-creators. They help them develop self-motivation in the form of will.

A quantum shift occurs when an organization enables people to work simultaneously from all three levels of function, being, and will. For example, projects can be designed so that functional work develops and expresses being and will—high-quality energy and morale and commitment to the pursuit of excellence in service to something larger than oneself. Morale is maintained at a high level when co-creators contribute their uniqueness to projects and grow their capacity to be self-regulating. Will is maintained when the projects are clearly seen to benefit others.

Not long ago, I was invited to help natural resource policy makers in British Columbia overturn extreme bureaucratic compartmentalization that has prevented the development of an integrated and systemic land policy. At our initial meeting, I joined a roomful of fifteen upper-level policy advisors, each from a different provincial ministry. I announced that I wouldn't be facilitating because my job was to shake them up and make them think systemically, not to enable them to stay in their comfortable grooves. I asked them, "What question will we have to ask to shift us from isolated functional roles to an inter-ministry perspective?" "Boy, that's a hard question!" they replied.

I intended to destabilize their state of being from the outset by asking a question that was both vitally important and impossible to answer from the perspectives they had brought with them, a nearly guaranteed way to awaken their wills! Usually, a facilitator starts a meeting by going around the room inviting all to introduce themselves and tell what they do and what functional roles they play. Right from the start, this traps the conversation in what exists. It's designed to encourage thinking from status quo and it almost inevitably results in the same old same old.

After they had been struggling in pairs for a few minutes to come up with questions, I could hear a rising hubbub. They were fully engaged. In fact, when I went around the room and asked them to introduce themselves and offer their questions, to a person they stated the question and how excited they were. I had to remind them to tell us their names and what ministry they worked in.

At a midpoint reflection, a deputy minister joined us, and the other ministers told her how they had walked into the room this morning assuming they would have to defend their departments and positions. Instead, they had shifted almost instantly from competing interests to a cohesive group responsible for a shared natural heritage. They had experienced a shift in *being* as a result of change in perspective. They had experienced a shift in *will* when they understood their roles as creating an integrated policy development process based on how nature defines itself, not how government establishes its jurisdictions.

In less than two hours we had gone from fifteen isolated functions to one integrated team. Even more inspiring, this team was setting out to plan for natural resources in a way that would contribute to their wholeness. There had been no special programs or incentives to motivate these people. What happened, happened naturally as it always does when whole individuals and whole teams work collectively in the service of a whole living system.

CONCLUSIONS

Excellent decision making is key to managing stakeholders as a living system. For excellence to become routine, organization must learn to think about how they are thinking. It's fun, it energizes creative decision making, and it helps people realize their potential.

Responsible Businesses foster nonhierarchical decisions, including those regarding sustainability and social responsibility, by making capability building a part of all educational and business endeavors. These businesses never stop learning. They apply regenerative systems thinking in every meeting; they reflect on their processes to assess whether they are generating new and more appropriate decisions and ways of making decisions; and they examine each program for whether it promotes and deepens internal locus of control and external considering. They engage whole people by connecting tasks to individual uniqueness and to what really matters to awaken will.

By thinking and operating from a systemic framework of stakeholder integration, the Responsible Business steps up to an entirely new order of work and value generation. Learning how to think about thinking is the foundation for excellent decision making.

Free downloads: There are three offerings for this chapter: (1) a graphic depiction of the five characteristics of a system, (2) a tool for assessing your personal agency for internal locus of control and external considering, and (3) a graphic depiction of the three levels of work. Go to the free downloads section at www.The-Responsible-Business.com.

PART THREE

Irresponsibility Happens: Reframing How Change Works

Almost without fail, when I speak about evolving Responsible Businesses and the magnificent transformation companies have produced, there is someone who will say, "What do you do about . . . ?"

The blank they fill in ranges from the "stubborn people who will not change" to the "leadership who gets in the way." It is sometimes assumed that evolving to responsibility is not possible in some industries or public or private companies; that it may not work in large, far-flung companies or small local ones; or that it may never fit with the culture of a non-Indo-European country. The premises behind the questions may even include the idea that people are ill-intentioned by the nature of being in a business context and that there is nothing one can do to change that. Then there is always the idea that they have already tried it and it did not work.

Although I understand the natural skepticism that arises when people have tried many programs and experienced as many setbacks or shortfalls, I can see some things they cannot. They are right that some people will not move immediately, but they are likely to be wrong about which ones they are—or that it is permanent obstinacy. For example, I often offer the executives who proclaim this restraint—usually before we have gone far—a suggestion that they write down the names of these recalcitrant individuals and seal the list into an envelope to be revisited in a few months. When we open it, the executive is almost always wrong about the specific names on the list because the process of building intelligence, connecting people with the market and corporate strategy, and redesigning work to awaken a personal experience of creative agency has not been a fragmented philosophy similar to other programs they have experienced. The people who had been "stuck" in previous change efforts are alive and moving by the time we review the list. On further reflection, one can see that among the people who had learned to work within the system of rewards and high-performance promotions, there is still a small number who are not comfortable with the requirement for exercising personal agency. It makes them uncomfortable when they are asked to initiate and lead from their own unique ideas about how to advance a business strategy. Yet although it may take them longer they will get there eventually. I love the look on the face of the executive when we open that envelope. Jaws drop as old assumptions fall.

The chapters in Part Three show the real challenges inherent in change processes and how to deal with them. Obstacles can range from leadership voids to one-size-fits-all pilot programs to corporate philistines who obstruct anything they haven't had a hand in developing. Evolving to responsibility includes finding ways through the obstacles by letting go of outworn axioms and learning to see the world anew.

Chapter Eight describes how significant shortfalls occur when the chain of logic described by the pentad runs backward, starting with investors rather than customers. Without intelligent design and ongoing commitment, entropy can be counted on to undermine a business's best work and intentions.

Chapter Nine describes how alternatives to traditional development processes are grounded in research and how these processes can foster creative transformation at every level of business. Chapter Ten explores six common hazards that threaten to derail development—just a few of the ways that entropy can undermine potential. Stories from successful companies show the pentad's potential to shift viewpoints and reveal previously hidden options.

CHAPTER EIGHT

RESPONSIBILITY RUNNING BACKWARD

We're lost, but we're making great time!
YOGI BERRA

The pentad depicts a chain of logic that begins with the living image of a customer and flows organically through co-creators, Earth, communities, and investors. This flow results in improved health and vitality for all stakeholders. Reversing it has the opposite effect.

More often than not companies turn the logic upside down and start from the wrong point, the investors. This initiates a degenerative process that I call *spinning the pentad backward*. When this happens, mental and creative energies focus narrowly on how to extract return from the system and the process becomes extractive rather than creative. Assets and value that rightfully belong to others are appropriated in an effort to subsidize a return for a single stakeholder group. This is unproductive and unsustainable.

Spinning the pentad backward has resulted in periodic collapses in the U.S. economy. Investment banks, savings and loans, corporate giants like Enron, and others have extracted inappropriate returns on investments through schemes that have left investors and ordinary people to suffer the consequences.

Not surprisingly, collapses of confidence often lead to community boycotts, lawsuits, or demands for regulatory enforcement, costly for businesses in terms of both dollars and brand equity.

Unbudgeted expenditures related to these community side effects then tend to push businesses into efficiency mind-sets. They cut costs in order to free up the financial resources necessary to manage a situation that is spinning out of control.

The efficiency mind-set eventually dooms a business to failure. Over time, it leads to efficiency-driven decisions that degrade the quality of resources and their uses and sidetracks any efforts to sustain ecological integrity. Once efficiency and value extraction have set in, employees and co-creators become just another cost of doing business. It's not long before there are programs to reduce the size and cost of human resources, contractors, suppliers—all of the entities within the co-creative stream. Naturally, this makes it increasingly difficult to attract or keep high-quality creative employees. All of this results in a business that no longer serves its customers. Problems start to pile up. Products degrade, deliveries fall apart, and brand identity deteriorates along with the company's public image. The airline industry, for decades the proud flagship of American capitalism, now shows up in surveys as one of the nation's least trusted industries. Talk about taking the eye off the customer!

A business is successful when it stands for something with integrity and constancy. Beginning anywhere on the pentad other than a full appreciation of the customer's life destabilizes that sense of integrity and continuity inside the company and immediately violates imperatives of the stakeholder just before it on the pentad. For example, beginning with best practices intended to protect Earth most often undermines co-creator agency and self-management. Spinning the pentad backward sets in motion a cascading series of degenerative processes. Not only does spinning backward take down individual companies, but it also can be contagious across an entire industry: for example, the Lehman Brothers 2008 bankruptcy triggered an international financial meltdown.

RUNNING FASTER IN THE WRONG DIRECTION

People measure what they pay attention to. When a business worries about how much profit it's going to return to investors, that's all it can think about. It is consumed by efforts to meet monthly, quarterly, and annual targets. These are broken into functional and sometimes individual targets and delegated with the intention that "it will all add up in the end." Similar to putting blinders on a horse, measurements tend to block out anything that might be distracting. They also block out context and the bigger picture.

A narrow financial focus blinds companies to many of its potential sources for value creation. It sees regulatory agencies and communities as annoyances and attempts to limit the effectiveness of laws designed to govern business activities. It sees the environment as a storeroom and environmental watchdogs as adversaries to be outmaneuvered. It makes employees and suppliers a cost of doing business and that diminishes returns. And finally it corrupts the customer, who becomes someone to be manipulated and seduced and whose buying decisions are guided by impulsiveness and unconscious consumerism.

Starting with investors and spinning the pentad backward inevitably does a disservice to all the stakeholders. Starting with customers and spinning it forward not only provides better returns to investors but it also benefits all other stakeholders along the way.

I helped intervene in a classic example of backward spinning in DuPont's titanium dioxide (TiO_2) business. Their mining operation was located in southeastern Australia. Their margins were tight and they were actively seeking to manage costs by preventing efforts to impose regulations on the disposal of mine tailings (residues) that threatened to increase production and cleanup costs.

Australians being Australians, local communities immediately rallied in opposition to mining that they perceived to be environmentally damaging. They set to work closing down DuPont's operations. Managing an unruly and angry community was not a natural part of the TiO_2 mining business. What was important to them was making sure that no one got hurt, a central aspect of DuPont's corporate essence. When protesters tied the company up in court and staged demonstrations at the mine, DuPont responded by diverting significant resources to ensure safety for everyone involved. They built barriers to separate protesters from sensitive mining equipment and sites that posed a danger to them. When one protester incurred an injury, the company took the traditional route of engaging in a public relations campaign to demonstrate its commitment to caring and safety, even though it had no direct responsibility for the injury.

DuPont continued to elaborate its defensive posture, doing everything it could think of short of changing mining operations. In fact their extreme measures to maintain operations while protecting public safety—new roads, additional trucking, and a host of other stopgap measures aimed at circumventing the impediments caused by community protests—were creating new environmental effects.

Employee overtime began to increase and contracting for security became a larger and larger percentage of the mine's operating budget. Temporary personnel were hired to manage operations that could be disrupted by protesters. To cut costs, teams were assigned to solve the problem of overtime and contracting expenses. Once the company broke trust with employees through layoffs and admonishments for overtime, employees began to offer information to the protesters, furthering the downward spiral.

Not surprisingly, the ability to get ore out of the mine on time and into the refinement cycle lost momentum. Quality varied due to focus on reducing costs. The management in Wilmington, Delaware, applied great pressure to meet standards and targets for margins and product quality. But with everyone's eye on cost, the customer's requirements slipped out of view. It was not long before shipments were returned and contracts canceled.

TiO_2 was at that time a commodity with low margins and the company found itself in constant bidding wars to stay competitive with other TiO_2 suppliers. With the spiral of escalating problems, it would soon cost more money to make the product than DuPont could sell it for.

As problems arose, management formed task teams to address each of the separate stakeholders but with very little coordination. Lawyers and PR people worked on the community problem. Operations and engineering worked on the problem of production and raw material sourcing. Human relations and management worked on the employee and contractor problem. Marketing, R&D, and logistics worked on the customer problem.

All this because DuPont had not taken time to reconsider production itself and generate creative ideas for reconciling community concerns about pollution with its own need for cost-effectiveness. No wonder the company began to question whether it wanted to be in the TiO_2 business at all.

A 360-DEGREE BUSINESS PERSPECTIVE

Fragmentation didn't originate with business leaders; Western culture tends to see things in parts and pieces. Environmental activists pressure management to work on whatever piece they believe is the problem. The community then pressures companies to deal with local economic, social, or environmental issues. Unions advocate for improved employment conditions and benefits. In modern times, the strongest influence has been investors who apply pressure with regard to profit-and-loss statements. The tendency of each stakeholder to approach a company from its own bias increases reactivity and reinforces fragmented approaches.

Ed Woolard, a creative, systemic thinker, became head of DuPont's global chemicals group during the time of the protests in Australia. He looked at the TiO_2 mess, said, "This is insane!" and began putting this business back on track.

Ed pulled together a cross-functional global core team and challenged them to look closely at the nature of TiO_2 and its effect in the lives of customers. "Let's work on the essence of TiO_2 and figure out how to make a better product that simultaneously cleans up all of these other problems." In short order this shift in focus led to the invention of a proprietary technology that enabled DuPont to develop a TiO_2 product with patentable properties highly differentiated from products available from other suppliers, moving it from a commodity to higher-margin specialty product and elevating DuPont into market preeminence.

Until this time, TiO_2 had been produced from high-grade ore in a mining process that generated mountains of rubble. As much as 90 percent of what was pulled out of Earth became waste in the form of highly regulated mine tailings. The new, patented technology made it possible to optimize low-grade ore, which resulted in a reduction of output from the mine to only 10 percent of what it had been before. The new technology also yielded a product with a much higher use value for customers.

By shifting focus from investors to customers, the company was able to involve employees and contractors in a creative process, the total redesign of its TiO_2 mining, transportation, manufacturing, and marketing. Most significantly, it removed the inefficiencies from its extraction process, dramatically reducing environmental effects and mollifying the protesters who had been advocating for Earth.

When the DuPont team changed the mining processes and opened new markets, they were able to increase their operations in southeastern Australia but with a different approach to all the stakeholders. It was astounding how quickly the community embraced them as employer, contractor, and generator of tax base. Instead of being the faceless and predatory corporate invader, DuPont became a member of the community, elevating life for everyone.

Finally, by taking itself out of the commodity game and positioning itself as a highly sought-after supplier of premium TiO_2, DuPont realized financial gains hundreds of times higher than they could have achieved by continuing down the path it had been on. This allowed the pentad to spin faster and faster in the unifying forward direction. DuPont extended the process to diverse stakeholder situations in other parts of the world, and eventually Ed Woolard became CEO of the company.

MAKE SOMETHING FOR SOMEONE

Highly skilled craftspeople, the manufacturers of an earlier time, were directly and intimately connected to their communities and customers, in many cases carrying forward generations-old family legacies. Contact with real people and places generates emotional connection and a sense of caring that naturally mediate the inherent destructiveness of toxic disconnection. Today nearly all relationships have become abstract, including those among and within corporate stakeholder groups.

When there is no relationship, there is little to prevent destructive actions. Without connection and the opportunity to observe the repercussions of behavior, humans don't experience the necessary stimulation needed to become socialized, empathic, and compassionate. For most people, newspaper stories about child labor may be shocking or disturbing, but they do little to inspire customers to stop buying products made by children because their effect is to increase the sense of alienation.

Most people base the majority of their decisions on mediated experiences and many have become dependent on third parties to manage their relationships. Financial advisors guide the purchase of mutual funds, creating several layers of disconnection between investors and the actual effects of their dollar. Family counselors manage parents' relationships with their children. Environmental experts manage individuals' relationships with nature. Physicians manage people's relationships with bodies. And designers manage their relationships to personal image and spaces. Some people even rely on third parties to assess their purchases and tell them which brands are "responsible."

Just as "disconnected" almost defines the modern individual, it also describes the modern corporation, which enables people to invest money at arm's length, distancing them from work and risk. Because of this, it hasn't been difficult to abandon the investor.

But just as people have to make a choice to be ethical in their private lives, investors also have to make that choice in their financial lives. To do so they have to reconnect, see through the fog of abstraction to what their money is actually producing. When there is no relationship between investors and the communities where they do business, negotiations becomes the purview of local governments and planning officials. But as populations have grown and representation has become diluted, city and county councillors may have been elected in ways that create no real connection with voters, and planning officials operate from a set of rules and regulations that distance them from the people they serve and even from the implications of the agreements they make with corporations that come to town. Many of the relationships between investors and communities end up being mediated by lawyers and courts. Individual humans experience them only through legal and financial instruments, which is to say hardly at all.

Backward-spinning businesses foster this pervasive disconnection. People invest with no sense that they may be exploiting a community of mineworkers, polluting coastal waters, or diminishing the livelihoods of third world coffee growers. These effects certainly don't show up in corporate annual reports where they might influence choices. Disconnection allows destruction of the social and natural fabrics of entire regions without ever evoking a sense of guilt or shame that investors would experience if they were causing it in their adjacent neighborhood. Very few people would demand that their neighbors be laid off so that they could have a bigger dividend.

FROM BACKWARD TO FORWARD SPIN

Over and over, people who hear my lectures and read my articles tell me that this is where their company is now, spinning the pentad backward. They all want to know what they can do about it. I tell them, "The answer is relatively simple. Start over again by reconnecting everyone with your customers and their real lives. Businesses need to engage in authentic relationships with their stakeholders by connecting them to the shared purpose that brings them together: *adding value to the lives of customers.*"

The critical point is to focus on real-life experiences, not abstract data. DuPont, Canada, had been using feedback aggregated by its customer service department to understand who its customers were. The purpose of the feedback was to help each group improve its performance but instead it focused everyone's attention on the bottom line rather than on making operations more effective for the customer.

Then DuPont engaged members of its team to become customer champions as part of a work system redesign. Each was part of a self-selected team who engaged with a particular customer and took full responsibility for that customer's success. This changed everything. The champions were even authorized to fly to a customer's site to help correct problems or to their headquarters to be part of their strategic planning teams. They were as deeply involved in their customers' businesses as they were in DuPont's.

They also worked beyond their own functions within DuPont to identify or resolve problems—ideally before they could negatively affect customers. Improvements took place rapidly. As part of their commitment to customer service, champions often stimulated or carried out the redesign of whole systems within the company. Customers reported that they felt DuPont's people understood their operations and were on board to help them succeed.

DuPont customer champions improved communications with customers well enough to figure out that breakage in the long sheet of fiber used in the production of airbags was not only a costly variance for its customers (airbag manufacturers) but also could cause airbags to fail in car accidents. Prior to this they had only received feedback when specifications hadn't been met, but that didn't tell them enough about how their fiber performed when it was actually in use. By reconnecting to the reality of their work and its implications, they were able to address the problem immediately.

Colgate, Europe, fell into the trap of starting from investors when it provided its sales and operating teams with numbers to tell them how they were meeting or falling short of targets for various distribution channels. The reports indicated the effect on share price for every variation that caused a bottom-line loss, usually because of a returned product. The numbers focused attention on the corporation and its investors, not on the customer.

As part of their work to learn the Responsible Business process, teams from Colgate, Europe, businesses developed a living description of their diverse buyer classes, their different ways of working, and the different requirements this placed on the company. Field teams drawn from across the organization were established to work with each of these buyer classes and became experts in their buyers' reality. Based on this expertise, they created distinctive sales and distribution systems and product packaging to improve marketability. Then they worked across field teams to find synergies and improvements in design and effectiveness that would support high-leverage pursuits. The return in sales and margins covered not only investment costs but also increased returns two to three times, making their former conversation about losses irrelevant. Real people in the Colgate operations were connected to the real experiences of their distributors and were able to see the differences between, for example, the needs of retailing giant

Carrefour and those of a mom-and-pop operation in a small village. This resulted in the transformation of responsibility from corporate motto to a felt experience when the Colgate, Europe, co-creators understood the effects of their actions on the success of others.

When Molly McNealy oversaw the IT operation at U.S. Bank in the Pacific Northwest, her group was responsible for making information technology available to advisors for the bank's retirement investment customers. They had been continuously harangued about their work's lack of quality, accuracy, and timeliness. The investment advisors had imposed fairly detailed measurement systems to track performance in these areas. It made the group's work disheartening; they were either on the mark or not, and there was no real way to take responsibility for continuous improvement. Because everything was managed in financial terms, they were constantly aware of the story the CFO would have to tell the board of directors, a typical corporate incentive to try to get people to improve.

Molly participated in a program I offered for small businesses and unit managers at Washington State University, where she learned about ideas like value-adding process and life-giving effects for end users. She took to these ideas like a duck to water. She began to reconceptualize the role of her group and set out to test the approach in her next set of events with department teams.

Through some quite wonderful engagements with the investment advisors, she convinced them to allow the IT operation to develop some understanding of the advisors' customers and what they needed. Even then it took a while; the advisors at first wanted only to provide her group with secondhand reports on customers. Eventually she persuaded them to let IT be part of customer round tables where portfolios were reviewed in depth to evaluate how they were managed and how they were serving the goals of specific retirement funds.

Molly's team came alive because they were connecting to people's dreams of retirement. They quickly figured out how to help advisors provide better guidance. As they continued to be involved in the round table briefings, they found more and more ways to support service to clients. And the advisors found themselves more and more interested in feeding back to Molly's group how particular lives were being changed by the work they did. The sense of responsibility for a person moving into retirement became the primary motivating purpose for a once-alienated IT group, reconnecting them to the meaning in what they did.

Conclusions

Business leaders who read this chapter may recognize a patterns of practices and behaviors in their own organizations that will have a strong tendency to spin the pentad backward. But the stories I've told here clearly show that it is never too late to reverse this state of affairs. There are two recurring themes in the methods for getting back on track. The first is to examine whether the business understands the stakeholder on each point of the pentad well enough to connect the stakeholder on the following point to it. For example, does the business understand its customers well enough for the co-creators to feel "fueled" with the spirit and inspired by understanding? Do co-creators want to serve customers and do they know what this service will entail? If the answer is no, then it is time to reconnect to the customer and reawaken co-creator spirit. The same test can be made for every point on the pentad: Is this stakeholder being well-fueled by the stakeholder on the prior point in order to build momentum?

The second theme is an almost foolproof way to address any problems that arise. Go back to the customers and reconnect to them as living people. In particular, reconnect to the uniqueness of each buyer group. Stop depending on surveys and get to know real people. A company that does this key work reestablishes the basis for forward motion.

CHAPTER NINE

OUR OWN WORST ENEMIES
Turning People Around

The range of what we think and do is limited by what we fail to notice.
  And because we fail to notice that we fail to notice, there is little we can do to change; until we notice how failing to notice shapes our thoughts and deeds.
R. D. LAING

I'll be more enthusiastic about encouraging thinking outside the box when there's evidence of any thinking going on inside it.
TERRY PRATCHETT

We have met the enemy and he is us.
WALT KELLY, CARTOONIST, POGO DAILY SYNDICATED CARTOON STRIP, ON EARTH DAY, 1971

On one occasion when Albert Einstein was asked how he discovered the theory of relativity, he replied, "I ignored an axiom." I have always understood him to mean that he questioned what he and everyone else was certain about. Each of the leaders of the Responsible Businesses I have written about let go of a truth and conceived anew how things work. The history of progress and innovation is full of such examples. But even profound insights such as Einstein's become barriers to discovery if they are allowed to crystallize into official truth.

What causes humans to persist in running their thinking backward? Why do so many companies engage in thinking and behavior that works so powerfully against their own best interests? Why do they spin the pentad backward?

The rapidly evolving field of brain science offers insight into these questions. The good news is that humans have lots of ways to engage with the world; the bad news is that they aren't always in charge of the choices they make. Humans are often blind to how their own brains deceive them. For the Responsible Business, this is not some esoteric study but an instrument for correcting errors and bringing self-direction to managing processes.

BRAIN WORKS

In the 1970s, Paul McLean, then director of the National Institute of Mental Health, made a profound discovery that provided an initial schematic for how the brain works.[1] He found that the human brain actually comprises three brains or three evolutionary stages of brain development. He observed that the base brain, which he named the *reptilian brain,* retains many of the characteristics and functions found in reptiles. The human mid-brain, whose characteristics and functions are shared among all mammals, he called the *limbic* or *mammalian brain.* He observed that the upper and largest part of the brain appears to be unique to humans, with functions that not even other higher primates share to any significant degree. This brain he called the *neo-cortex,* the new brain.

The reptilian brain regulates the ability to sense the environment. When one responds rapidly to an oncoming car, the reptilian brain is doing the work.

The mammalian brain is enacted when mammals nurture their young until they are able to live on their own. They form some version of family or clan—prides of lions, dens of foxes, and herds of elephants—that helps them to survive and prosper collectively. This mammalian tendency allows humans to form friendships and teams that can do more together than they could ever do alone.

The neo-cortext brain is characterized by the so-called right- and left-brain functions that are unique to humans. It enables the use of complex language and the creation of culture and art. It lets humans project into the future, envisioning better lives for themselves and others. It enables them to stay on course or to assess whether a change of course is necessary. It integrates emotions and thinking as a way to discern what paths are likely to be most successful.

Since McLean's discovery, brain science has advanced rapidly, beyond what will be useful for the purposes of this book. However, I use his idea of three brains metaphorically as a way to understand the developmental potential of human beings. My aim is to show how the differentiation and integration of the three brains—the frames of reference they enable and the intelligence associated with each—can promote business success.

THREE-BRAINED DECISION MAKING

Jonah Lehrer, a brilliant neuroscientist and journalist, has focused on communicating to a lay audience what science is discovering about decision making. (He blogs at The Frontal Cortex, http://scienceblogs.com/cortex.) In his newest book, *How We Decide*, he tells a story that illustrates the profound interrelatedness of brain function.[2] He shows that the three-brain process is far less neatly separated than McLean described it. He also explains how emotions are integrated into good decision making.

In Lehrer's story, a patient named Elliott walked into the office of neurologist Antonio Damasio in 1982. A few months earlier a tumor had been cut out of Elliot's cortex near the frontal lobe of his brain. Before his surgery he had been a model father and husband. Since his surgery, IQ testing had found his intelligence level to be fundamentally unchanged. But he now had one psychological flaw: he was incapable of making a decision.

This impairment made normal life impossible. Elliot was unable to choose what to wear, eat, buy, and do. Outings with his wife and children became intolerable. He lost his job and eventually his family. Though he was a man of normal intellect, he was no longer able to decide anything.

Through a series of tests, it was determined that Elliot was also unable to experience emotional responses. When he was shown pictures with violent or grotesque content, he had no reaction. He was trapped in the emotional life of a mannequin. His pathology suggested that emotions are a critical part of the thinking process. Up until this time, most people had believed that emotions were irrational. But if that were so, Elliott actually should have been able to make better decisions because his thinking was uncorrupted by emotions. In fact, a brain that can't feel can't make up its mind. Lehrer summarizes that the frontal cortex is involved with emotions and calls on them to make its decisions. Metaphorically, one might say that it reaches down into the mammalian and reptilian brains to do its work.

Good decisions depend on the integration of the whole brain, including its emotional capacities, and the Responsible Business intentionally fosters such integration. By contrast, the standards and procedures common in most companies are designed to take emotions and therefore emotional intelligence out of work. A company fosters better and more integrated decision making when it uses framework-based dialogues to encourage wholeness in thinking. Systemic frameworks stimulate questions and interactions that call on diverse mental processes—including experiential and intuitive understanding—and then correlate the unfolding dialogue into an evolving decision. The self-organizing nature of this work fosters the inherent capacity of the human brain to explore and make accurate and rapid decisions.

TRIAD OF MENTAL FRAMES

At the same time MacLean was formulating the three-brain model, Charles Krone, a major contributor to the pioneering work at P&G, was developing an analogous theory. Krone proposed three levels of mind-set or mental frame through which humans interpret the world—reactive, relational, and purposeful—and described processes for understanding and developing them. These mental frames correlate to the three brains but sidestep the conceptual difficulties raised by imagining the human brain, a highly integrated system, as three separate parts.[3] Understood as an integrated whole, Krone's mental frames provide a comprehensive basis for understanding the functioning of human behavior and values.

In Krone's theory, all three frames are working all the time, but a lack of adequate mental development means that their influence occurs primarily outside conscious awareness and control.

This means that most people are unable to tap their full mental potential. According to Krone, it is critical to develop the capacity of the more encompassing, more complex frames of mind because without this development they end up pressed into the service of the more primitive defensive and territorial systems of the reptilian brain. With development, the relational and purposeful mental frames automatically integrate the reptilian, reactive aspects of the brain into higher-level thinking functions, employing all three frames to their best advantage.

REACTIVE MENTAL FRAME

The reactive frame of mind is conservative by nature and seeks habituation, permanence, and stability. It correlates with the stimulus-response mechanisms that behaviorists study in animals. However, even these automatic responses can be guided, directed, and modulated when put into the service of relational and purposeful frames. For example, when one has a purpose, one builds and maintains relationships relevant to that purpose and reacts to appropriate stimuli while ignoring what does not advance both the purpose and the relevant relationships.

RELATIONAL MENTAL FRAME

The relational frame of mind maintains all physical and emotional bonds among individuals, families, and societies. It has responsibility for dreaming, visioning, and intuition. When engaged in integrated mental functioning, it assists in determining when reactivity is called for, distinguishes true emergencies or threats from false, and provides an expanded context for deciding on appropriate action. Unless the relational frame of mind is honed, reactivity can usurp its emotional powers, causing an individual to be carried away with fear or other intense emotions. The relational frame can also help individuals overcome competitiveness when appropriate and design cooperative efforts when needed.

Thus, properly developed, the relational frame of mind enables reflective governance of the reactive aspects of human character. It is powerful; it encompasses the capacities for scheming, predicting, and controlling other people and the environment, philosophizing and waxing poetic, inventing and emoting.

Purposeful Mental Frame

The purposeful frame of mind has the inherent capacity to enhance the potential of both the other mental perspectives. Managing them requires only a small amount of its energy. Its real work is to enable the mind to evolve and constantly revise the constructs it holds of the universe and reality.

When the capacity to engage the purposeful mental frame is inadequately developed, the mind tends to revert to defensive or emotional postures and is forced to fall back on the reactive and relational perspectives. Because these mental functions use so little of the energy available to the mind, it begins to starve from lack of stimulation. Too little challenge at the purposeful level will cause the mind to lose the ability to access this kind of mental operation.

Unfortunately, most work design fails to tap the real potential represented by these three mental frames. In part, this is because Western culture as a whole has done a poor job of differentiating, understanding, and developing the appropriate relationships among them. For this reason, a business can't afford to simply "put the minds of its people to work," because the default for most people is to start from the self-preservation emphasis of the reactive frame of mind, with relational and purposeful modes playing only supporting roles.

Business cultures are rife with mechanisms that reinforce reactivity in co-creators. Fear and threats are used in subtle or explicit ways to motivate or control employees, triggering strong reptilian responses. Procedures attempt to manage behavior and end up driving intentionality and creativity out of the workplace. Incentive programs promote self-serving behaviors over the values of belonging or altruism.

Some effort has been made to introduce more relational intelligence into the workplace. However, these programs fail to develop the guiding capability of the relational perspective, and the overdeveloped reactive mind usually takes charge. For example, organizations do team-building exercises to foster camaraderie and trust, but the results tend to be short-lived as soon as day-to-day stress and pressure reassert themselves.

Development of the purposeful mental frame is given short shrift in education, society, and business. Because it has become a shared blind spot, even a little work in this arena can yield spectacular results. This was the driver in so many of the success stories described in previous chapters. Imagine the potential of a leader, industry, or nation that commits itself to developing all three mental levels!

FAMILIARITY IS THE ENEMY OF CREATIVITY

Locked perspectives or paradigms can be insidious and self-reinforcing. There are three reasons for this. First, the brain likes familiarity; indeed, it likes familiarity so much that when it encounters something it recognizes, endorphins are released. The brain's biological preference for the familiar can easily dispose it to see what it expects rather than what is really there. It takes mental effort and discipline to "see things new."

Also, the brain more readily forgets things that are unfamiliar. One may have had experiences that would contradict one's assumptions, but over time memory selects for what is familiar. This is especially true when one is simultaneously receiving evidence that reinforces some other part of what is familiar. For example, the marketing and customer research people at Seventh Generation were trained in business school to understand customers based on particular research methods ranging from focus groups to consumer market surveys that relied on asking questions and observing people using a product. The understanding these methods yielded was always partial because the focus was on the use of the product rather than on the living customers themselves.

Gerald Zaltman, a professor of Marketing at Harvard Business School and a fellow at Harvard's interdisciplinary Mind/Brain/Behavior Interfaculty Initiative (MBB), points out, "Eighty percent of all market research serves mainly to reinforce existing conclusions, not to develop new possibilities. As a result eighty percent of all new products and services fail within six months or fall significantly short of forecasted profits."[4] As a consequence of falling into this trap, Seventh Generation was surprised when they got apathetic market responses from customers to what—based on the evidence they had from research—were great ideas. The research methods continued to be used even with poor-quality results because the methods were familiar.

Paradigms are also reinforced by the tendency to ridicule and demean anyone who challenges a familiar understanding. Kingsford was being watched by other parts of Clorox as it involved its workforce in research and development projects. In the larger Clorox culture this nature of work was considered sophisticated and prestigious, and lots of jokes were flying about letting the inmates run the asylum, that is, until the product development and process improvements began emerging from the manufacturing division of Kingsford. They set a new standard for the rate of revenue-generation improvement, exceeding all growth projections for any division and for the company as a whole. Take note: It always looks wrong when "we" didn't think of it.

Unless one makes a conscious effort to engage in dialogue with perspectives that are unfamiliar, disorienting, or even threatening, it is difficult to shed light on that which is partial and unexamined in one's own understanding. In a striking parallel to the Clorox experience, I once brought a group of senior managers from the DuPont facility that produced TiO_2 to visit the Kingsford charcoal plant in Belle, Missouri. The contrasts were so extreme they were comical. TiO_2 is a white, powdered mineral that makes paint opaque, and charcoal is a product made from black powder. The DuPont guys were well-dressed, button-down engineers in white shirts, walking through a plant covered in black dust being led by operators in t-shirts and red suspenders.

The Kingsford charcoal team giving the tour asked if the DuPont group would give them an example of a safety assessment. DuPont is recognized for its attention to safety. Its engineers were so conditioned to thinking in these terms that they couldn't walk through a facility without automatically engaging in assessment, and they were happy to accommodate the Kingsford operators. At the end of the tour, they spent an hour walking them through the details of what they had seen on the site. There was much room for improvement. The Kingsford workers took detailed notes, still asking questions as they followed their guests back to the van.

As we drove away the DuPont engineers gave me a dressing down. "Why did you bring us to such a backward place?" they wanted to know. "We thought you said we'd learn something here!" They catalogued everything they saw wrong with the facility, including that the plant manager had not even bothered to attend.

"Did you see anything that might be useful?" I asked them. They swore there was nothing. I asked, "How important was it that the operators asked you for a safety assessment, knowing that's what they could learn from you?" They grudgingly acknowledged that this was pretty smart. I asked them, "What did you observe about the level of commitment to change? Didn't they use every last minute to ask every question they could think of to better understand what you were telling them?"

Then I said, "And about the plant manager, he was there the entire time. Why do you suppose he chose to be invisible and give responsibility for the visit to the operating team? Not the managers, the operators!" But I couldn't get through to them. Their minds were made up.

Two months later, Moose and Eric, two of the operators who had led the tour, asked if they could come to Delisle, Mississippi, and share with the DuPont team how they had applied the input from that visit. Not only did Moose and Eric report back on the fully executed change in their safety program, but they brought a set of principles that they had gleaned from the DuPont leaders that would enable Kingsford to continue to improve.

The DuPont managers were invited to reflect on what they heard from Moose and Eric. After an embarrassed silence of several minutes, the DuPont plant manager, who had not been on the original tour, said, "In my experience, no client, supplier, or even internal DuPont system has ever executed a safety program to the level of skill and commitment that I have just heard." One by one the managers who had attended had to admit that what Kingsford had learned from them represented a systemwide commitment that exceeded their own capacities.

I then asked the managers what they surmised about how the Kingsford business must have operated to have internalized and changed its systems so rapidly and completely. One responded, "I can't imagine how you design a work system so that you can have a couple hundred people in a month change how they are working. I'd like to learn how you design that." Another said, "I don't understand how you could build a whole safety system from the bottom up, without the plant manager having mandated it. I now want to understand that." Yet another said, "I don't understand how the two men standing in front of me could make the technological, organizational, and production changes needed without professional engineers to design them for them. I now want to understand that." And Eric and Moose said, "Come see us again." Three months later we made another trip, and DuPont was finally able to hear the story of the important transformations at Kingsford and understand how important they would be for their own business.

INCENTIVES NARROW THE MIND

The design and implementation of incentive programs unintentionally and almost inevitably trigger only the reactive, reptilian mind. Such programs are intended to produce specific, predictable responses and results. For example, they incentivize competition and meeting targets and disincentivize cooperation and exploration for better ways to serve customers. Though the designers of incentive programs hope to provide encouragement and self-esteem to their winners or recipients, the lack of relationship to purpose and the unintended relegation of some people to the role of "loser" tend to foster a sense of threat among the majority of organization members.

An organization that works on the development of all three mental frames creates a culture that will enable the full development and expression of the value people are capable of generating. The ability to choose an appropriate frame of mind makes possible a whole set of behaviors guided by an intelligence that is capable of *effective* thinking. Only purposeful mental activity supports the kind of evolution on which healthy and enduring businesses depend.

Narrower Frames of Reference Cause the Pentad to Spin Backward

The majority of goals driving the senior management of companies come from the return on investment expected from shareholders. This sets up a reptilian, reactive response throughout the organization. Instead of being an uplifting and inspiring force for spinning the pentad forward, most strategic planning processes are driven by the need to meet shareholder expectations.

Once return on investment becomes the organizing principle, a business goes on the alert for anything that reduces return. The relational frame of mind is focused on who's a friend and who's not; for example, within the relational frame, the mind expends a lot of energy distinguishing the high performers from the low. From the purposeful perspective, the mind is left with nothing to do. Corporate culture, especially in top management, becomes one of "every reptile for itself."

By contrast, starting with the customer connects a business with real lives, thus activating the frontal lobe's essential purpose—to create a better world. The mind with purpose will go to work to discover the leverage points that are most likely to create that better world. Inviting an entire organization to be in service to the lives of customers creates spirit as well as an undying loyalty from customers.

In this context, the co-creator becomes a beneficial, tribal-relational concept, uniting employees, suppliers, contractors, and others around the shared intention of contributing to the customer. A purpose-driven tribal effort is one that the purposeful mind can lead without politics or fear. This results in a return that is fair and significant for all stakeholders, including shareholders and those who invest their time, labor, ideas, and all the other necessary ingredients for making a successful business.

Leading from the Purposeful Mental Frame

Here's what a Responsible Business looks like, one designed by fully developed and integrated human brains. First, everyone in the organization envisions and works toward a better future for all stakeholders using a critical and evolving self-chosen role. Making the business's constant organizing principle "A better future for all" awakens purposeful intellectual engagement. When co-creators people are directed to look into the future toward an invigorating outcome, they learn to control their reactions and look beyond instant gratification.

Second, in the Responsible Business everyone is asked to serve the customer in a way that makes a unique difference. This awakens caring. It enables one to experience oneself within a kinship network, part of a larger whole that is an interwoven and interdependent system. One is no longer separated by tribe or territory and has become aware that it takes everyone for anyone to prosper. Caring is critical to the Responsible Business because it cannot connect co-creators to stakeholders in a sustaining way if co-creators cannot develop relational intelligence within themselves.

Third, in a Responsible Business all co-creators are stewarding the whole. All are responsible for the company and for themselves and all receive the support it takes (including challenges) to achieve the contributions to which they have committed. This builds a strong sense of accountability for shared purpose and develops the capacity to tack into the wind, facing restraints and using the whole brain to go under, over, or around anything that stands in the way. It is the source of what many people call discipline, tenacity, and perseverance, precisely those qualities that managers often say are missing in their workforce.

The new research around the role of purpose, described by Daniel Pink in his book *Drive*, indicates that the responsibility element cannot be activated until caring and sense of purpose are fully present.[5] In other words, people do not rise to challenges that are not embedded in the vision of a better world to which they can make unique contributions.

It is important to understand that it takes several years to deconstruct deeply entrenched thinking patterns and learn to lead from purposeful intelligence. The Responsible Business makes this its mandate and embeds it into work design, building the skills needed to be guided by a fully developed, integrated brain.

PERSONAL DEVELOPMENT AND CRITICAL THINKING SKILLS

Even from events that didn't succeed, people can learn and grow. The often-touted mandate of Total Quality Management—"Get it right every time"—makes it difficult to consider growth and learning as a natural process. Working practices that build reflection into operations are inherently developmental and are core to the Responsible Business.

Humans are blessed with flexibility of mind and spirit, but with them comes volatility. I can wake up any morning full of life and spirit and go to bed the same day down and depressed. I can engage with another person in a way that brings us both to new creative and inclusive places or I can diminish the synergy generated between us the day before. Without effort and consciousness, I am at the mercy of my environment and my conditioning. What brings hope to the human situation is that we can actually develop the capacity to manage this fluid and flexible nature to produce more predictable and regenerative outcomes.

This is accomplished by developing the capacity to understand and manage one's own emotions and intellect. When people can look into themselves and choose the selves they need to be in particular situations, they become masters of their own destinies. Without this they are at the mercy of their environment. Through critical thinking and personal development, one can create possibilities that would not otherwise exist and realize potential that would not be recognized without a mind that penetrated beyond what is visible to the naked eye.

The personal development that was embedded into my monthly sessions with Seventh Generation enabled its teams to overcome a major obstacle to success. Because of the nature of its mission, Seventh Generation attracted very compassionate souls who wished to work for a company that cares about people and Earth. This culture of caring had a hidden downside: a tendency to be overly gentle with one another and to walk too carefully around difficult financial, market, and corporate responsibility questions. By introducing frameworks and learning self-observing and self-managing practices, the teams improved their thinking and interaction skills. This led to dialogues that were no longer personal but focused on the effects the business was after. These rigorous dialogues led in turn to rapid financial and market growth.

CONCLUSIONS

Spinning the pentad backward creates momentum like a runaway train. One of the reasons for this momentum is that the human mind loves to follow familiar patterns. Without development to use its full emotional and mental capacities, the mind will take the course of least resistance. Many philosophies and spiritual traditions have warned against this automatic way of living. They advocate becoming conscious of one's own thinking and being in order to develop the capacity to be purposeful and make good decisions. Unless people cultivate intelligent awareness and work within systems designed to keep them awake, old patterns become the inevitable default. The hallmark of a Responsible Business is its commitment to building a future based on conscious choice.

 Free download: A graphic depiction of the three intelligences at work with the three brains can be found in the free downloads section at www.The-Responsible-Business.com.

CHAPTER TEN

CAUTIONARY TALES
Design for Prevention and Cure

We learn wisdom from failure much more than from success. We often discover what will do, by finding out what will not do.
SAMUEL SMILES

When I speak in front of audiences, I'm often asked whether the developmental business systems in my stories still exist. Is it still possible to go see them? Some do and some don't. But my initial answer to these questions is, "The work always stays alive in the people who were part of it, and they spread it through the way they live their lives: the nonprofit boards they serve on, the families they raise, the businesses they build, and the next level of leadership they take on, even in another company."

There's an obvious hope and longing in the question but also an implicit misunderstanding. The organizations described in this book aren't machines—they can't be turned on and expected to do the same thing year after year. More important, entropy is real. Products lose their markets; people retire and new people come in. What was a brilliant insight in 1990 will be very old news in 2015.

A better question might be, "Which of these systems continued to evolve and learn, and what was required for them to be able to do that?" The learning and transformation that these stories depict has to be regenerated again and again. Continuous development is a lifelong process and a way of life for people and for organizations. Not everyone has the discipline to keep at it. In order to keep this work alive for years and decades it's important to understand how things can go wrong and what to do about them when they do.

SIX COMMON HAZARDS

The following six hazards show just some of the ways that entropy can get the upper hand in an organization that's trying to transform itself. It's important to balance the inspiration to create a Responsible Business with some consciousness about the restraints that will inevitably be encountered along the way.

HAZARD ONE: LEADERSHIP VOIDS

A business that commits to becoming a Responsible Business undertakes a change process that carries real hazards. The highest level of hazard comes from a change of leadership at the top, especially if it happens too early in the process or if too many committed leaders leave at the same time. Visionary and selfless leadership is necessary for a significant cultural change, especially if the goal is a self-organizing company in which hierarchies would evaporate. Business schools don't prepare leaders for this kind of work, and the culture in most companies weighs against it. But there are extraordinary human beings, far more than most people would expect, who want to undertake business transformation and are willing to do so if it makes business sense.

Although significant results can be achieved within six months, the internalization of this radically different way of doing business takes a minimum of three to four years to become fully established. It is important to maintain consistent leadership over time, but there are two primary challenges.

The first challenge is internal. On initially encountering this new paradigm for running a business, it can be easy to underestimate how different it really is. There is a strong tendency to interpret the new way of working through past experience—"been there, done that." A leader's will, or the will of those she reports to, can be strongly tested when it finally dawns on her what she's committed to.

The second challenge has to do with turnover. New leaders generally want to prove themselves in a new situation, and without a concerted effort to bring themselves into a deep understanding of the nature and importance of the change process, they will almost always undo it. This is true of sensitive and well-intentioned leaders. Even after P&G established its revolutionary prototype at its Lima facility, it faced this challenge every time a new generation of leaders came in.

In one company I worked with, when the original business leader left, the new leader came in with a strong desire to place his own imprint. He was smart and experienced and had developed clear beliefs about business during the course of his career. What he encountered when he came into this radically unconventional organization offended his sense of what was appropriate and responsible. He was particularly startled to see people at lower levels participating in significant product decisions, a violation of what he considered to be professional standards. He mandated that only those whose training gave them the needed degree of excellence and experience (in this case the marketing group) could be involved in any discussions about product development. This immediately began to unravel the purposefulness, camaraderie, and creativity that had energized the workforce.

When another business I had been involved with was sold, its new management team was never able to understand that up until this time work had been self-organized by those who were to do it. Roles emerged organically as needed from within the teams and could evolve and change as the market or daily tasks required. No external authority was needed to delegate and assign tasks. The business operated like a functioning household. People didn't really need an efficiency expert to give them assignments; they just did what made sense and was of particular interest to them.

A decade of working in this way had created a highly capable and self-reliant workforce, which regularly exceeded industry and market expectations. Blindness to this fact on the part of the new management caused it to dismantle much of what had been accomplished. For reasons of efficiency, workers were divided into clearly demarcated work groups and supervisors were installed. It wasn't long before attrition became a serious issue. People who had never experienced a developmental approach replaced the original workforce and the developmental system quietly faded away.

Companies that experience remarkable improvements in performance as the result of the introduction of a developmental way of working see their performance decline when they abandon it. Occasionally a company will recognize its error and bring in someone who can reinstate a developmental approach. More typically, though, corporate culture dictates that new managers have the freedom to run businesses as they see fit. When this happens, the lessons die out in the company as a whole, living on only in the individuals whose lives have been transformed by them.

DuPont, Canada, found an effective way to maintain consistent leadership. Though it was working on only two of its businesses in depth, it immersed the entire organization in an education process around the new way of thinking. This meant that managers could move across businesses without experiencing a cold entry into a completely unfamiliar culture. In time, Canadian managers moved into the United States and Europe, bringing with them an understanding of what it takes to lead a developmental organization. DuPont, Canada, and Kingsford intentionally developed managers who could become available to systems beyond their own. Kingsford held many cross-company forums, particularly in the manufacturing groups, where there was a high likelihood of rotating managers.

This attention to leadership continuity is very important. A change process this profound affects the spirit of everyone who works in the business and therefore it changes the level of contribution that a product line, business, or company can make. A company should not start a process like this unless it is willing to commit to it for the long term. Otherwise, the loss of spirit, morale, hope, and sense of personal creativity can be deeply disruptive. People don't necessarily stop using what they have learned or actualizing who they can be in the world, but the collapse of the developmental environment often drives them out of the company or causes them to segregate work into an unrewarding corner of an otherwise rich life. Managing this hazard is critical for a company in order to ensure that it gets the long-term return on its investment in change.

HAZARD TWO: HOMOGENIZED HUMAN RESOURCE PROGRAMS

Once a company has decided to change, it has a natural and healthy tendency to want to know what's possible. People in the company survey what other companies are doing, read the latest books, attend conferences and workshops, and seek out motivational speakers.

But people who are good at running a business are not necessarily also good at assessing programs to improve the running of a business. Every program is based on a set of assumptions about how humans and human systems work, and many are based on patently inaccurate but enduring myths. Added to this, human resource departments are often delegated to carry out the assessment. Although there are many excellent human resource professionals, in my experience it is the field of expertise most contaminated by unvalidated assumptions. Popular programs such as 360-degree feedback and reward and recognition have never been validated by scientific studies and are not proved to produce the desired market results. In fact, Daniel Pink reports that the research suggests the opposite.[1]

Also, human resource programs are frequently compensatory; they seek to redress bad or improper management practices. For example, human resources will create extensive review programs to stimulate and guide improvement in managers who don't relate well to other people. Then these programs become universalized to all managers, including those who are good at relating and giving guidance. Such programs reduce effectiveness by addressing problems as if they were systemwide when they are not and limit options for even great managers, producing the opposite of what was intended. They particularly diminish agency and initiative on the part of employees.

Contradictory approaches to human resources and development create confusion and antipathy toward improvement efforts. Companies will often borrow techniques without noticing that they are incompatible with intended effects. The resulting double standard can be crazy making. It can get really bad when a human resource department cannot see that it has introduced programs that work against one another (for example, it preaches self-direction but practices performance reviews or peer feedback). Because false human resource assumptions are so pervasive and familiar, it takes a concerted effort to replace them or block their introduction.

However, this can be accomplished through an examination of company philosophy. Doctors ask for details about diet and exercise in order to ascertain that a lifestyle is healthy. In the same way, the Responsible Business must ferret out the underlying assumptions of any proposed change program to ensure its compatibility with the company's overall direction. In my experience, this is much harder to do than it appears. Many of these programs are actually toxic, but toxicity is undetectable when it has become the norm.

For the entire first year that I worked with one company, I was undermined by the good intentions of an acting human resource manager. She had twenty years of experience in organizational change and management, most of it as a consultant, and she had a tool kit of programs from which she had built her reputation and professional life. To her, these programs were "additive" to what we were doing.

For example, she wanted all managers to learn to delegate better. Meanwhile, we were in the process of building self-reliant and self-disciplined individuals who could guide their own work. She wanted to use an enneagram as a personality test, classifying every employee into one of nine types. Meanwhile we were working to overcome previous classification efforts and institutionalize the idea that every person is unique.

She insisted that she had seen these programs succeed in the past but she couldn't see that they were actually counterproductive to business development. A program intended to make something that doesn't work, work better probably indicates the wrong starting place.

In my time with this woman, I often felt that the problems she wanted to address were genuine but the proposed solutions had nothing to do with—and in fact were antithetical to—the creation a self-organizing, essence-based Responsible Business. I often felt like a military police officer trying to fend off the dozens of programs that were proposed as "support" for what we were already doing. I knew that they would steal momentum and divert us from our true work, and I wanted to prevent the dissonance that would almost certainly be created by mix-and-match programs. Unfortunately, this came across to her as intolerance to her perspective.

I worked in an overseas company where a U.S. manager had been brought in because of his success at creating what he called *high-commitment work systems*. He believed in his approach and expected it to enhance our efforts to build a Responsible Business. He was particularly interested in setting up pay systems tied to customer satisfaction rates as a way to keep operations employees' "eyes on the ball."

The dissonance this approach introduced came from two sources. First, pay systems activate the reptilian brain; they speak to people's survival instinct. The mind turns inward, focusing its attention only on the narrowly defined indicator it's been given. This draws all of the attention away from the uniquely human neo-cortex with its potential for the purposeful management of complex wholes.

Second, this pay system focused the entire operation on an abstract number—the percentage of satisfied customers—without any meaningful connection to what was happening in those customers' companies. The group was measuring its performance against a number pasted on the wall. There was no activation of personal will other than to pay attention to the number. It became virtually impossible to recruit customer champions from the section of the organization where this U.S. manager was working. And the section repeatedly had the lowest customer satisfaction rate for the region. But by their own internal measures they were managing to produce the yearly, targeted incremental improvement, which resulted in incremental pay increases. It appeared to them that the system worked exactly as it was intended.

The really sad part of this story is that this manager never could see the limits he had imposed on his teams through tying pay to customer satisfaction numbers. The rest of the company tried to show him the deleterious effects of the program but he just didn't get it. Eventually he returned to the states and the new manager eradicated what he generously called a "misstep." This produced a significant turnaround not only in the group's performance but also in its spirit.

I cannot emphasize strongly enough how detrimental an inconsistency in philosophical approaches in an organization is. I don't mean that everything has to be done exactly the same way. It's more that the beliefs behind an approach actually send a stronger message than the approach itself. When an organization does not line up its philosophy with its practices, it makes itself vulnerable to clever manipulation, unimaginative excuses, and confusion about what is really the right thing to do. Lunchroom conversations are peppered with phrases like "mixed messages" and "speaking out of two sides of his mouth." This drains energy away from what the organization really wants to achieve.

In 1992, I was working in Germany with Colgate, Europe. Companies with businesses in multiple European nations were under pressure to adapt to changes brought about by the newly forming European Union, including the unified monetary and regulatory systems. Our task was to integrate all of Colgate's European businesses into one, optimizing all their functions, and to do this within eighteen months. Business leaders and operators in nine nations speaking twelve languages worked together to radically redefine the company. We often had six national Colgate companies in the room working through simultaneous translation and learning how to think about redesigning a business as the redesign was happening. For years, they had operated independently, but the stakes were high and the competitive threat, should they fail, enormous.

These companies used a variety of models and platforms for working on everything from product development to human resources to work design to management. They made an effort to be inclusive and please everyone as they negotiated their way toward integration. I pushed hard to get alignment on beliefs and philosophy as a means to reconcile what were, from my perspective, radically different worldviews. This change effort was the history of Europe replayed.

For a couple of months I watched dedicated people strive to be inclusive at the same time they were defending their territory. Finally, to stimulate dialogue, I wrote a paper about how to distinguish what would achieve direction and what would not.[2] I wanted to give them guidelines to discern when philosophies were in conflict and when they were aligned.

After I presented my paper to the Colgate group, the process moved away from brainstorming, a completely unstructured process. The teams switched to the development of objectives and principles with which they could assess the ideas they were generating. This curbed their tendency to be overly solicitous and gave them a higher platform for reconciling competing philosophies and practices.

Next they taught themselves how to assess the effects of any suggested work process. With a set of overarching guidelines and a strong desire to achieve meaningful results without diversion and lost time, it became much easier to quickly evaluate whether an idea was consistent with the objectives and direction of the group. The teams learned that programs are not neutral in their effect on human and organizational behavior and that a dialogue to evaluate every new program and practice lifted the organization's capacity to lead itself.

Companies should not be seduced by inappropriate, flavor-of-the-month programs no matter how popular they might currently be or how well they fit the biases of particular people. A company can learn to assess and even create the program that best suits its essence, its direction, and its context. The trick is to make a wise first selection that starts the evolution toward self-organizing systems.

HAZARD THREE: PILOT PROGRAMS

I have no quarrel with trying things out and learning from experience, but the idea of pilot programs is based on a bad assumption—that what has proved to work well in one place can be made to work everywhere. This assumption is the antithesis of the mind-set of the Responsible Business, which dedicates itself to designing live and in the moment.

There are two good reasons why pilot programs inhibit real change, which boil down to "it wasn't invented here." First, what is learned in one effort won't necessarily be applicable or relevant in a new context. Second, people will correctly point out the differences between themselves and the pilot group and they will refuse to adopt what was learned. But even against overwhelming evidence, managers often insist on the bad practice of the pilot experiment.

I learned the "no pilots!" lesson the easy way, by listening to colleagues and professors who were launching consulting ventures. Most of these colleagues began with the assumption that pilot projects were the right way to introduce change into organizations. But they were soon complaining that they were unable to scale their work into whole companies because nonpilot groups invariably rejected the best practices developed in the pilot groups. When they would attempt to design a program that everyone could agree to, they ended up with compromised and generic results, the "design-by-committee" phenomenon.

Even as a young professor I could see that the very idea of finding one right way was flawed. The "not-invented-here" reaction seemed to me a completely natural response, an organization's immune system defending it from an attack on its core identity. Though I often suggested to my colleagues that each business or group should be engaged uniquely, the idea was so unfamiliar that it fell on deaf ears. Because I was still naive, I had the courage to challenge these pervasive assumptions and find my own path.

The recipes produced by pilot programs are mechanical, and Responsible Businesses need to dedicate themselves to overcoming mechanicalness in thinking and behavior. In the beginning, it is important to disrupt every tendency toward formulating and proselytizing the "one best way." A good way to prevent mechanicalness is to work in at least two business systems (three or more is better) at the same time. This guarantees that a business will recognize how profoundly different its options and approaches can be, given the uniqueness of its businesses and workforces. For smaller organizations, working in a business strategic planning series with other small organizations is a good way to accomplish the same thing.

This does not mean that a corporation needs to transform all of its businesses at once, but it does need to work on more than one at a time. It cannot afford to play with a single, isolated pilot project. To change the corporation as a whole requires thoughtful and simultaneous initiation at multiple leveraged points (for example, divisions or businesses that are significantly different from one another). Otherwise, the business is in danger of fostering the development of an internal business so radically different from the parent that it ends up being rejected.

In the case of Kingsford, we actually worked with two businesses simultaneously—charcoal and food products—though I've only described charcoal in this book. This allowed the two businesses to learn from and support one another and stand strong in the face of challenges when outsiders questioned their seemingly unorthodox approaches.

This notion has caused endless problems for business, society, and planet Earth, and the primary task of the Responsible Business is to act as an antidote to it. Growing a Responsible Business is not about installing a packaged program. It is about growing the capability to continuously create relevant business processes and offerings and to evolve strategies as situations change. The Responsible Business invents relevant and effective practices that are unique to each situation and system.

HAZARD FOUR: PACKAGED PROGRAM OF THE YEAR

Years ago, I had an extraordinary opportunity to observe two parallel but very different approaches to the use of systemic frameworks. At the same time that I was working in Kingsford and DuPont, I was an embedded but peripheral player in a massive top-down change effort at a giant utility company. At Kingsford and DuPont, a set of sophisticated concepts and frameworks were growing organically within each organization, whereas in the utility company they were introduced as a set of packaged lessons.

Although I was part of the team at the utility company, I could see that one of the primary problems with the venture was that it was designed to be a controlled or mechanical process. The principle guiding the introduction of content was "never deviate from the package." In my own consulting endeavors, the principle was "never create a package. Design based only on what is relevant at the moment." This experience of being pulled in opposite directions revealed more clearly than I'd ever seen before what really creates change.

The packaged effort had many shortcomings but none more detrimental than the idea that one can prevent variances by making learning mechanical. The top consultants created a package, trained people to deliver it, and then introduced everyone in the organization to the same material in the same way. People inside the organization coined the term *sheep-dipping* to describe their experience. The concepts, which required thoughtful and reflective internalization of their meaning, were completely incompatible with this approach.

For example, one concept worked on being able to better manage one's behavior. People were taught the differences among reactive, ego-driven, and purposeful behaviors. When this discernment is introduced in a way that invites introspection and self-discovery, it becomes a powerful instrument for self-management. However, if it is introduced and then processed as if it were a math lesson requiring learning by rote memorization rather than understanding, the likelihood increases that people will feel accused of behaving improperly and fear that they will be evaluated on the basis their behavioral patterns.

In contrast to the more organic approach that fosters internal locus of control, a packaged learning process almost inevitably results in a conditioned state of external locus of control. In the Responsible Business, consciousness of different modes of behavior is an instrument for self-directed self-development. In a packaged training program, it's just one more set of external ranking mechanisms. In this large organization, a group of people who were particularly fearful of its use as an evaluation tool succeeded in completely destroying the program and did so very publicly.

Top-down, sheep-dipping programs are every bit as destructive as pilot (*toe-dipping*) programs. Both of these extremes come from the same root fallacy: assuming that one right way will work for everyone.

Most consultants would prefer to enter a company through its most senior leadership, thus gaining the authority to institute a program through every corner of the organization. This is the path of Total Quality Management, reengineering, Six Sigma, and a plethora of other approaches to business efficiency and effectiveness. I agree that an entire organization should share a consistent philosophy from which people take guidance and manage themselves. But I am totally opposed to the idea of one-size-fits-all, packaged programs that seek to make people's behavior uniform.

Packaged and mechanical change processes do not build the capacity for responsibility; they build capacity for compliance. The very idea of the Responsible Business carries self-direction within it. A change process related to responsibility must nurture self-governing and self-determining human beings who exercise their own will and creativity toward improving and evolving the world of their stakeholders. Only individual responsibility can grow societal responsibility.

HAZARD FIVE: CORPORATE PHILISTINES

Many people would say that corporate America is full of greedy, self-interested people and is destructive by nature. But I've had a really different experience during the past thirty-five years. I have found the corporate world filled with visionary leaders who believe that business is a way to do something good for all and a powerful platform to accomplish things that could happen no other way.

Nevertheless, I've also experienced executives who seek to kill anything that does not serve their interests or fit their personal models of how things should be. I have seen people go to great lengths to undermine a change effort, even in the face of enormous evidence of its effectiveness. I often suspect that this very effectiveness is the source of their antagonism. It's somehow intolerable to see something succeed that they didn't invent. The sad reality is that not everyone will accept an invitation to engage in personal development and to serve something larger and more meaningful than themselves. One always hopes that they will come around, but a wise leader will be prepared for the occasional saboteur.

One particular case stands out in my mind. As part of a political gambit to gain control of a company, a small group of leaders worked with board members to undermine an exceptionally successful and profitable program. The old leaders were fired and new people were brought in to dismantle the work system. The explanation offered was that hard times were predicted and new hard-line leaders were needed. Eventually, the creative spirit of the business was broken.

It was frustrating to watch a product development powerhouse turned into a mediocre business. My best guess was that this was the result of a secret power struggle over who was to be the next CEO. The person who prevailed did so by discrediting his competitor and frightening the board. This beautiful little business was a casualty in a much larger chess game.

More interesting, though the developmental process had been killed within the business, it continued to live in its co-creators. Some found ways to carry on within their new, more limited roles. Others went on to create new and very successful businesses or to become executives in other companies. One guy joked with me that when his colleagues got together to reminisce, it reminded him of people who constantly relive their high school glory days. But he had to admit those five years before the business was disassembled were the best years of his life, too.

There is no guarantee that a successful change effort will be recognized and accepted. Building a Responsible Business is not a task for the faint of heart. The leaders described in this book knew that what they were aiming to create was both powerful and fragile and that they would need to protect it while it proved itself.

In another organization, a small group of leaders were driven by fear to collude in undermining the change effort. They found themselves deeply challenged by the new insistence on fully revealing their thought processes. For whatever reason, they had difficulty expressing how they had arrived at their conclusions and they were uncomfortable simply acknowledging this fact. In particular, one key leader consistently refused to participate in personal development and lacked the self-reflective skills to know how to deal with his own strong emotions in the face of the challenge.

The group argued that the focus of the work was on changing people rather than on making functional improvements and that this was inappropriate. In this regard, they were half right: the emphasis was on growing people, but a business only grows by developing its people. They also argued that recent improvements were not the result of the change process but were an accidental consequence of forces that had nothing to do with growing new capacity to work differently. Though they were a small minority in the company, they eventually prevailed because senior leadership was distracted, worn down, and either unwilling or unable to transform the conflict.

Humans can be political animals and there is always the possibility that one or more people will act willfully and sometimes dishonestly to undermine change. That is one of the primary arguments for a top-down approach, when all executives in all businesses are required to engage in the change process from the beginning. I actually support this idea of starting from the top and find it more successful as long as it builds will and understanding and isn't force-fed. In the absence of a universal mandate from the top, executives who choose to initiate such an endeavor should be prepared to deal not just with naysayers but also with willful disrupters.

From one point of view, people who have given up on corporate America are right. There are some philistines who don't care what the evidence says and who will pursue their agendas without regard to reason or conscience. But they are wrong. Humans have enormous capacity for change and growth, and one can't know the mettle of people if they're never given an opportunity to prove it. Bad apples are no excuse for failing to seed and grow more responsible ways of doing business. The world needs courageous leaders who will stand up against petty malice, whether in government, the military, or business.

HAZARD SIX: UNDEVELOPED CO-CREATORS

Many people would say that personal development has no place in professional settings. In organizations where personal development is undertaken without a commitment to building responsibility, I might be willing to agree. But responsibility requires conscious understanding and intention about choices at every level. Responsible Businesses cannot develop without growing the sense of personal and collective responsibility in every co-creator.

Personal responsibility requires the capacity to reflect and to see the effects of actions. This hasn't been a part of most people's education unless they had unusual mentors or parents. Without this capacity, by the time a person enters the work world, his ability to self-manage and self-direct is seriously underdeveloped. When a business aspires to have responsible people in every function and role, it discovers that personal development is essential.

Companies seeking change find that people generally resist altering their behavior. These companies often resort to incentives and disincentives to accomplish what people seem unable to do for themselves. I've come in behind several corporate Six Sigma initiatives and have heard from the leaders that until they set up disciplinary procedures and incentives for those who weren't getting with the program, they were unable to accomplish full implementation. Clearly these leaders had missed the most important element—the capability of people to see the effects of their own choices and actions. No intentional effort had been made to build consciousness capacity.

This work is most effective when individuals initiate it from the contribution they want to make to the business. A clear sense of contribution focuses personal growth aims and guides reflection on progress. Mandating personal development becomes unnecessary or less important when people have their own strong sense of personal will. They know they need development to accomplish their promises-beyond-ableness.

For a Responsible Business this is core work but mandated participation in personal work can easily feel like an invasion of privacy. Handled poorly, it can be interpreted as someone else deciding what is good and right and something one must do to avoid being ostracized or fired. It's one thing to make personal responsibility for growth and development a condition of employment; it's another to impose the process from above. The Responsible Business walks a fine line. In order to bring about real change, it requires extensive growth and development of its co-creators. But this must be accomplished by processes that evoke personal agency and self-determination.

I once knew an executive who blew it in this regard. He had a passionate desire to share his own personal growth experience with everyone in the business and mandated that they participate in a development process. Unfortunately his co-creators did not share his powerful realization that the evolution of the business depended on the growth of them all. His insistence on personal development generated strong resistance in those who felt coerced by the boss to participate. What he had intended as a gift became a battlefront.

What was missing here was a preliminary process that would allow key leaders in all departments to experience for themselves the powerful effects of personal development. Without this they had no way to envision how a well-implemented program for universal personal change could transform the company. In the end the hasty but well-intentioned mandate undermined a core element of business growth and development.

I cannot repeat this often enough: it is not possible for a business to grow without growing people. Any organization that thinks it can do so is blind to human nature. A Responsible Business must make personal development an underpinning of business development and how it does so makes all the difference.

AN OUNCE OF PREVENTION

Several measures can help companies avoid the pitfalls described in these cautionary tales. The right people with the right mindsets are the surest way to prevent worst-case scenarios. Though I'm confident that other useful guidelines are available, I know from experience that the following five will help ensure success for any change process, especially the development of a Responsible Business.

Systems umbrellas are people who agree to shield fragile innovations in the same way that gardeners shield early seedlings from heavy rain. These people run interference when potentially disruptive forces threaten the change effort, which is especially important for changes in businesses that are part of larger enterprises. At P&G, Bob Sykes served as such an umbrella to protect the fledgling detergent business in Lima from the flood of proscriptions that would have flowed in from its more conventional parent. Without his intercession, the business development there would not have been systemic and would not have generated sixty years of buzz.

Purposeful leaders should be identified and cultivated to fill every leadership position. These must be people for whom the success of the business is more important than personal reward. In *Good to Great,* Jim Collins calls these *level five leaders.*[3] I call them *purposeful leaders*; they are committed to the purposes of the business stakeholders rather than to their own personal gain. Ken Wessel, the business development leader for P&G, Lima, had already proved himself in his career. As he put it, "I had satisfied my ego needs prior to leading this start-up." He was more interested in creating a legacy than in making a name for himself.

Managing principles should be established early and reflected on often. They should be designed to endure, operating independently of any particular person or specific role. As principles they are intended to guide decision making rather than control behavior and to become the basis for building shared culture. They are used to manage transitions when new leaders take over from founders or previous leaders.

When Johnson & Johnson was founded two hundred years ago, a statement of credo and values was written to guide it through its ongoing life and evolution. The original founder used these documents repeatedly as a way of developing every manager in the organization and reminding them what was to govern their decision making. The first principle on his list had to do with making patients and their caregivers the primary influence on all decisions within the company. Another principle stated that the company would have decentralized management but would offer its businesses the resources of a large system. These were not just platitudes on a wood plaque at the entrance to headquarters. They were used from the beginning and they continue to be used to reduce ego-driven results and create continuity through time.

Ongoing education and development will allow a business to nourish and regenerate the culture needed to buck convention and keep its unique ways of working alive. Ongoing education includes regular reflection on the progress the organization is making in living up to its beliefs, philosophy, and principles. When such reflection is a recurring conversation, it becomes the familiar way of viewing the world rather than the alternative way.

Success stories must be told immediately and often and they should be published far and wide. This reminds the organization of what it is creating and how important its work is. Also, as P&G discovered to its chagrin, when other people tell the story they distort it—they haven't lived it and they don't really get it.

Broadcasting the story makes it more difficult for philistines to make a case against it. This is part of the genius of successful companies such as Google and Apple—they manage their media extensively and successfully but they also tell their stories internally to remind one another who they are and who they aspire to be. At Kingsford, Will Lynn and John Kabler, leader of manufacturing, never entered a meeting without asking people to tell them how things were improving, how people were growing, and what results they were producing. They always asked that these stories be written down so that they could use them to maintain a steady flow of reassuring information to the board of directors. This helped them play the role of systems umbrellas to protect the developing innovations.

CONCLUSIONS

No doubt by now the reader has noted the degree of effort and challenge involved in creating a Responsible Business. At first glance, programs like Total Quality Management and Six Sigma seem easy by comparison: packaged solutions that just get plugged in for results that get cranked out. But anyone who has worked with them knows that most of the cautions I list here also apply to these programs. The human tendencies and failings that underlie these tales are universal and any program will need to address them. The good news is that developing the Responsible Business is worth the effort because it so consistently outperforms most other improvement programs.

 Free download: "Six Common Hazards" and "An Ounce of Prevention" can be downloaded in a graphical format from the free downloads section at www.The-Responsible-Business.com.

PART FOUR

THE BIG PICTURE OF RESPONSIBILITY

To people in the trenches, responsibility sometimes seems impossible. When we take a tally, there seem to be more shortfalls than successes. More oil spills than revitalization of watersheds. More accidents in mines and foreign factories than attempts to improve the lives of workers. More communities that lose control of their own destiny than ones who are supported in their uniqueness by businesses. It's hard to tell if we're making progress or falling further behind every day.

In the Responsible Business, measuring progress includes assessment based on the concept of ROI, *return on the investments* of capital by stakeholders. In Part Four, Chapter Eleven focuses on a responsible view of capital that goes beyond the traditional definition of a financial-only investment. It seeks to express in a single unifying picture the systemic understanding of stakeholders that we have built in previous chapters.

Chapter Twelve describes application of the Responsible Business framework in an assessment process that any company can implement. To demonstrate its utility, I engaged two dozen business leaders intimately connected to a few of the currently most acknowledged innovative companies. We used fifteen indicators of responsibility, three each for the five stakeholder groups. It was enlightening for the executives involved and resulted in a useful instrument for their own future use.

Chapter Thirteen extends the concept of responsibility from the level of the business to the levels of corporation and then industry, describing the unique roles that corporate leadership will play in the evolution of the Responsible Business, the Responsible Corporation, and the Responsible Industry. To illustrate these roles, I describe three alternative business approaches, including two that take on issues of corporate governance, and I touch on responsible investing within the current legal framework.

CHAPTER ELEVEN

A RESPONSIBLE VIEW OF CAPITAL

Not everything that can be counted counts, and not everything that counts can be counted.
ALBERT EINSTEIN

Each part of a living system has its own self-interest, but also works within the interest of the larger whole that contains it. In a mature system, every level expresses its self-interest, so that negotiations are constantly happening towards co-operation.
ELIZABET SAHTOURIS, EVOLUTIONARY BIOLOGIST AND FUTURIST

Capital is accumulated wealth that can be used to build new wealth and a better future. The word is derived from the Latin *capitilis* meaning *head*. The number of head of livestock had long been an indicator of wealth, which could be increased through careful husbanding. The narrower and more recent financial meaning suggests that those who invest financial wealth stand at the "head of the line" in front of other, nonfinancial interests.

For better and for worse, the history of the modern era has in large part been defined by the emergence and development of the phenomenon of capital and the powerful energies it has unleashed. The benefits and the abuses of capital have generated technologies, economies, ideologies, revolutions, and global wars. Clearly, capital is an instrument for great creativity and great destruction.

My work in the business world suggests to me that in and of itself capital is not the issue, although its use for score-keeping tends to obscure its real nature. The problem comes from defining capital too narrowly in financial terms and accounting only for effects on one's own returns. One of the most powerful insights I have derived from the stakeholder pentad is that all stakeholders are investors. Each contributes a form of capital essential to a business's enduring success.

I believe that this insight may provide new ways to understand capital and to imagine capitalism as well as a means for addressing capitalism's degenerative tendencies. In recent decades the concepts of natural and social capital have been advanced by various economists and ecologists attempting to make economic theory more holistic.[1] The stakeholder pentad extends this thinking to include five forms of capital, one for each stakeholder, and suggests some ways to build this enlarged perspective into successful business practices.

Stakeholder Return on Investment (ROI)

All stakeholders are investors—although they invest different forms of capital—and each expects some kind of return on investment. *Return on investment* refers to the future increase in value that is expected when the initial capital contribution is made, commensurate with the delayed gratification and risk involved. Stakeholder investors are willing to postpone enjoying the use of some portion of their accessible wealth in the hope of having more to enjoy later. Co-creators, for example, are willing to invest intelligence and creativity that they might otherwise spend in their own personal activities if they are reasonably ensured that doing so will upgrade their creative capacities. ROI is the output from providing one's capital to another for use over time.

Many companies already recognize the importance of their investors' intangible expectations. Brand equity and goodwill equity are both taken into account in valuation exercises. Reframing these intangible or systemic sources of value as forms of stakeholder ROI makes it easier to grow them in a disciplined, coherent, and value-adding way.

Figure 11.1. Stakeholders' Stake in the Responsible Business

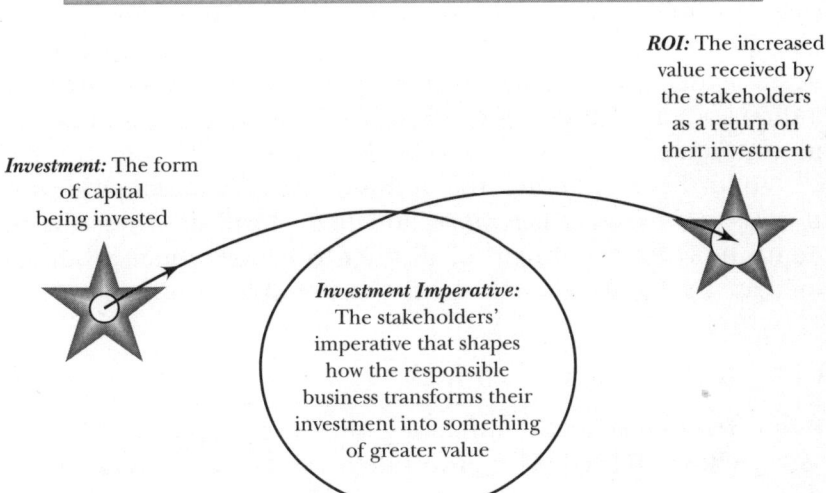

Stakeholders' Desired Effect—Reason for Investing

ROI: The increased value received by the stakeholders as a return on their investment

Investment: The form of capital being invested

Investment Imperative: The stakeholders' imperative that shapes how the responsible business transforms their investment into something of greater value

Figure 11.1 shows the relationship among key dimensions of stakeholder investment in a business.

As the diagram shows, a stakeholder group invests in a company for a desired effect. This is their stake and their reason for investing. *Investment* is the *form of capital* a particular stakeholder invests in a company. In a Responsible Business, capital is understood to extend far beyond the financial resources provided by shareholders to the resources provided by all five stakeholder groups.

The company transforms the investment through activities that are consistent with the group's *investment imperative*. The resultant ROI embodies *the increased value received by the stakeholders as a return on their investment,* a return that becomes meaningful in terms of the stakeholders' desired effect when they integrate that value into their individual lives.

For example, co-creators act from worthy motives or inspired purposes to make differences that really matter. This is their stake and their desired effect. Their *investment* is the intelligence and creativity that they bring to all aspects of their work. Their *invest-ment imperative* is the evolution of a working culture of personal and professional development within which they can make contributions based on their unique, creative capabilities. Their expected *ROI* is increased creative capacity. That is, every one of a Responsible Business's employees and each of its supplier businesses expects to become capable of higher levels of creativity as a direct result of the actions they take to serve the business and its customers.

To further clarify the three terms of the investment process—*investment, investment imperative,* and *ROI*—I will now describe in depth how the investment of distinct forms of capital produces increased value for each of the five stakeholder groups.

CUSTOMER CAPITAL AND ROI

When customers make purchases, they are in pursuit of their stake, a life well lived. They invest their capital, which is an *aspiration for integrity along with personal and business distinctiveness,* in order to acquire what they are unable or unwilling to create for themselves. Integrity is the state of being whole, entire, and undiminished; it refers to the coherence of one's life as much as it does to the ethical uprightness of one's character. Customers aspire to integrity in their lives and they rely on the integrity of the companies they do business with and the quality of their products. Customers and businesses also seek ways to express their distinctiveness, which is reflected in unique and appealing business offerings. Figure 11.2 depicts the journey of customers' stake through the Responsible Business.

The absence of integrity causes customers to experience disruption and missed opportunities and may even prevent them from achieving the goals they desire in their everyday lives. Customers trust companies to be what they say they are and to stand behind their activities and offerings, and they evaluate the effects of businesses on all aspects of their lives. Thus, when a product or service fails to live up to expectations or when a company shows up in a bad light in the media, customers suffer a loss on their investment.

Figure 11.2. Customers' Stake in the Responsible Business

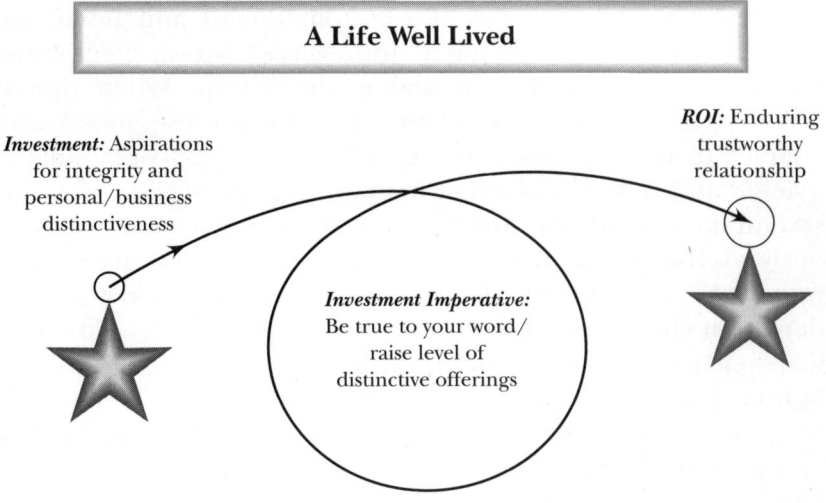

For example, in 2009, Toyota experienced widespread problems with accelerators on its cars, which compromised its integrity and caused loss of customer confidence in Toyota's absolute reliability that had been built over decades. Toyota was forced not only to recall thousands of cars but also to lower prices and increase the warrantees and offerings associated with their products in order to reestablish confidence. Some research suggests that longtime Toyota owners found themselves in a defensive position with regard to their personal choice. The loss of customer capital is clearly reflected in the drop in sales in the first six months following the headline news. It now appears that customer capital may be even further diminished by decreases in resale value of the many of the recalled models.[2]

Customer ROI or output is a *trustworthy relationship* with a business and its offerings. The less vigilant buyers need to be in order to ensure that their purchases meet their expectations, the more they experience a return on time and energy. These days customers also increasingly assess ROI in terms of businesses' effects on their communities and the environment. Customers are less willing to tolerate oil spills or other detrimental environmental effects.

Dependable companies win customer trust and build customer ROI. At a critical moment, Johnson & Johnson exemplified the skillful development of trustable relationships. When Tylenol was tampered with in the 1980s, the company responded with characteristic integrity. Three people died from contaminated Tylenol and reports of further tampering gripped the nation for several days. Suddenly, America's open retail system felt dangerously at risk. Johnson & Johnson made the costly decision to remove 100 percent of its Tylenol and many other packaged products from shelves because at that time it had no way of knowing whether the tampering had occurred in manufacturing or distribution or in the drugstores themselves.

The company instituted a significant testing program and in about ten days had refilled the shelves with products that it could ensure the public were safe. It also bought back any products that customers had purchased at any time. This had a powerful effect on the markets. The public and investors could see Johnson & Johnson reacting swiftly and with great skill to take care of them. This, along with the obvious sacrifice of profit, had the effect of building relationship capital and preserving—and even strengthening—trust that might otherwise have been lost forever. Tylenol's brand equity increased and so did Johnson & Johnson's goodwill equity.

In the case of the customer, the real meaning of capital is the aspiration to be in an agreement of integrity and to have it result in the capacity for a trustable relationship. Just as personal relationships grow through series of interactions and exchanges, so do customer relationships with a company. Trustable relationships develop over time as the result of exchanges that reflect the authenticity of a company's people or its capacity to bring the highest level of integrity to exchanges. But they can be lost almost instantly, as shown in the 2010 recall of Tylenol and other Johnson & Johnson products. It will take some time to rebuild the company's integrity. Whenever there are shortfalls—intentional, unintentional, or even ones for which the company is blameless—the openness of the relationship determines whether it is strengthened, weakened, or broken. Openness requires a great deal of effort and in recent years some companies have convinced themselves that brand loyalty is not possible. I suspect what they really mean is that the effort it takes to maintain a high level of authenticity and integrity is too difficult for their current organizational structure to manage. This emphasis on relationship has an old-fashioned sound to it, but it is the basis for the longevity of some of America's most venerable companies, those built on caring for the customers they serve.

The Responsible Business doesn't draw hard and fast boundaries the way more conventional companies do. It dissolves the sense of inside and outside, us and them. It doesn't distinguish the kind of care and character one brings to one's family from the care and character one brings to one's customers. The Responsible Business understands that its actions affect how business as a whole is viewed. Johnson & Johnson certainly had its own self-interest at heart, but it understood in the 1980s how to reconcile that self-interest with the interests of society as a whole. It could have minimized its short-term financial loss with a much less generous response but this would have cost a loss of public faith in its own industry as well as in the capacity of businesses in general to protect customers in the face of negative circumstances. Johnson & Johnson seems to have forgotten this when in 2009 it cut out the unit responsible for making this level of care an embedded way of working in their organization. The company and the industry are paying a price in trust because their customers and the public in general now see them as less trustworthy.

Co-Creator Capital and ROI

The co-creators stake is to make a meaningful difference for people or purposes they care about. They invest their capital— *intelligence and creativity*—which is more than their existing knowledge or capability. Capital always expects to grow, and co-creators hold the perfectly reasonable expectation that work should grow their capabilities and give them increased opportunities to be creative. Their real capital is the power of their minds and character to make something distinctively new. This capital is threatened and ROI is diminished by standardized work procedures, didactic training, hierarchies of control, and uninspired

FIGURE 11.3. CO-CREATORS' STAKE IN THE RESPONSIBLE BUSINESS

Making the Difference That Matters for Systems of Which One Is a Part

Investment: Thinking/being capability—intelligence and creativity

ROI: Increased creative capacity

Investment Imperative: Create a working culture of personal and professional development, in which they can be distinctively additive to teams and offer unique, creative contributions

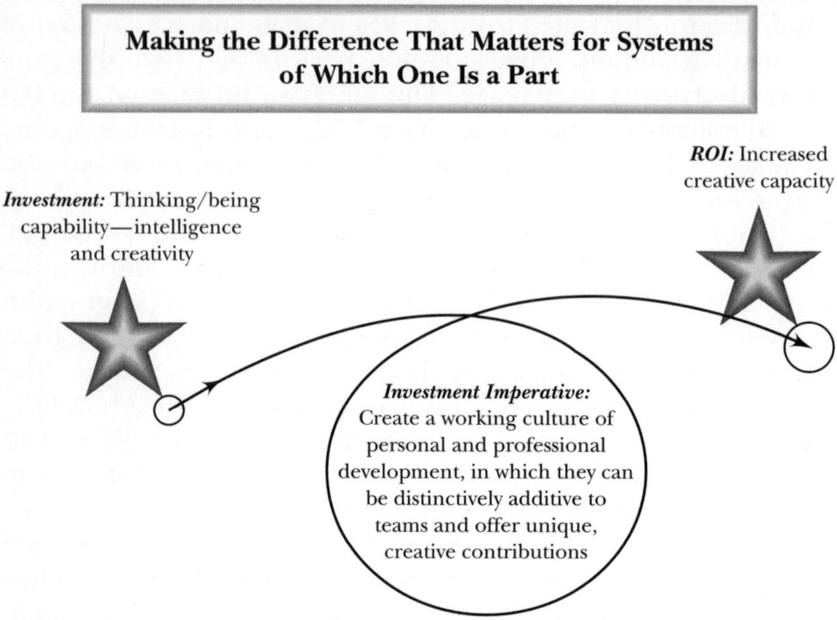

direction. Figure 11.3 depicts the journey of co-creators' stake through the Responsible Business.

Co-creators invest intelligence in order to make their futures more secure, advantageous, creative, and meaningful. One of the biggest draws a business has for attracting new top-of-the-class graduates is the promise of further training, education, and stretch experiences. When forced to choose, high-quality recruits will choose intellectual adventure over salary and benefit incentives. People have a natural tendency to cast themselves into the future because that's where possibility exists.

The ROI that co-creators expect is the increased intelligence and experience that will allow them to invest in the next, more challenging application of creativity. For these stakeholders, one of the most valued dimensions of the corporate relationship is the feeling that in each moment there is an opportunity for learning and personal development that can make the next set of tasks easier, more productive, or more personally rewarding.

The simplification and proceduralization of work and supply chain practices through programs such as ISO Quality Standards works against the development of this form of capital. Such programs assess performance based on whether employees follow unchanging procedures and punish those who don't follow them. This shifts the emphasis of assessment from rewards for improvement in every action to documenting compliance.

Internal and external procedures and standards make things more replicable, but after their newness wears off they reduce the opportunities to grow, be innovative, and meet new challenges. When companies understand that innovation is something that must be continually evolved, good product quality arises organically from the creativity of people rather than from management. People seek wisdom that comes from unpredictable experiences, especially when they can use those experiences to make a meaningful difference.

In the late 1960s, *The Peter Principle* made the ironic observation that there is an upper limit to what people can achieve and that often, for political or other reasons, people are promoted beyond their limits.[3] By contrast, the notion of co-creator capital is based on the understanding that human beings are open-ended in their capacity for growth and development, especially when they are guided by a self-directed pursuit, a self-chosen contribution, and a self-specified learning aspiration.

I named this stakeholder *co-creators* rather than employees and suppliers because these other terms fail to capture an important dimension. The Responsible Business views its employees, contractors, and suppliers simultaneously as members of its team and members of society. They move back and forth between the organization and the rest of their lives where they lead communities, houses of faith, and families. People aspire to lives that matter. A Responsible Business strengthens society by strengthening the citizens in its system, which it accomplishes by providing an engaged, developmental workplace. Through this process co-creators are empowered to take what they have learned and apply it outside the workplace.

In order to keep its people engaged in an upward spiral of growth, the company has a responsibility to grow itself and continuously elevate what it believes it can do. An organization's rapidly growing creative energy will force it to adapt and the best way to accommodate new energy is to evolve strategic direction and increasingly demanding pursuits. Mike Brand of Tektronix developed a company principle to move all new technologies as quickly as possible into the public domain. This forced the company to continually push its boundaries into new territory and stay on the cutting edge, an elegant illustration of the collective evolution of intelligence capital.

EARTH CAPITAL AND ROI

In pursuit of the capacity to regenerate itself infinitely, Earth invests the capital of *resources that support living processes*. Earth provides working capital for the nurture and evolution of the human species as well as for all other living systems. It does so through the differentiated raw materials, landforms, climates, ecosystems, and cultures that make the planet so diverse and lively. Business activity is a small subset of Earth's larger natural economy of reciprocal exchange and maintenance. Figure 11.4

FIGURE 11.4.   EARTH'S STAKE IN THE RESPONSIBLE BUSINESS

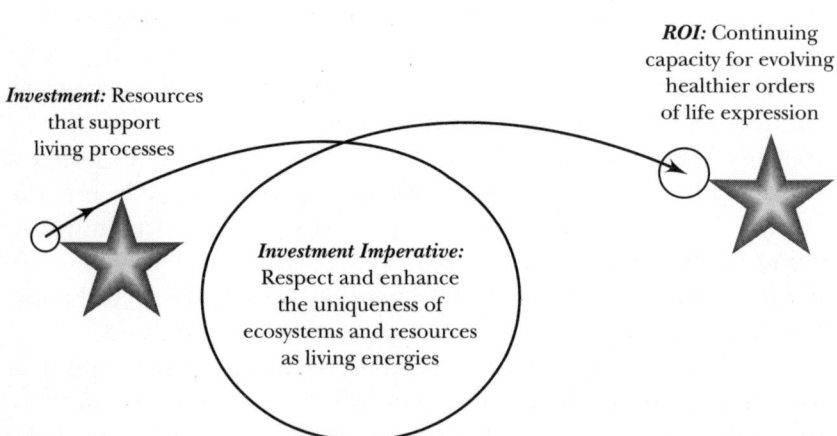

depicts the journey of Earth's stake through the Responsible Business.

Humans and their organizations and countless activities have a role to play in sustaining and elaborating Earth's living potential by understanding and co-creating with the raw materials they use and the places they inhabit. For all the green, sustainability rhetoric out there, the real work is to measure Earth's ROI by Earth's yardstick: resiliency, diversity, connectivity, complexity, and capacity to evolve an increasingly complex web of higher-order ecosystems. In return for its incalculable investments, Earth seeks to increase its capacity to sustain and evolve life, including the dreams and creative endeavors of future generations of human creators.

The key to working on ROI within the context of Earth's living networks is to understand that raw materials are highly differentiated expressions of unique places on the planet. Specific raw materials can strongly influence how a place expresses its identity, so it is important to take a deeper look at how the Responsible Business comes to know and work with these materials.

Working on the essence of a material shifts the mind to seeing it as a unique gift that is received from Earth. Once a material has been considered in this way, it becomes a living energy with a significant part to play in the process of transformation. When the operators in Colgate, South Africa, danced and sang the song of diatomaceous earth, they were singing it back to life. Their songs began to be sung on the lines and out in the townships as a way of reminding everyone who handled the product that it was a living contribution with very special properties. Having witnessed this, I'll never be able to look at a tube of toothpaste the same way again.

The Responsible Business seeks to bring the life of Earth's contributions back into the consciousness of all who receive their benefits. It ensures that they are returned to Earth for recycling, renewing, regenerating, and as a result regifting.

Regenesis, an ecological planning company based in Santa Fe, New Mexico, makes a useful distinction between environmental and ecological thinking. By definition, an environment is the context within which something exists. Environment contains an "us" and a "not us" in its meaning. Ecology, by contrast, sees all aspects as part of a working dynamic whole—it's *all us*. Humans are engaged by Earth to serve an ecological purpose, even if they don't always do a good job of it. From this perspective, many of the planet's ecological and social problems arise from the false perception that humans and nature are separate.

For Regenesis, understanding the potential of natural capital begins with the premise that every place on the planet is a unique expression of geophysical, climatic, biological, and cultural influences. No two places are alike. Everyone knows that Paris is different from New York and Yosemite is different from Death Valley. What is less commonly understood is that those differences are written right into the DNA of the landscape and the qualities of the materials it produces. This uniqueness is expressed in a continually changing, living way and is the real source of natural capital.

COMMUNITY CAPITAL AND ROI

In pursuit of their stake in the vitality and viability of the places they live, communities invest the capital of *unique identity and vocation manifested through social and cultural web of relationships*. These webs and communities' distinctive relationships with local ecosystems are what make possible the unique work of a particular place. They comprise the understanding, symbols, collective wisdom, and ways of conveying these things that together make up a local culture. They also give rise to the unique economic potential that attracts people to a community and from which it can manifest unique business offerings. Figure 11.5 depicts the journey of communities' stake through the Responsible Business.

From an ecological perspective, social capital is a special case of natural capital. It derives from the distinctive roles that humans play within the living systems of a given place, roles connected to their unique capacity for consciousness.

A healthy community endeavors to create a context that will enable the fullest possible expression of potential for each of its members, consistent with the needs of its collective life. Each community has unique work to do based on its place in history and its landscape and on the distinctive raw materials that source

FIGURE 11.5. COMMUNITIES' STAKE IN THE RESPONSIBLE BUSINESS

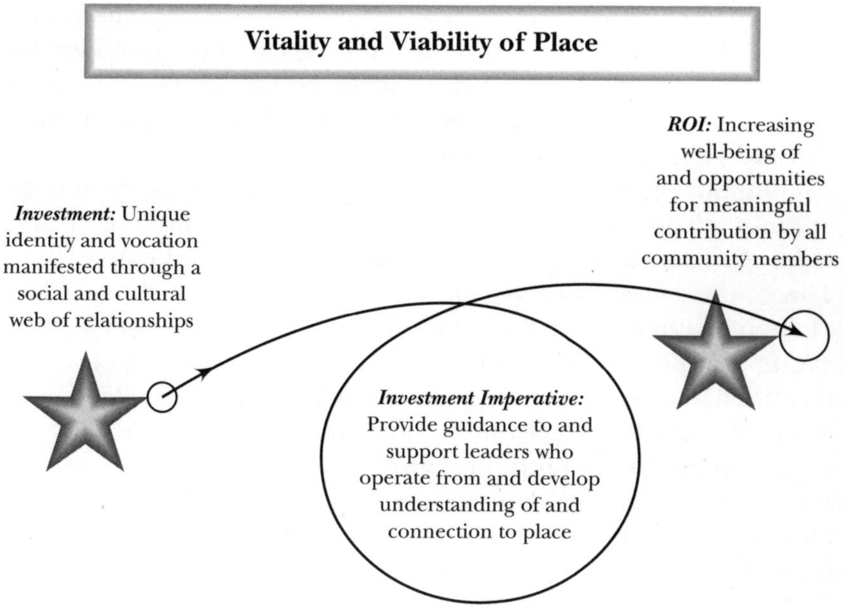

Vitality and Viability of Place

ROI: Increasing well-being of and opportunities for meaningful contribution by all community members

Investment: Unique identity and vocation manifested through a social and cultural web of relationships

Investment Imperative: Provide guidance to and support leaders who operate from and develop understanding of and connection to place

its economic life. The Middle East offers different work from British Columbia because each context is different. Each has to find its unique identity and vocation, its brand and its place, within regional and global economies.

Most social programs are actually efforts to mitigate the side effects of the disconnection from place. For example, business failures increase in places where people have lost their traditional connection to the local identity and resource base. Portland, Oregon, is holding up better in the 2008–2010 recession than Los Angeles and has rebounded faster at least in part because of its community's strong business and personal connections to place. Communities with living connections to their places naturally value all of their people, create place-based economic growth, and preserve and evolve unique local cultures. Living connection to place was once ubiquitous. It is now rare and as a result communities are fragmented and vulnerable.

The growth of a community's capital requires conscious development of the identity and vocation of place as a means to renew its authenticity and create a base for business development and growth that is consistent with local ecological and social imperatives. A revivified understanding of place unifies people across every social, demographic, and political line because place is what all local people have in common.

Organizations produce a return on community capital by operating from an understanding of and connection to place and helping others develop the same understanding and connection. There was a time when businesses were widely revered as pillars of their communities; they shared with their neighbors a deep caring for place. That role is still available to businesses that reawaken to it, and businesses can become leaders and role models in movements to redevelop love and understanding for place.

A community's ROI is the *increasing opportunity for the well-being of and meaningful contribution by every one of its members.* This ROI is measured by the integrity of the social fabric. When there are great disparities in opportunity, the entire community suffers. When all members, including the youngest, find ways to contribute, then a community is gaining ROI from its economic and social endeavors.

Communities maintain and strengthen their social fabrics by pursuing economic development that authentically reflects their unique characters. Regenesis uses the concept of place to help people understand the dynamic exchanges that are always occurring between people and nature in a specific community. The idea of place gives communities a way to move into the future—through settlement, social programs, cultural endeavors, and business development—consistent with the natural patterns and cultural stories that make them unique. Regenisis calls this *Story of Place*. Communities that find this distinctiveness or brand and attract or develop businesses consistent with it are more resilient after economic downtimes. They also stand apart in the world because of their unique contributions to the regional or global stage. South Africa has played that role with regard to truth and reconciliation, as has Curtiba, Brazil, with regard to the elimination of poverty.[4] Both of these communities realized an extraordinary ROI in the face of great hazard and great opportunity.

Curitiba is a large provincial capital city in southeastern Brazil with a population of roughly 2.4 million inhabitants. It is not known for any exceptional landmark; there are neither beaches nor wide, bridge-spanned rivers, and it rains quite often there. *Favelas,* or shantytowns, have sprouted up around the city's edges and roughly seventeen hundred new peasants migrate from the countryside to the city every month. Its population has skyrocketed over the past fifty years, doubling four times. Its city resources have been scant.

Given all of this, it is a small wonder that Curitiba has not followed in the footsteps of most other burgeoning third world cities faced with similar dilemmas. But rather than becoming an urban metropolis overrun with poverty, unemployment, inequity, and pollution, Curitiba and its citizens have instead seen a continuous and highly significant elevation in their quality of life. Many, including the United Nations, have in fact lauded the city of Curitiba as a leading model for ecological urban development and planning. The statistics show why:

- The amount of green space per capita in the city has risen in the past thirty years from a dismal half-a-square meter of green space per inhabitant to over fifty square meters per inhabitant. In fact, nearly one-fifth of the city is now parkland.
- Over 1.5 million trees have been planted by volunteers along streets and avenues.
- Curitiba's fast and efficient bus system carries more passengers per weekday than New York City's and runs with an 89 percent approval rating.
- Auto traffic has declined by more than 30 percent since 1974, despite the fact that Curitiba's population has doubled and there are more car owners per capita in Curitiba than anywhere else in Brazil.
- The city of Curitiba has the highest percentage of citizens who recycle in the world. More than 70 percent of all the city's trash is now recycled.

- Curitiba's thirty-year economic growth rate is 7.1 percent higher than the national averages, resulting in a current per capita income 66 percent higher than the Brazilian average.

What makes these accomplishments even more astonishing is the fact that all this was achieved through the means of a very limited civic budget. Many of Curitiba's programs are designed to help pay for themselves, to address multiple civic issues at the same time, and to systemically coordinate with and enable the working of other programs.

Curitiba's success was based on many of the same principles and practices behind the Responsible Business. The planning team started by developing an understanding of what was unique about the city and how one could build a sense of community and vocation in the world based on that uniqueness. Because the city was both poor and smart, it sought ways to make highly leveraged investments and coined the term *urban acupuncture* to describe interventions designed to get mega-multiplier bangs from its scarce bucks. Every project had to meet rigorous criteria for being "fast, cheap, simple, and systemically effective." The city had a strong orientation to improving the lives of every one of its citizens (its "customers") and emphasized building self-determination and self-management throughout the population. Ideas were expected to be obvious enough that people could readily see their relevance.

Just one of the thousands of creative programs the city put in place was designed to address sanitation in the favelas, which were emerging spontaneously, with no central planning and no utilities, built from whatever materials lay at hand. As a result, garbage collection was impossible, and disease, rats, and other problems became acute. The city offered to pay residents to separate their trash and bring it to collection and recycling areas on the periphery of the favelas. Residents were paid in tokens that could be used to access the city's excellent public transit system or to buy food at local farmer's markets. With this simple program, the city was able to clean up the garbage, build acceptance for recycling, provide access to good food and support for local farmers, and improve employment opportunities by enabling very poor people to use public transit. Not coincidentally, children from the favelas were able to use their bus tokens to spread out and clean up the rest of the city, becoming valued and contributing citizens at a time when vigilante groups in other cities in Brazil were shooting street children.

The creativity and holism that Curitiba's leadership team brought to everything it did was remarkable, not only because the group was so innovative with such limited means but also because it was able to sustain its quality of thinking over decades and through many changes in political leadership. This required a significantly different way of thinking than that provided by conventional training for city planners or managers. It also required a continuous planning process rather than a single annual planning event. Every morning for the last forty years, the city's management team has met at the campus of the Free University of the Environment to "dream forward." It spends its mornings in the world of ideation and possibility, and its afternoons managing day-to-day operations—and is very clear that it could not afford the costs of doing it any other way. This has nourished the spirit of the leaders while generating an endless supply of ideas to be tested and implemented. The corporate world would do well to learn from Curitiba's story.

In another compelling example, John Knott demonstrated the interrelatedness between reconnecting to place and the economic return to a city. Noisette, South Carolina, a suburb of Charleston, has become the home of a visionary joint public-private venture between the city of North Charleston and the Noisette Company. The Noisette Company has funded the master planning for the conversion of a 3,000-acre former naval base in addition to a community-involvement process that was conducted over thirty months and involved hundreds of meetings with thousands of citizens.

John Knott said, "We need to restore our intuitive connection to the natural world and better integrate the design and operation of our human habitat within it. Our failure to understand our buildings and communities as systems that directly impact and are impacted by our natural world is at the root of many of our building failures and our current global crisis."[5] This process at Noisette involved documenting twelve thousand years of human and natural history. The planners discovered the condition of the natural systems before human settlement and overlaid them with the existing urban infrastructure. This analysis showed that it was possible to reconnect about 70 percent of the natural systems without taking over private land and to improve the storm water performance of the community.

The Noisette project sparked the revitalization of an impoverished area and opened the Cooper River to the North Charleston community for the first time in more than a century. Between March 2001 and October 2005, home ownership in the area rose from 32 to 45 percent. Housing values boomed from $54 per square foot, a value that had remained flat or declining for twenty years, to $140 per square foot. Average time on the market decreased from 270 days to 30 days. Commercial land, which traded for $50,000 per acre in 2001, rose to $250,000–$500,000 per acre in 2005. In areas where there had been no investment for thirty years, more than two thousand new housing units were started. More than eight hundred new professional families with children moved into existing housing and changed neighborhood and school dynamics. Gentrification was avoided by increasing infill rather than forcing out existing, less economically advantaged residents. More than twelve thousand new jobs were attracted to this previously ignored area.

One of the most unusual integrations of business, community, and ecology regeneration is emerging in the Middle East. During fall 2009, I began participating in a new endeavor initiated with a conference in Beirut. The focus was on integrating the work of business with improved sustainability for the region while building economic development. Twenty Arab nations and over one hundred businesses participated in a gathering sponsored by the Arab Federation for Environment and Development (AFED) to launch the process.

In the future, the intention is to move forward with a set of six industries, changing them from commodity industries to value-adding industries based in Story of Place. In each of these industries, including oil and agriculture, there is a new opportunity to understand the essence of the molecules and places involved as well. This kind of focus on the value-adding possibility is how W. L. Gore built a business. Understanding the unique working of a molecule and how can it be engaged in a regenerative way can also regenerate Earth and communities involved. A consortium of AFED leaders believe they can accomplish this shift to value-adding businesses and improve the vitality, ecology, and stability of the region. Imagine the power of Story as a starting place for the regeneration of these ancient communities and ecosystems.

But currently no businesses in the Middle East are engaging with natural resources as parts of living systems. Instead they are harvesting them according to conventional extraction models and pursuing efficiencies in survival mode. As a result, community economies, cultural history, and ecologies are all in diminishing positions.

In cooperation with the United Nations Foundation and the OPEC Foundation, the intention is to reinvigorate the Mediterranean and Gulf regions by building capability to think in a systemic mode across government and industry. New capabilities will be needed to reverse trends and build a strong connection to the story of this place that cradles so much of what we call the civilized world today. But to take on the idea of reframing all these places of antiquity is one of the most exciting opportunities to demonstrate the power of such thinking. The United Nations Foundation and OPEC Fund believe it will make a difference. YouTube offers some of the talks regarding the new venture and its possibilities, including those of Mohamed El-Ashry of the United Nations Foundation board of trustees and Selieman Al-Herbish of the OPEC Fund for Development.[6]

A Responsible Business becomes a member of its communities, joining with them to reweave the webs of cultural relationships and connection to place. This reestablishes the sources of community creativity and supports the economic viability of both community and business.

Investor Capital and ROI

Investors pursue their stake—the value that flows from supporting other's manifestations of creativity and steadfastness—by contributing the capital of *accrued equity*. There is a natural tendency in all living systems to reinvest; nature does not hoard. Investors know that a changing world will diminish the value of equity that

FIGURE 11.6. INVESTORS' STAKE IN THE RESPONSIBLE BUSINESS

Value from Supporting Manifestations of Creativity and Steadfast Growth

ROI: Growth and income; returns for all stakeholders; improved value by others for the industry and workability of capitalism for benefit of all

Investment:
Accrued equity

Investment Imperative:
Durable returns consistent with articulated principles and paradigms

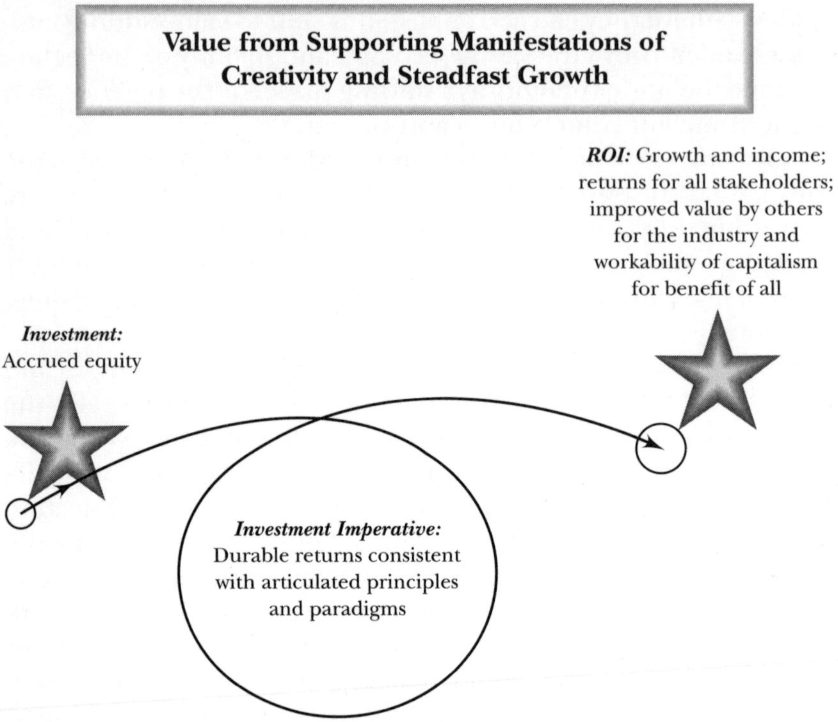

isn't reinvested. Figure 11.6 depicts the journey of the investors' stake through the Responsible Business.

Investors of financial capital expect and count on businesses to use their resource with the same care and thoughtfulness that they exercised to accrue it. They prefer consistency and rely on companies to operate from sound principles and paradigms. They lose confidence when decisions or actions are inconsistent with articulated principles and paradigms. Investors are most likely to lose their equity when leadership fails to exercise the systemic rigor and discipline required to use its principles and paradigms as meaningful guides to decision making.

Return on financial capital can be measured at three levels, only one of which is generally reflected in the annual report. The first is functional, related to growth and income, and is the generally accepted understanding of ROI.

A Responsible Business also accounts for a second kind of ROI: the return to its other stakeholders. This return on other kinds of capital extends the meaning and nonfinancial consequences of the financial investment. Without this kind of accounting, investors have no way of knowing whether or not their passive income has been generated from value-extracting or value-adding processes. This is not the same as reporting how much was spent on social or ecological contributions because these contributions may have little to do with a real return on nonfinancial capital. Only measures of increased ecological and community health qualify at this second level of return.

The third nature of return occurs when a business improves how investors and capitalism are perceived in the world at large. This is measured by the confidence of the citizenry in the role business plays in fostering a healthy society and planet.

Thus, financial capital moves to a new platform in terms of how return is measured. The Responsible Business is no longer content to report financial return without considering the investment of other stakeholders. It seeks to understand and report on the outputs or effects of its investments on increasingly healthy communities and ecosystems. It also seeks to measure specific effects along with its value-adding process from Earth to Earth— that is, from resource extraction to product recycling, reuse, or disposal. These effects show up in the form of improved economic viability of communities from which materials are purchased. The watersheds and bioregions where its physical facilities are located become demonstrably healthier as a result of its presence. Its workers undertake to educate the local population, which results in a functioning political system.

In order to produce the kind of stabilizing force that builds investor confidence and pride of ownership, business leaders begin by working with boards of directors to formulate meaningful principles to guide governance and management. These are designed to address the global imperatives for all stakeholders and can have a huge effect on the relationships a company depends on for survival.

CONCLUSIONS

A healthy and evolving business environment requires that all five stakeholder groups continue to invest. This comes about when all parties recognize the systemic nature of their connections and the contribution that businesses can and should make to an increasingly vibrant world.

Continued customer investment depends on the reliably life-enhancing qualities of business offerings. Continued co-creator investment depends on working environments that foster growth and creativity and enable the pursuit of worthy aims. Continued Earth investment depends on a steadily growing capacity of natural systems to support life for all. Continued community investment depends on increasingly harmonious and equitable social relationships. And continued financial investment depends on durable returns from endeavors that advance the well-being of society as a whole.

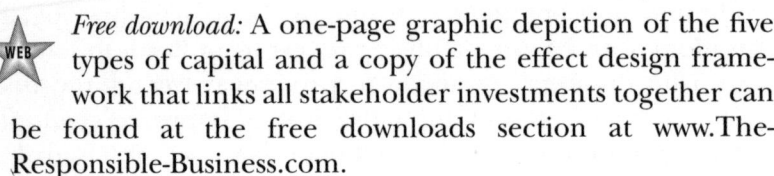

Free download: A one-page graphic depiction of the five types of capital and a copy of the effect design framework that links all stakeholder investments together can be found at the free downloads section at www.The-Responsible-Business.com.

Chapter Twelve

Assessing Responsibility

There are three things extremely hard:
steel, a diamond, and to know one's self.
Benjamin Franklin

I often wish I knew the degree of responsibility practiced by the companies I do business with. I particularly wish I had this kind of understanding when I make investment decisions. Although some companies are transparent and even forthcoming about their business practices, current rules and executive mind-sets make it difficult for most people to really know the businesses they invest in and buy from.

In preparing to write this book, I engaged with business leaders from a variety of industries to assess two of the most popular, esteemed, and innovative new businesses of the past three decades—Google and Apple—using a set of indicators based on the stakeholder pentad. These leaders included twenty-four executives from companies that have interacted with Google and Apple as customers, suppliers, consultants, and even competitors. Each of these executives has amassed a wealth of understanding from their direct experience. What I wanted from my conversations with them was a better sense of how well both companies are developing as Responsible Businesses. My aim was to demonstrate that any company can use systemic responsibility indicators to assess and improve itself as it evolves toward responsibility.

Many of the executives had been my clients and all were familiar with the ideas offered in this book, although none of them were among the executives profiled in earlier chapters. I engaged them in small-group dialogues, the same method I recommend for companies that wish to do their own self-assessments. All the participants wondered aloud what Google and Apple would have to say about themselves and this helped guide our exploration. As we talked, they offered examples of responsible business practice from other good companies, with a particular emphasis on W. L. Gore, and I've included those thoughts as well. In what follows I have summarized the small-group dialogues, honoring my agreement to keep participants anonymous.

What is offered here is not intended to be a scientific or rigorous analysis. Instead, it is meant to provide an example of reflective thinking and dialogue among business leaders who are deeply engaged in developing Responsible Businesses. It might be accurate to say that they were also assessing and developing themselves as responsible leaders as they conducted the assessment of Google and Apple.

SYSTEMIC RESPONSIBILITY INDICATORS

There are fifteen indicators, three for each of the five stakeholders, to ensure that all stakeholders are benefited simultaneously without trading one off against another—an important criterion for the Responsible Business. During our conversations, the executives discussed how they felt a given company performed with regard to each of the indicators and where the company appeared to be heading over several years.

CUSTOMER INDICATORS

The following indicators assess how well a Responsible Business enriches the lives of its customers.

1. *The Responsible Business honors the uniqueness or distinctiveness of the user experience delivered by its product or service offerings.* A Responsible Business provides offerings that only it can deliver and that serve its customers in ways that are distinctive and enriching. Uniqueness is expressed and extended continually.

2. *As a result of the Responsible Business's offerings, customers experience better lives than they could with competing offerings.* Customers do not compare companies; they compare experiences. They are attracted to offerings that improve and enhance their lives by improving their overall well-being (including their health and the health and functioning of their communities). Customers are not in the market for offerings that are simply less bad than the alternatives.

3. *The Responsible Business's offerings are reliably and distinctively value-adding and ethically created even in the face of market and economic hazards and opportunities.* Customers shop for offerings and companies that actively seek to understand and improve their lives without fail. The Responsible Business never lets users down by being unstable or unresponsive.

The executives discussed these three indicators in an interactive way as they applied to Google and Apple. They found them to be good guidelines for developing understanding about events and activities that they had not previously thought of as indicators of responsible actions and decisions. They highlighted arenas where there were shortfalls even in great companies. Businesses using the indicators to guide their own assessments may be surprised to discover how their everyday decisions concerning finance, business model development, management structure, and work with regulators (to name a few examples) have multiple, ongoing responsibility implications.

Reflections from the Executives
The executives first of all observed that user experience drives everything that Apple and Google do. Google states explicitly that if a customer has difficulty using its offerings, it is Google's problem. Google commits to reading the minds of its users by tracking patterns in their entries, much as a spouse learns to finish a partner's sentences. It interprets the ways words are spelled so that users don't have to spell their inquiries correctly in order to get help. Google doesn't ask its users to change; it continually changes itself to anticipate what they need and give them better service. ("I want a husband like that," said one of the female executives.)

How is this possible? Although everyone agreed that Google competed vigorously to hire brilliant minds, there were clearly other factors that enabled it to "adopt a customer's problem" as its own. This sets them apart from Microsoft and other software providers. Microsoft customers load software onto their own computers. Customer problems are addressed every two to three years when new versions of software are released. Some solutions and improvements are provided as electronic files that customers must be prompted to accept and download.

By contrast, Google can correct a problem within weeks or days because management of its software remains entirely in its hands. There is no reason for the user to modify or upgrade to a new version. Ongoing, continual service to the customer remains uniquely seamless, even invisible. This is an act of responsibility to its customers. Amazon and salesforce.com have also developed strength in this arena, but each of the executives named Google as the preeminent leader in responsibility to customers.

Google has also mastered the ability to manage multiple levels of offerings. A user can enter an endless variety of questions into a Google search box (including math questions) or go to Google Wonder Wheel to find information organized in a new, simpler, and more convenient way. Customer management of such complex software on their own computers would require many disks and multiple user manuals, but Google makes their diversity of sophisticated searches immediately available with no impediment. A single portal that works for users at different levels of sophistication makes layers of questions and multiple levels of background possible.

Apple also strives to debug problems before they reach the user and to address them as soon as they appear. The company films people setting up each new system to see how they go about it. Its teams try to make the system "not work" to reveal flaws in the design and operations. This dedication to effortless interface demonstrates a commitment to be better than competing offers in terms of the customer's experience. It yields something unique in the categories Apple competes in: *fail-proof from the beginning*.

Another aspect of Apple's uniqueness is the *elegance and essentiality* of its offerings. One executive contrasted this with Intel and Microsoft's informal partnership. Intel had been advancing the speed of processors and their ability to rapidly handle increasing degrees of complexity. Microsoft in return was creating more complex software with more sophisticated features. Microsoft believed that Intel would always solve the complexity problem with its next CPU and so it never considered complexity as a restraint to design. When the software finally did exceed the CPU's ability to manage its complexity, it created a great opening for Apple.

Apple took a different path. It focused on offerings that were elegant in design, user friendly, and targeted to what consumers were actually trying to do with computers. When the Windows debacles began to multiply, Apple stepped into the breach. With its computers and mobile interactive devices (iPod, iPhone, and iPad) introduced each succeeding year, Apple created a system of products that were *intuitively useable* and highly effective in their results.

This *seize-the-moment approach* fits with Apple's philosophy that although market research might serve to confirm successes, it can never be a source of creativity. For Steve Jobs, this is rule number one. Do not ask people what they want. They don't know. Give them what "wakes them up" to what is possible, over and over again. In fact, this is Apple's default principle. *Surprise people with new possibilities.* Buyers look forward to the surprise. They count on it. This shows a high level of being responsible to customers compared with commodity offerings, which do not serve conscious consumers in the market with fewer products with more elegant multitasking capability.

Google clearly offers customers better life experiences by assuring them that whenever they make a mistake, someone has their back. Users do not want to be educated or sold on how great something would be if only they could learn to use it. Google and Apple offerings do not require user manuals. If a product is not intuitive and even surprisingly more useful than the customer expected, it is not leading to a better life. All the executives felt that both Google and Apple excel at producing these kinds of offerings and are inherently dedicated to getting continually better.

A former ranking Microsoft executive said that he had been aware—even as he sought to corral all the permutations in search and software products that engineers might dream up—that Apple was right in a couple of critical ways. First, they developed a core principle to guide the design of each product, specifying what the product was to do and how it was to do it. This development of a core principle for every product made it easy to reject brilliant ideas that did not serve it. Such a rejection was not personal; it was principle based. As a result it led to better thinking and better design. By contrast, in design sessions at Microsoft rejections were often felt personally, and this inevitably discouraged creative thinking.

Second, Apple did not distribute design decisions. A core principle for a particular product focused people's creativity and kept them aligned. Microsoft felt decentralization of design was important but didn't necessarily build the capabilities required to decentralize in a ways that produced superior customer offerings.

W. L. Gore, manufacturer of Gore-Tex, was also described by the executives as a company that ranked exceptionally high with regard to these customer indicators. W. L. Gore is a brick-and-mortar operation that generates material products. From the executives' perspective, it has been uniquely able to understand the essences of chemical molecules and use them to serve customers. Through its chemical precision, W. L. Gore provides reliably distinctive and value-adding products that leverage the success of customers in industries with very precise requirements.

All the executives felt that Google, Apple, and W. L. Gore are each true to themselves, continually exploring who they are and how they work. Google's product design approach is different from Apple's, which is different from W. L. Gore's, and each would consider it inauthentic to try to copy someone else's best practice. Thus, they are able to maintain fidelity with their customers and themselves.

The executives' overall reflection was that beyond ensuring responsibility to the customer, performance in these three customer indicator arenas was core to a business's doing well in the market. As one executive group wrapped up their discussion, a participant laughed and said, "Of course, that's what being a Responsible Business should mean: be unique and relevant, be better at improving life."

CO-CREATOR INDICATORS

The following indicators show how Responsible Businesses enable all of their co-creators to reveal and express essence in their work.

1. *The Responsible Business enables unique contributions and opportunities for employees and suppliers to bring something of value to other people's lives, including to customers.* The greatest loss in the Industrial Revolution was the ability of individual workers to experience directly the effect of their work and the value their creations brought to users.

2. *The Responsible Business ensures individuals the opportunity to complement the work of one or more teams. At the same time it helps them develop their own unique potential.* Many team-based systems turn workers into interchangeable robotic parts with no connection to customers. Training and development are most useful when they are provided within the context of contributions a person commits to make to a strategy and global imperative of the business.

3. *The Responsible Business honors the worthiness of all members of its organization, ensuring the expression of their creativity.* The whole is diminished when any one person is excluded from the creative process. (This is one reason layoffs hurt the people who stay as well as those who leave and why great care is taken in this regard by Responsible Businesses.) Rewards and incentives create losers and undermine the natural tendency and value to be a contributing team member. Recognition is more meaningful when it is self-initiated as the result of making good on a promise-beyond- ableness.

Reflections from the Executives

Both Google and Apple seem to have grasped the fundamental truths that connection to customers is what allows a co-creator to flourish and that the connection originates from the co-creator not from delegation. Both companies enable creative people to connect to the experience of the customer—the real source of excitement in a job. Google tests and tracks continually to interpret for its search engine users what they want and how they can access it. This gives Google engineers direct access to and involvement in the customer experience, fostering their passion for the work they are doing and their role in the business.

At Google, product engineers are product managers. A couple of engineers known to some of the executives had mixed feelings when they went to work for Google—not about the company but about being brought on with no defined role and expected to find where they fit. They liked the idea that if they were square pegs they would not be required to operate in round holes, but the sense of contribution and fulfillment that comes from teaming seemed delayed. For each of them it took about nine months to find a home where he knew he would belong. Each suggested he wanted to design a way to evolve the entry process while preserving the motivation and character building it offers.

Google is not a heavily managed company and it encourages the expression of uniqueness in its engineers. Microsoft is heavily hierarchical, with four to six direct reports for each manager. This makes for many management levels in large teams—on average, five managers for every twenty-five people. At Google, forty to fifty people report to each manager. Google counts on a bottom-up approach for innovation and offers its engineers 20 percent open time to pursue their own areas of research or inquiry. This dedicated open time has yielded major contributions to its search engine, YouTube, the Android operating system, and its marketing.

Yet the open-time practice has caused some problems. Although it promotes entrepreneurship, enables responsibility to the customer stakeholder, and provides co-creators with opportunities to contribute, it has also resulted in too much innovation, too fast. The large number of engineers at Google, combined with incentives to launch new ideas and get awards, has expanded both the number and frequency of new ideas. In one brief period there were so many launches that customers become confused. So a few years ago Google began revamping the open-time practice to focus on key strengths of the businesses.

Though executives appreciated Google's open-time approach to encouraging bottom-up innovation, they also criticized the way it separated creative time from "real" work rather than integrate creativity into all aspects of co-creators' work. Some members referred to their own experiences with promises-beyond-ableness, which made ideation (the process of generating useable ideas) widespread among co-creators and delivered high returns on time invested. (Promises-beyond-ableness are described in Chapter Six of this book.) They pointed out that it is not just freedom and autonomy that count but also the meaningful contributions to colleagues and customers that freedom enables. They also noted that actively engaging all members of an organization, not just the engineers as in Google's case, honors the worthiness of every employee and cultivates the unique contribution each can make.

All the executives agreed that the secrecy surrounding Apple makes it hard to know how its workforce is managed. But the company has faced criticism for several deaths and illnesses among contractors in China, and this has opened doors to efforts to improve its co-creator relationships. The executives inferred that caring was not built into the sourcing process for Apple, and none of the executives felt that the company was doing a particularly good job of enriching the lives of workers beyond its direct employees.

However, Apple does intentionally foster a wider creative community. It creates opportunities for many creative entrepreneurs to make a living and has more openness to new ideas from outsiders than any other hardware or software business in its categories. A couple of the executives currently are leading new ventures that partner with Apple. They have found the people there to be great team players, generous and creative in helping their businesses succeed. But these are large ventures with income-producing potential for Apple. It is unclear how well partnering with Apple would work for smaller ventures.

The executives perceived many open-ended opportunities for Apple workers to contribute, except in one arena—product concept. At Apple, concept development is held by a small, closely bonded group that engages in a tightly focused process. Steve Jobs currently leads the group, but others are increasingly taking on the leadership role.

Once a concept has been created by the small group, it is turned loose so that everyone at Apple can work on designing it. A design is judged by whether it has manifested the elegance of the original concept. People have learned that if they want to contribute to a design, their ideas must start from an improvement in the experience of the users and their lives. This is a criterion that many of the executives had built into their own organizations but they agreed that Apple is the master. They noted that the perception that Steve Jobs and the small team responsible for original conceptions make all creative decisions, excluding anyone not in their inner circle, is a misunderstanding of the process that shapes the concept and eventually the offering itself.

The executives also observed that at W. L. Gore, team members are expected to be intimately connected with the customers' fields of experience, whether it be mountain bikes or surgical units. The team members' goal is to solve problems and create opportunities for customers before they even know they need them or think to ask for them. Those who knew the company intimately wondered whether it completely understood the brilliance of what it had created.

Though the founder, Bill Gore, has been gone for over two decades, his business philosophy has continued to nourish the company's culture and success. He believed that individuals who have an idea for a project or product should have to convince others to join with them in its development. This recruitment process builds a deep sense of will and motivation and fosters the development of individual and team potential. Those who commit to an idea continue to gather others until the full complement of talent needed for the work has been assembled. The idea of layoffs has not been a part of the culture at W. L. Gore because they have not had to face it. Similar to promises-beyond-ableness, the work systems at W. L. Gore build strong offerings that match almost precisely the needs of their customers and inspire co-creators to devote themselves wholeheartedly to inventing and discovering such offerings.

One of the executives also offered the example of Starbucks, which appears to be moving toward an overarching commitment to increase the wealth of all of its suppliers. All of the executives agreed that Starbucks needs to go further and they proposed that connecting to each supplier as a co-creator with unique capabilities and offerings was a promising way to strengthen their entire field of operation. Other consumer product companies, including Patagonia, Clif Bar, Green Mountain Coffee, Walmart, and Whole Foods Market, were mentioned as businesses working to buy more from local producers as a way to support a broader range of small suppliers and diverse products—an encouraging, albeit nascent, development.

EARTH INDICATORS

The following indicators show how Responsible Businesses serve Earth by evolving the unique potential of ecosystems and natural resources.

1. *The Responsible Business discovers how each of the ecosystems it affects and each of the natural resources they provide are unique and how they work as living systems.* Modern science and technology treat resources in isolation from the ecosystems they are parts of and this leads to fragmented and formulaic sustainability programs that obliterate the integrity and working capacity of living systems—and even their ability to function as systems. In Responsible Businesses, co-creators are aware that each Earth mineral and biota invested in the business's success has a unique purpose within the ecosystem and that understanding the reciprocal working aspects of all of the life in the ecosystem is the prerequisite to creating appropriate returns on investment to Earth.

2. *In the Responsible Business, co-creators experience themselves as Earth citizens, embedded members of their ecosystems, joined with and supporting the expression of the ecosystems' essences and workability.* The Responsible Business's deep care, connection, and respect for natural resources and ecosystems arises from the understanding that each is a living whole with a unique essence. In Responsible Businesses, co-creators do not speak of *environments* because the term indicates something separate from themselves. Consciousness of their contributing role and the effects of their actions on local ecosystems and Earth as a whole is pervasive.

3. *Where they work and live, the Responsible Business's co-creators participate actively in evolving ecosystems in their production processes, productive capacity, and capacity for regeneration.* They base their

participation on rigorous observation and reflection. They understand that although reducing harm is important, their role is to regenerate and secure the health and vitality of a living planet. Interventions and actions are not designed to "minimize the damage." Instead all interactions with ecosystems are conducted to create a net positive effect.

Reflections from the Executives

The executives found only limited evidence that Google, Apple, or any of the other businesses we discussed were engaging with Earth at this level. All of the businesses have some technological and behavioral initiatives to arrest the level of damage they do. Google focuses on building more energy-efficient servers. Apple has definitely taken a big step with mercury-free and energy-efficient batteries. But clearly there is plenty of room for improvement when it comes to growing businesses that add continuing value to the capacity of ecosystems.

COMMUNITY INDICATORS

The following indicators show how Responsible Businesses help communities develop their inherent potential and unique identity.

1. *The Responsible Business fosters and develops human systems to evolve the uniqueness and vitality of communities.* A Responsible Business is evolved from an understanding of a given place, people, and context rather than from standardized and mechanical approaches that are universalized across different cultures and landscapes.
2. *The Responsible Business seeks out, develops, and supports communities that develop initiatives to integrate many diverse perspectives.* A Responsible Businesses actively supports community efforts to reconcile multiple perspectives and opinions rather than perpetuate divided interests and polarized confrontations.
3. *The Responsible Business supports and promotes community governance based on the rights and obligations of all living beings to contribute to and participate in societal and ecological health.* Although we are a nation of laws, not everything is best

accomplished through legislation. Healthy communities also require tolerance and the capacity for thoughtful reflection, qualities that are better nurtured through education, including experienced-based learning at work and within social and faith organizations.

Reflections from the Executives

One story about Google especially illuminated the subject of community consideration. In 2009, during its conversion to a digital format, the Federal Communications Commission (FCC) auctioned off the frequencies that previously had been analog. This was expected to bring $10 million into the U.S. Treasury. It was the FCC's job to benefit taxpayers by getting the highest possible bids. In theory this was an open auction, but it was likely that the bandwidth would be bought up by existing carriers in cable and wireless services in order to shut out competition. The bandwidth was auctioned in packages, and established carriers appeared to control the whole process. Ordinarily, Google would not have been one the parties to the auction, but because the conversion would affect all Internet users, Google decided to act on their behalf, without certainty at the time how the company might benefit.

Currently, a wireless customer cannot participate directly in the use of bandwidth but can only access it though a carrier who licenses and controls use. Google saw an opportunity to change the rules and asked for legislation to that effect. This new rule would offer a spectrum of bandwidth within which wireless service customers could go anywhere. In return, Google announced to the FCC that it was willing to bid at a higher rate to set a higher minimum, thus serving the FCC's mandate to return value to taxpayers. Google succeeded in getting the FCC to change the rule for a part of the bandwidth, even though they did not win the auction. They are credited with single-handedly moving FCC regulations in a new direction and opening up arenas for innovation that would serve communities.

This act of community service grew out of Google's culture of fostering diverse perspectives, pushing limits, and enabling community access to vital information. It had the added benefit of creating a new playing field, one in which Google is likely to succeed. The lesson from this is that responsibility is embedded in how this company does business rather than only in isolated, nonsystemic programs.

Google uses its "Ten Things We Know to Be True," a statement of values, as guiding principles in the way they do business. One principle states, "You can make money without doing evil."[1] In this context, the executives noted Google's explicit disallowance of ads that are not directly related to the entered search terms. Google wants everything on a search results page to be relevant to what the search is about; otherwise it refuses the ad and gives up the revenue. Google offers additional transparency with its overt specification of advertised information as a "sponsor link" just below each ad.

INVESTOR INDICATORS

The following indicators show how Responsible Businesses generate systemic wealth and promote conscious capitalism.

1. *The Responsible Business provides durable returns from investment in the creation of wealth for all stakeholders.* Responsible business leaders work with their investors to be conscious capitalists. Such investors understand that they are engines for the creation of systemic wealth, not just for their own personal wealth. They do not assume that there is a need to trade off among stakeholder interests. Instead they understand that reconciling apparent conflicts among stakeholder interests is a source of creativity and wealth for themselves and other business leaders.
2. *The Responsible Business advances the industry's character and capacity while building asset value.* Ensuring the viability and vitality of an industry is self-serving for the investor but also has the advantage of fulfilling a capitalistic imperative on which larger economies are based.
3. *The Responsible Business understands divergent and destabilizing forces in governing processes, economies, and markets. It leverages these forces to create world-changing effects and stakeholder evolution.*

Reflections from the Executives

Most business people think of responsibility as something that a company pursues separately from its usual business and that it is related to social and environment concerns. This exclusion view is especially true when it comes to dealing with regulators or making decisions about how to advance shareholder value. But in the case of the FCC bandwidth auction described previously, Google was able to distinguish between what it perceived as responsible and irresponsible forms of capitalism. Irresponsible capitalism was focused on keeping the use of airwaves under corporate control and limiting the amount that would be paid into the public treasury. Responsible capitalism sought to create the greatest advantage for all stakeholders, including Internet users (customers) and taxpayers (in this instance, the investor), which would have been underserved without Google's intervention. Google seized the opportunity to evolve a responsible capitalistic approach in a changing event that destabilized the regulation process and creating an opening.

Recommendations from the Executives

The executives found that Google and Apple showed high levels of responsibility in several areas. The set of fifteen systemic responsibility indicators made for a rich assessment exercise, enabling the executives to identify where responsible development was incomplete and develop four recommendations that would help the companies evolve more responsible business systems.

Evolve Responsible Partners and Suppliers

The executives observed that co-creators had developed high levels of responsibility with regard to their own employees but had neglected the potential to help suppliers and contractors evolve Responsible Businesses. They suggested basing purchases from suppliers on responsibility factors as well as pricing. They noted that high-tech suppliers and partners who are regarded as fully enabled members of the Google and Apple teams often treat their low-wage workers as interchangeable and expendable cogs.

Further, there is opportunity for Google and Apple to draw on the creativity of partners and suppliers in the product creation process and to help them increase their own sense of business direction. This would also increase the wealth-building capacity of suppliers within their communities and as a result communities would be strengthened as well.

Evolve Responsibility to Earth

The biggest downsides for both Google and Apple were revealed by the Earth indicators. Both companies will advance their responsibility as they find ways to engage all of their employees and everyone in their co-creative streams in efforts to understand and apply the indicators to assess the sourcing of materials and people practices with resources in their operations. In particular, employees could be engaged to explore the essence of the materials work with and their relationships to the ecosystems from which they are sourced. The intention would be to create understanding of the ways in which business activities—for example, product development, extraction and production operations, and investment decisions—affect local ecosystems and Earth as a whole.

Advance the Understanding of Communities

Because of the diversity of their cultures and places, communities are a nearly limitless source of new potential, both as markets for offerings and as sources for creativity and far-reaching new ways of thinking. By developing increasingly nuanced relationships with the communities in which they operate, both Google and Apple have significant opportunities to work with them and to access the value they have to co-contribute. Google in particular is beautifully designed to become a powerful community-building tool through collaborating with community leaders using its mapping and information services.

Evolve Investor and Industry Responsibility

The position that Google and Apple hold as public companies at the top of their game will make it possible for them to continue to make innovations in investing and educating their own investors. Based on the evidence of their quarterly analysts' reports, neither company currently relates to their investors as becoming potentially more responsible stakeholders. Executives who participated in the assessment and who are investors in Apple and Google strongly suggested that the companies should provide education and information to help realize investor potential as a conscious stakeholder.

The executives also noted that W. L. Gore has a great opportunity to better understand its management framework and, working with the indicators, to enable all co-creators—employees, suppliers, and partners—to make contributions based on the uniqueness of their customers and employees. They felt that the company is in a great position to adopt the responsibility indicators and to spread the word throughout its industry that doing so makes for far more effective business practice, as they have already demonstrated.

Much that has been written about W. L. Gore does not adequately describe the company's underlying philosophy and the paradigms that have made it successful. When other companies seek to copy from the W. L. Gore success, they have no way to learn from the foundational practices on which it is based. By becoming consciously committed to responsibility and articulate about their work, W. L. Gore could make itself a model of alternative business practices in the same way that P&G, Lima, has served as a model for hundreds of other companies during the past five decades.

The executives were clear that they were not suggesting judging the work of others and labeling it right or wrong. Instead they were advocating teaching companies by example to make better business choices. This is an act of responsibility that goes beyond Earth and communities to improve the integrity of industries and to foster the highest expression of capitalism.

CONCLUSIONS

In a Responsible Business, all stakeholders engage in practices that contribute to the ongoing evolution of increasingly more effect business practices. Responsibility is pervasive throughout. My conversations with the executives ended

(*Continued*)

with expressions of surprise that Apple, Google, and so many other companies that are highly esteemed and valued are still focusing on pockets of well-defined responsibility, apparently unaware that opportunities exist to make responsibility systemic.

All of the executives suggested that the indicators are valuable instruments that can help change the conversation into one that brings deep understanding of the ways a business affects all of its stakeholders and how the stakeholders are intricately connected with one another. They vowed to engage their own organizations in assessments based on the indicators and to do so regularly in order to keep the them alive and active in their daily business practices.

 Free download: A graphic of the assessment indicators can be found in the free downloads section at www .The-Responsible-Business.com.

CHAPTER THIRTEEN

THE FUTURE OF RESPONSIBILITY

Learn from yesterday, live for today, hope for tomorrow.
The important thing is not to stop questioning.
ALBERT EINSTEIN

As the stories in this book suggest, the business unit, which has direct responsibility for all of the activities that affect stakeholders, is often the most effective organizational level from which to engage in work on corporate responsibility. At the business unit level, where there is a direct connection between managers and the results of their daily decisions, responsibility can become systemic. Decisions affect shareholders, and they make further choices that all stakeholders live with.

At the same time, there is a unique role for corporations in the evolution of a more responsible business culture in the world. They must lead the way to the future of responsibility. The nature and legal structure of corporations enables them to provide the level of infrastructure needed to engage with regulatory agencies, interface with the investment community, and build a broader consensus with regard to ethical business practices. Corporations establish the overarching principles and philosophy that can guide individual businesses in their development and operations.

As Chad Holliday found when he finally had responsibility for the whole of DuPont, the scale and complexity of a major corporation made it difficult to directly affect the financial, social, and sustainability goals of individual businesses, but it gave him an important platform from which to create dialogues that shaped thinking and behavior choices globally. Chad worked with other business leaders and the United Nations to found the UN Global Compact and to discover what would move industry toward responsibility. He and others observed that corporations begin to evolve toward responsibility when they commit to creating cultural containers or chartering entities for responsible practices at the level of industry and national government.

Chad also wrote books to help inform the broader dialogue. Along with nine other leaders he helped found the American Energy Innovation Council, which seeks to move public policy toward more responsible practices. He sought changes beyond what individual companies are able to effect in the climate and contexts in which businesses operate. That was a unique and critical role for a corporation, and I think we will see increasingly more of this kind of leadership in the future. The Responsible Corporation will prepare the ground for creating and nurturing responsible businesses, industries, and governance.

GETTING FROM HERE TO THERE

The hardest shift a business must make as it becomes increasingly responsible and regenerative is to educate itself in thinking and working systemically. Fragmentation has become so ingrained in business and in the culture at large that it undermines the practice of responsibility and of business itself. The programmatic approach that comes out of fragmented thinking can never deliver the systemic results needed by the planet and society.

To be effective, responsibility work has to be done while doing business. It cannot be bolted on but must be built in. When businesses settle for doing less and less bad they fail to take on the really interesting and necessary challenge of fostering the health of the whole, of making a meaningful contribution to the ability of stakeholders to pursue their own systemic responsibilities.

In each of the case studies in this book, power came from adopting a new approach and a new paradigm for business. The primary role of the Responsible Corporation is to change the conversations across businesses and between the corporation and its collective stakeholders. Business cannot do this efficiently. The following are a set of responsibility-based directions through which corporate leaders can begin to leverage the work of Responsible Businesses into the creation of Responsible Corporations.

1. Engage broad communities, including businesses not yet pursuing systemic approaches, in enlivening public conversations about what it means to go beyond sustainability and corporate responsibility as they are currently conceived. (The work of the United Nations Global Compact and the American Energy Innovation Council are good examples of this kind of conversation.)
2. Engage business leaders and governments in dialogue and other reflective processes in order to articulate global imperatives and give businesses a richer source of support to guide and evolve their own development.
3. Report progress toward enterprise-wide responsibility in annual reports rather than in separate corporate social responsibility (CSR) reports in order to foster public dialogue.
4. Use quarterly meetings to educate investors and the investment community as a whole on the global imperatives of society and Earth; clearly describe intended actions to develop portfolios of responsible businesses. Encourage investors to learn how it is possible to develop systemic wealth (wealth for all stakeholders) and how their own future and enduring returns are tied to the development of systemic wealth.
5. Work at the global level to help evolve business practices in their own industries in order to evolve Responsible Industries.

ALTERNATIVE BUSINESS APPROACHES

The evolution of Responsible Corporations and Responsible Industries from Responsible Business will become increasingly the role of corporate leaders in the future. The need for sustainability and corporate citizenship officers will simply disappear into the work of all leaders. Responsibility will have become completely integrated into corporations' engagement with their businesses at all times. And responsibility will no longer be a cost issue because evolving Responsible Industries will be pulling businesses forward.

In researching this book I found several new and meaningful efforts that can help change the face of business in the future. The first is a growing trend toward cooperatives sponsored by cities and regions to foster economic growth and employment stability. The second is the development of engaged shareholder advocacy, a new form of responsible investment. The third is a set of adaptations to the legal nature of corporations that make it easier to embed responsibility into by-laws and tax structures.

COOPERATIVE BUSINESS MODELS: CLEVELAND, OHIO

Cleveland, Ohio, in the heart of the rust belt, is home to an innovative new approach to the cooperative model of business. Up until the 1960s, Cleveland had been second only to New York City as a home to Fortune 500 corporations. The city was particularly hard hit by the shortsighted strategy of shifting U.S manufacturing to overseas sites, leaving Cleveland to slowly and steadily decline. After the collapse of its manufacturing base, the city was left with little else than legacy or anchor institutions such as hospitals, colleges, utilities, and arts organizations.

Ted Howard, a native Ohioan, had been working on changing the process of wealth building for communities from his seat at the University of Maryland's Democracy Collaborative. The collaborative believed that people needed a localized experience of democracy before they could exercise it at a larger level and that they needed stable jobs and communities before they could take on larger social concerns. So Ted and his colleague Gar Alperovitz began to conceptualize cooperatives as a way to link economic development to increased capability to practice democracy.

Since the 1970s Gar had been working in the field of cooperative and employee ownership. He had tried to create worker-owned businesses as a way to save the Youngstown steel industry, an unsuccessful effort that generated a lot of regional interest and experience with regard to what this alternative approach to ownership makes possible. Later, he established the National Center for Economic Alternatives with a primary focus on democratizing wealth. An author of many books, including *America Beyond*

Capitalism, Gar points out that larger institutional change is certainly necessary.[1]

In May 2005, Ted and Gar partnered with the Aspen Institute on a forum, "Enterprising Organizations," which for the first time brought together experts and leaders of community wealth-building models and innovations from around the country. The dialogue was productive, engendering many high-level proposals to advance the wealth-building movement.

Ted and Gar turned to John Logue, the head of the Ohio Employee Ownership Center at Kent State University, for advice. John had been inspired by Gar's work in Youngstown decades before and was now a leading national authority on worker ownership. Together Ted, Gar, and John conceived of a Cleveland "Community Wealth Round Table" that would bring together the leaders of legacy anchor institutions, city officials, local foundations, community activists, and the local business community (including employee-owned companies). For a day and a half, some fifty Clevelanders and a handful of wealth-building leaders from other cities explored new approaches to rebuilding the economy of Cleveland by leveraging the local assets.

With the flight of business and people from the area during the previous decades, most manufacturing and many services were outsourced to other towns, many outside the state. In some respects, Ted saw parallels between Ohio and a country like Ireland, which had seen a diaspora of millions of its people. This led to a rapid and catastrophic loss of an educated population and wealth-building capacity that took generations to replace.

Following the round table, the Cleveland Foundation, the nation's first community foundation and the largest philanthropy in northeast Ohio asked Ted and his colleagues to help devise a strategy for leveraging Cleveland's anchor institutions to create jobs and equity in the city. This resulted in the Evergreen Cooperative Initiative, a network of small cooperatives built around work that was needed by the anchor institutions and was now being outsourced beyond Cleveland. In other words, they started with customers and worked the pentad forward.

Institutional laundry was a huge activity for all these organizations, especially local hospitals and nursing homes. After eighteen months of planning, the Evergreen Cooperative Laundry was launched. The greenest laundry in the region, it was designed to employ fifty residents of nearby low-income neighborhoods, all of whom would be owners of the business. Like any new business venture, it took some learning, but the laundry co-op is now working well.

Evergreen is democratically run and provides above-industry standard wages and free health care benefits. Each year a percentage of its profits goes into employee accounts, possible because there are no external shareholders to compensate. Evergreen has launched a solar energy installation and maintenance cooperative that also carries out energy audits and weatherization for local homeowners. A large (five acres under glass) hydroponic food production greenhouse will soon open, producing four million heads of lettuce for the local market. Other cooperative businesses are in the pipeline, each with a triple-bottom-line mission: profitability, environmental sustainability, and economic and social stability for the community.

Ted was drawn to this work early in life. He watched his own father, who worked for Standard Oil, be laid off simply because a younger worker could be hired at a lower salary. From his perspective it seemed companies just threw away people. He grew up in Kent, Ohio, and although his family had left long before May 1970, he was shaken to the core by the violence at Kent State University, where the National Guard fired on unarmed students protesting the war in Vietnam. This shocked his conscience and led him to leave his work as an aide to a U.S. senator. He eventually returned to help Cleveland and other communities rebuild and discover value-adding activities that could benefit everyone.

Ted's enthusiasm for co-ops comes from the fact that they are such a viable means for creating stakeholder value.

- Co-ops represent a tighter integration among stakeholders. The customers often are co-workers and investors. Local values are built in, creating a more tightly knit shareholder pentad through a circle of shared intentions.
- Much of the wisdom about how to do things well in the world now belongs to organizations—including businesses.

The cooperative model fosters stakeholder reciprocity in a way that helps ensure that this wisdom is shared in a transparent way.

- Cooperatives move the pentad toward value-adding and away from value-extracting. In contrast to employee stock ownership plans (ESOPs), which rise and fall independently with the industry and markets, cooperatives experience greater flexibility in economic cycles because they generally work as a cooperative of cooperatives. Workers move from one co-op to another when there are swings in demand or innovation opens new doors. This flexibility provides a more sustainable profitability, economic vitality, and reduced vulnerability to market volatility and enables economic recovery that is more predictable and therefore easier to guide and manage.

ENGAGED SHAREHOLDER ADVOCACY: NEWLAND SOCIAL INVESTMENT

Most people seeking to bring about change work from a two-force model of the world. There is the "right way" and there is the "wrong way." To get others to see the right way, they advocate, demonstrate, lobby, and interfere. Although there are certainly times to use these approaches, when they become a steady diet people tune them out. The two-force, wrong-way–right-way view results in an increasingly uncivil discourse and distressingly polarized characterizations of all subjects of importance, including the way mainstream media and politics attempt to grapple with urgent social and planetary issues. "There is global warming." "No, there isn't." "Capitalism is bad." "Capitalism is the only economic model." "Health care for all." "The public health insurance option is a socialist prescription for bankruptcy." These debates continue but very little really changes.

There is another model that introduces a third force of shared values through which differences can be reconciled. This third force always seeks a higher ground from which both sides in a conflict are recognized, valued, and integrated. It usually depends on seeking common purpose in serving some larger good. Strong and enduring relationships are grounded in the recognition that everyone does better when they look beyond narrow self-interest to something larger and more important.

I am impressed by a recent movement, called *shareholder advocacy,* that uses this reconciling approach. Shareholder advocacy requires a great deal of knowledge, critical thinking, and commitment to third-force interventions. One exemplar, Newground Social Investment, led resolution challenges at Albertsons, DuPont, Intel, and McDonalds to bring issues of concern to shareholders before their boards of directors, offering them the opportunity to vote for responsible change. With each of these challenges, Newground sought reconciliation between the desire to maximize shareholder value and the desire to "do the right thing" through introducing the third force of brand integrity in the public's perception (personal communication with Bruce Herbert and Larry Dohrs, April 10, 2010).[2]

In 2000, Newland guided a small group of shareholders at the market chain Albertsons to persuade the corporation to take responsible action to protect their investment, successfully linking *Do what is right* to *Do what benefits the investor.* They had become aware that the grocery giant was shelving tobacco products at the backs of stores where they were effectively unsupervised. Not surprisingly, this resulted in a high theft rate, in particular by teenagers. Albertsons was not especially concerned because all of the tobacco companies agreed to repay distributors full value for losses due to theft. It was "no skin off Albertsons' back," so to speak.

With the help of Newland, some knowledgeable shareholders set out to do something about this. According to Security and Exchange Commission (SEC) guidelines, when shareholders file a resolution, it must be presented to the shareholders at large for their consideration. In other words, when some members of the community of investors have a concern, they have a right to bring it to the attention of the whole. But there are exceptions. If the resolution concerns an item that affects less than 5 percent of the company's sales, the company does not have to put the issue before shareholders.

Tobacco sales fell below this 5 percent threshold and so when a resolution was introduced Albertsons' management informed the filers that it was not appropriate to make it public to the remaining shareholders. After several attempts to gain the attention of the board of directors, this small group became increasingly certain that the existing leadership didn't understand the implications to the Albertsons brand. They rightly worried that the public might think that Albertsons made it easy for teenagers to get access to cigarettes.

The concerned group prepared a report, not a threatening, haranguing blast but a well-reasoned argument about the potential effects on share value and customer loyalty if such a perception took hold of the public. They were not seeking to damage the Albertsons brand; they wanted to increase the brand value and preserve the long-term loyalty of shoppers.

That did the trick. All of Albertson's management and the board of directors agreed that this was a value-creation and -retention question and a concern that the leadership of the company shared. Until that point, company leaders had narrowed their thinking to whether the resolution came within SEC guidelines. They were also concerned about the expense of rearranging stores. But the equation shifted when the value proposition could be legitimately described.

The same approach was used to get Intel to address its overuse of water in Arizona. Supported by Newland, a small group of its shareholders advanced a compelling argument that connected business performance to doing what is right. And in 1999, DuPont was persuaded to avoid undertaking a fifty-year strip-mining operation along the entire eastern border of the Okefenokee National Wildlife Refuge. DuPont ended up donating the land in a way that will prevent anyone from mining it in perpetuity. Finally, the same method persuaded McDonald's to work with suppliers to reduce pesticide residues in potato production. Though the company initially took the stance that this was the purview of its suppliers, it changed its mind when an institutional investor, Bard College, said it wanted to explore the effects on the security of its investment.

In each of these cases, it was not the threat of exposure and lawsuits that transformed policy but a real and meaningful demonstration of the possible effects on stakeholder trust and brand equity. Trust and equity are the means through which investors gain a secure return over time, and their vigilance in protecting them is a contribution to overall corporate health.

This kind of vigilance serves not only the interests of stakeholders but also makes an essential contribution toward overall corporate responsibility. Because so many boards of directors and shareholders have abdicated their education and self-accountability role, it has fallen increasingly to activists. However, most activists lack a basic understanding about how corporate change really comes about. Without it, their road is likely to be long, painful, and full of disappointment, regardless of how honorable or righteous their cause.

Bruce Herbert and Larry Dohrs, the founders of Newground, evolved their version of this reconciliation-based strategy out of their own personal histories. As a young man, Bruce traveled abroad to study meditation. He learned to be present in the moment without judging others, and he believes that all human beings have a nature that wants to be and can be transformed. Larry has dedicated himself to the Free Burma movement, which is similar to the South Africa efforts to overcome apartheid. Both he and Bruce have a deep commitment to doing what is right without calling others evil. They know that there are unifying values and imperatives that are bigger than the differences that divide the world and they work diligently to find a reconciling approach.

Newground's mission is to harness the power of business in service to the human yearning for strong and resilient communities, a healthy and clean environment, and a robust, sustainable, and locally determined marketplace. Its approach goes beyond ethical screening to active investment in local ventures, particularly those that have traditionally been denied access to capital and other banking services.

Newground also puts a great deal of attention on shareholder advocacy, moving from advocating *to* shareholders—telling "them" what to change—to advocating *as* shareholders. Though Newground is a major player in the shareholder advocacy movement, its work might more accurately be called education and exercise of agency because advocacy implies already having the answers. Newground seeks open dialogue to find more creative approaches and ensure that shared values are considered. It does not attempt to intervene in how companies are run; that is management's job. Instead it brings attention to the effects of decisions and practices on all stakeholders, particularly shareholders.

The key here is that Newground is *invested* in businesses. It cares about its investments and believes it is in the interest of business as well as of society as a whole to advocate for what produces broad-scale health and success. This requires businesses to find the place where shared values meet, often in brand equity and in sustainable returns and growth through time. If a brand is damaged, then stock value is threatened as well. Newground works to find solutions that always increase the value to future investors and customers, which requires businesses to be contributors to social and planetary health.

EVOLVING THE LEGAL INFRASTRUCTURE: B LAB

Newground's less direct approach—linking responsible actions to the preservation or increase of brand equity and share values—is necessitated by the current structure of corporate law, particularly with regard to publicly traded companies. However, not all corporations are bound by exactly the same regulations. Besides the familiar C corporation, the form taken by publicly traded companies, a variety of other legal structures are designed to serve specific needs (S corporations, limited liability corporations, and professional partnerships, for example). But none of these structures specifically favors building a Responsible Corporation, which means that only hardy pioneers have been willing to buck convention and try to figure it out. The restraints embedded in the legal infrastructure have seemed insurmountable until recently, when a new generation of innovative social entrepreneurs set out to make responsible practice accessible to everyone.

Jay Coen Gilbert, Andrew Kassoy, and Bart Houlahan are the founders of B Lab, a nonprofit dedicated to creating the infrastructure for a new kind of corporation, one that takes all of its stakeholders into account.[3] Friends since their student days at Stanford University, where they had spent long hours talking over their values and aspirations, these three pursued independent and successful careers in investment management and as entrepreneurs.

Eventually each of them realized that he had failed to adequately integrate his values with his work. Jay and Bart were the cofounder and president, respectively, of AND1, a basketball footwear and apparel company that also worked to use sports to change the lives of kids. They were bitten by the social entrepreneurial bug and after selling AND1 joined forces with Andrew to solve the problems involved in using business to address social and environmental problems.

They found three impediments. First, it appeared that governing by-laws in most states disallowed or discouraged corporations from considering anything but shareholders. Second, increasing numbers of businesses were jumping on the "good business" bandwagon and claiming to be sustainable, green, and responsible even when they were not. Because green-washing was rampant, it was increasingly difficult to tell good marketing from deep practice. Third, mission-driven companies had more trouble getting the capital they needed to grow.

To address these impediments, Jay, Bart, and Andrew founded the nonprofit B Lab, initially with their own money and later with support from the Rockefeller Foundation and the Halloran Philanthropies. Their intention was to establish a new and meaningful business standard that would encourage and reward companies that offered "true benefit to all stakeholders." Their process enabled socially responsible investors and customers to make informed choices and allowed companies to brand themselves through participation in a credible program. This way, investors who sought authentic and socially responsible opportunities would actually know what they were investing in.

B Lab established a certification program with a clear threshold that could be measured and made available for all to see. For a company to get the seal of approval as a Certified B Corporation (*B* is for *benefit*), it must meet comprehensive and transparent social and environmental standards via the "B Impact Rating System." It must also agree to be transparent to the entire world about its effects on all stakeholders. This sets a benchmark that distinguishes "good companies" from "good marketing"—or as Seventh Generation's Jeffrey Hollender likes to say, "Separating the real thing from the pretenders."

A Certified B Corp must also amend its governing documents to formally recognize the interests of employees, community, and environment. The company is provided with a legal roadmap and help as needed to make these changes. When these values have been embedded into what B Lab calls "the corporate DNA," they are far more likely to survive changes in investors, management, and even owners. This builds an enduring and trustable culture and structure, one that investors can support with confidence, and encourages the flow of capital toward worthy businesses.

This certification model differs from other industry-driven certifications, which tend to focus in a segmented way on specific issues or stakeholders, for example, meeting organic standards or ensuring fair trade. B Corp certification says that a company as a whole has met standards of responsibility across all designated stakeholders and thereby increases the value of the brand.

To get started, B Lab focused on thirty states that have constituency statutes that allow for the B Corp stakeholder language under existing law. But B Lab wanted to go further and create a new corporate form that would enshrine in law expanded corporate purpose, transparency, and accountability. On April 14, 2010, Martin O'Malley, Maryland's governor, signed a historic bill that created the nation's first Benefit Corporation. Vermont immediately passed similar legislation, and soon after New York, Pennsylvania, New Jersey, and Michigan introduced legislation. North Carolina, Colorado, Virginia, and Washington are considering making similar changes.

Currently, B Lab's focus is on privately held companies. Eventually, one of these companies is likely to go public or be bought, slowly moving the B Corp concept into broader public awareness and acceptance.

Andrew Kassoy believes that larger sustainable businesses, such as Burt's Bees or Ben & Jerry's, which are subsidiaries of public companies struggling to make the connection with their new consumer base, might opt for a B Corp certification. Other subsidiaries or companies may want to become B Corps in order to be distinguished by their transparency. When any of these do become B Corps, the innovative legal structure that's built into them will position them to affect the rest of company.

Andrew further suggests that there are multinational corporations that are interested in cleaning up their supply chain, following in Walmart's footsteps, but they have no method for measuring, comparing, or rewarding their suppliers. A few companies, such as Whole Foods Market and Home Depot, have internal standards, but most do not. They might choose to require B Corp certification as a means to establish and maintain social responsibility standards, improving the performance of suppliers while creating enhanced credibility for themselves.

The B Lab approach offers financial and risk management institutions an impartial and credible way to evaluate companies for certain kinds of risk. In the aftermath of the financial meltdown of 2008, one thing is almost certain: more and more investors will demand responsibility as a basic criterion for investment. This growing demand for opportunities to invest in "trustable companies" is not likely to disappear any time soon. And neither, therefore, is B Lab.

Early supporters of B Lab included Seventh Generation, Numi Organic Tea, and White Dog Cafe, all pioneers in the world of corporate responsibility. Now there is a new generation of entrepreneurs for whom the B Lab approach seems obvious and natural. One example is Ryan Martens, a successful serial entrepreneur in the information technology world based in the green haven of Boulder, Colorado. Ryan's newest company, Rally Software, is funded by private equity, and he keeps a tight hold on the reins to ensure it honors its commitment to his investors.

Ryan initiated Rally Software with a responsible business commitment and he practices the 1/1/1 model of philanthropy, in which a company agrees to donate 1 percent of its employees' time, 1 percent of its equity, and 1 percent of its product to philanthropic endeavors. He developed strong values as a Boy Scout, pursuing merit badges on community and the environment, and found them verified as an adult when he read *Natural Capital* by Paul Hawken, Amory Lovins, and L. Hunter Lovins.

Rally Software sought certification as a B Corp for tactical as well as social reasons. By consolidating purchases with other for-benefit companies, Rally accesses discounts that it could never leverage alone. These discounts free up funds for increased investments in corporate social responsibility efforts that would otherwise be beyond a fledgling company's means. Investors get the brand value of ownership in a proactively ethical company with no increase in risk or reduction in return.

One of Rally's investors, Brad Feld, originally encouraged Ryan to jump into the 1/1/1 model, even knowing it would dilute his own shares. That initial 1 percent equity donation from Rally provided seed funding for the Entrepreneur's Foundation (EF) of Colorado, an affiliate of the national EF organization, and gave both Ryan and Brad a strong voice on the board.

Ryan believes that a stronger community makes for a stronger company, a foundational idea for B Corp members. Like salesforce.com and Google before it, Rally plans to go public with its 1/1/1 model, propagating its values and way of doing business while building public good will.

Responsible Investing Within the Current Legal Framework

As many progressive entrepreneurs are working to create new corporate structures, still others are finding ways to evolve Responsible Businesses within the current legal framework. Or some might say they are doing what was always possible but lost in the rush to make it a program. More and more business leaders are challenging the prevalent myth that companies cannot pursue socially responsible actions because such actions favor ecosystems and communities over shareholders. Their work is also helping to dispel the common misperception that investors have interests that contradict those of customers, co-creators, Earth, and communities.

Rebecca Hendersen of Harvard Business School is an acknowledged authority in corporate governance, strategy, and management practice. Her wisdom strongly contradicts conventional belief. In a recent conversation she suggested to me that businesses are empowered to do social good when they follow three simple principles.

Taking Care

When managers and management teams focus on improving the long-term value of their companies, they are said to be caring for the investment. It is reasonable to take socially or ecologically responsible actions that are likely to increase the value of a company in the same way that it is wise management to train workers, upgrade manufacturing facilities, engage in research and development, build a brand, or work to enter new markets. None of these are certain to produce short-term gains, but all are likely to produce long-term improvements in the value of a company. Using a systemic framework to upgrade brand position, viability of suppliers, relationships with communities, and the sustainable health of resources is a strategic investment like any other. And there are strong business track records that prove it. Managers cannot be sued for pursuing systemic responsibility if they can demonstrate the care they are taking for the investments of shareholders.

Candor at All Times

The relationship between a company and its shareholders is a civil agreement governed by law. As with any other civil agreement, the expectation and legal obligation is for truth and openness in all dealings. A manager who lies to investors can be sued. Responsibility to investors requires precisely the same level of impeccable honesty as any other aspect of business life. Keeping the transparency process alive through education increases the opportunities for candor and helps prevent inadvertent misrepresentation. It could even be argued that not informing the investor of the more extensive effects of the business's efforts could be a "sin of omission."

Loyalty

Self-interest on the part of an executive should never override the interest of the shareholders. Executives are expected, indeed required, to operate on behalf of shareholders. This expectation is secured by the equal expectation that the CEO will do everything necessary to ensure the health of the business and is reflected in the practice of rewarding executives with options and shares in the company. When executives work on their own behalf by improving the share price of a company they are keeping faith with their larger responsibilities.

Living up to these principles not only protects a manager from being successfully sued, as has been demonstrated repeatedly in investor law, but it also creates a platform for the work of Responsible Corporations. Risk of being sued should no longer be used as an excuse for postponing this work. When doing what is good for all stakeholders will improve long-term share value, then that becomes a company's primary obligation. I strongly believe that socially responsible investors will get far more traction with companies and boards of directors when they learn to make this case.

CONCLUSIONS

This may sound strange, but I can hardly wait for the corporate responsibility movement to run its course so that businesses can get back to being responsible by nature. Making responsibility the purview of a department or program is the best way to make it fragmenting and ineffectual.

I began this book with a story about P&G, whose pioneering accomplishments with regard to responsibility arose directly from the way one of its businesses was designed and the kind of values that were built into its founding. When that same business was visited by outsiders, they were able to see the obvious teaming systems and flat organizational structures but they missed the underlying ethos of responsibility, systemic thought, and conscious reflection that made it work. If there is one message I hope this book clearly conveys it is that one cannot copy the practices of other companies. The most important work, not only for acquiring responsibility but also for business success, is educating a new mind, one that acknowledges the lives of co-creators, communities, and Earth and understands how all beings are deeply connected and caring. As this mind evolves, I have every confidence that my readers will invent ideas that are even better and more creative than those presented here.

(Continued)

P&G's ideal of creating a craft or artisan culture as a way of working in the detergent business helped it to connect in a caring way to the lives of its customers, the communities where it operated, Earth that provided resources for its creations, and the investors it depended on. The detergent business experience taught a major corporation how to strip things down to essentials and remove the fragmented complexity associated with so many corporate responsibility programs. Much of what they accomplished can be boiled down to an ethic: *Design to evoke caring, systemic critical thinking, and personal growth, and you cannot go wrong.* Good advice to any business seeking to become responsible, to any corporation seeking to develop a portfolio of Responsible Businesses, and to any corporate leader seeking to participate in the evolution of Responsible Industries.

Epilogue: Developing Capability for Responsibility

Democracy is a device that ensures we shall be governed no better than we deserve.
GEORGE BERNARD SHAW

A Responsible Business aspires to grow responsible individuals. Indeed, it can't achieve its full potential if it doesn't. Working with the pentad is more than just good business; it is a means to sustain healthy democracies and a healthy global community.

For democracy to work well, people must participate in government—and just voting is not enough. Citizens are truly citizens when they seek to improve government, refuse to become compliant or apathetic, and engage in civil and thoughtful discourse about the best possible future. This capability for participatory democracy is built in organizations, starting with schools and extending to workplaces and beyond.

I am fortunate to live in an amazing time and place. I enjoy the benefits of a democracy in which I have a say in how I am governed and how I earn my living. I see many ways that this democratic system is threatened and I see real problems, many of them created—as often as not unintentionally—by corporate practices. I have faith that there is much that companies will do to strengthen society and address the world's problems, just by the way they conduct business, if they rise to the challenge to grow responsible individuals. It is not a separate piece of work to be responsible for society. It is the work we do when we do business responsibly.

THREE CAPABILITIES UNDERLYING RESPONSIBILITY

Three capabilities underlie the thinking woven through this book: *agency, ableness,* and *affectiveness.* When I refer to self-determination, self-direction, and self-management, I am describing the practice of agency. When I talk about development of capacity or capability, I am describing ableness at higher and higher levels. When I advocate standing in the shoes of others, enriching their lives, or caring for the evolution of living systems, I am invoking the idea of affectiveness.

Developing these three capabilities is fundamental to the realization of human potential, individually and collectively. Though the capacity for them is inherent in all people, not everyone has done the work to develop them. The Responsible Business builds its development into the way it thinks and operates and thereby into the way democratic societies think and operate.

AGENCY

Agency is the inner motivation that individuals and collectives exercise when they become conscious of intentions and can manage themselves to achieve them. Agency is the ability to be accountable for one's own effects and effectiveness. It combines internal locus of control and external considering. Even very strong-willed and passionate people can expend a great deal of life energy without making a real difference. Until they develop the ability to guide their own thinking and action, they are impotent to bring about change.

The thing that worries me most about organizations that attempt to become responsible through nonsystemic, noncaring–based practices is that they often diminish agency. For example, they combine hierarchical delegation, standards, procedures, and external evaluation by others, all of which squash agency and actually foster learned helplessness.

A sense of agency is critical to reversing political apathy, grievance, frustration, and helplessness and unless it is exercised, it will atrophy. Unless it is exercised, this capability will atrophy. Its development is fundamental to the Responsible Business.

Ableness

Ableness is the exercise of a skill or capacity at will whenever it is needed. One may have knowledge or training in particular skills but unless one is able to pull them together in a meaningful way in real time and under pressure, one cannot be said to be able.

To grow ableness, a Responsible Business pursues two kinds of human development. First, it builds people's capacity to manage their own state of being—their attitudes, behaviors, and ability to remain purposeful. The result is people who work productively in group settings toward shared goals. Management of one's personal state of being is not a typical item on the human resource agenda but it is critical to business and urgent for democracy. Without it, emotional reactivity severely limits people's ability to engage in civil discourse and societal governance.

A Responsible Business next seeks to develop deliberative dialogue and critical thinking skills. Critical thinking is the ability to see a situation, entity, problem, or opportunity from a systemic view. Rather than simply treating symptoms or accepting issues the critical mind operates in an enlarged playing field— seeing underlying dynamics and reconciling seemingly impossible conflicts. Using systemic frameworks at work has helped a large and diverse array of people learn to guide, discipline, and improve their own thinking and to carry that capacity back to their homes and communities, where its benefits are even further enlarged.

Democratic systems only work effectively when they move beyond the idea of there being only two sides to an issue. All living systems are complex and multidimensional. Converting all conversations into a dyadic, polarized set of options diminishes the capacity of citizens to think in more encompassing and reconciling ways. The media's insistence on representing conflicting views has the effect of dumbing down public discourse and reinforcing polarized thinking throughout society. Critical thinking skills benefit corporations but they are even more urgently needed for democratic governance processes based on deliberative dialogue.

AFFECTIVENESS

Affectiveness is the ability to engage emotionally, empathetically, and in terms of the effects living beings have on one another. It allows people to experience the world as it is experienced by others, including nonhuman others. The noun *affect* is defined as "an observed or expressed emotional response."[1] Affectiveness is the ability to experience and reflect back a sense of meaningful connection.

Affectiveness depends on reading and experiencing other people and their emotions. I believe that the modern tendency toward distance and objectivity has undermined this basic ability—in business, in society, and in relation to Earth. When I speak of abstraction, I refer to the reliance on mechanical instruments and third-party intermediaries such as market research to provide objective information about the world. These exclude the felt, subjective, and therefore directly connected experiences of fully engaged individuals.

It is difficult to experience caring for other beings without connecting to them directly and seeking a deep understanding of their uniqueness. The absence of authentic caring leads to genericizing (one size fits all), homogenizing (it's really all the same), and commoditizing (compromising on the lowest common denominator). Even planning and measurement become self-referential, more concerned with stated goals than with living realities. The work systems, planning processes, product development strategies, and community and ecological connections built into the Responsible Business are designed to reconnect these lost links.

I live in a small community on the north end of Seattle that still has a gathering place for community dialogue. We come together and discuss subjects that require collective agreement, sometimes with elected officials and sometimes as active and interested citizens. We do this face to face. Although sometimes our debates are heated, they are always characterized by a sense of respect and consideration for all our neighbors.

Granted, we are a small town, which makes an experience of personal connection easier, but far more important is the presence of a shared meeting place, known as "The Commons," where deliberative dialogue can take place. Because this dialogue is not structured as political debate, it allows us to express civil and yet passionate thought and to consider ideas that might start out feeling alien to us. A growing number of communities and groups are attempting to foster such deliberative dialogues but their numbers and influence are still limited.

The pentad offers corporations and the businesses in them a systemic instrument for making their work holistic. By using the pentad all stakeholders and the system as a whole can become increasingly wealth generating. It builds ecological and social consciousness from the inside without the need for ideological debates and policy-driven mandates. Using the pentad is a way to grow healthy communities liberated from the need to defend against destructive corporatism and boom-bust economics. Best of all, it helps provide a basis for increasingly ordered, enlightened, and successful community governance.

A Final Reflection

My friend Daron Byerly is a brand manager at Seventh Generation and one of the original leaders of the change process there. He also coaches Ultimate, a game of extreme Frisbee, at the University of Vermont (UV) and plays with a Montreal, Canada, Ultimate team that has won many national championships. This gives an idea of the intense passion with which he approaches life.

Daron's UV teams have repeatedly qualified for regional playoffs. They practice a "ridiculous number of hours" (but it's fun, they say). They use principles to develop their practice, set insane stretch goals, and always work on preparedness. Many sports teams do that, but there is something truly different about playing Ultimate. Sportsmanship, respect, fairness, courtesy, grace, and having fun are considered integral aspects of Ultimate play, even when competition becomes intense. For example, Ultimate rules define a *foul* as contact "sufficient to arouse the ire of the player fouled" and referees have never been part of the game (personal communication from Daron Byerly, April 10, 2010). All Ultimate matches, even high-level playoffs, are self-officiated. Ultimate Frisbee seems to demand an ultimate level of agency, ableness, and affectiveness.

This last story, along with the stories of other business leaders in this book, offers plenty of evidence to support a theory I've developed over the course of my life. Whenever people are developing their ableness and potential, directing themselves using principles calling for personal agency and responsibility, and working creatively in the service of higher purposes that they care deeply about, *they are living the ultimate life.* They are doing work they value, making contributions that matter, and living in communities and nations that give them the freedom to make a real difference with their lives.

> I wrote *The Responsible Business* for corporate leaders, but a number of individual readers have asked me what they can do to apply its concepts. In response I have created "Exercising Personal Agency," a guide for reflection and action to increase the level of consciousness in personal and family life. It is available free at www.The-Responsible-Business.com under "Personal Agency."

> I also hope that this book will become a useful contribution to conversations at high schools, community colleges, colleges, and universities, both public and private. Perhaps nonprofit and community organizations that are dedicated to social justice and a responsible relationship with Earth will also find it valuable. Free study guides are available at www.The-Responsible-Business.com under "Study Guides."

Often organizations that I have worked with form study groups to carry on without me. The Responsible Corporation Dialogue Network supports their ongoing efforts. Introductory material is free at www.The-Responsible-Business.com under "Corporate Dialogue."

 Finally, for reading groups, a free guide to help spark discussion is available at www.The-Responsible-Business.com under "Reading Group Guide."

NOTES

Prologue

1. Scott Lee, CEO Walmart, Second Quarterly Environmental Strategy Meeting, Walmart Headquarters, Bentonville, AR, July 12, 2006.
2. A. G. Lafley and Ram Charan, *The Game-Changer: How You Can Drive Revenue and Profit Growth with Innovation* (New York: Crown Business, 2008).

Introduction

1. Paul Hawken, Amory Lovins, and L. Hunter Lovins, *Natural Capitalism: Creating the Next Industrial Revolution* (New York: Little, Brown, 1999), p. 129.
2. Maurice Berns, Andrew Townend, Zayna Khayat, Balu Balagopal, Martin Reeves, Michael Hopkins, and Nina Kruschwitz, "The Business of Sustainability: Findings and Insights at the First Annual of Business Sustainability Survey and the Global Thought Leaders' Research Project," *MIT Sloan Management Review Special Report*, 2009, http://sloanreview.mit.edu/special-report/the-business-of-sustainability (accessed July 18, 2010).

Chapter One

1. United Nations Global Compact, www.unglobalcompact.org/AboutTheGC/index.com (accessed August 10, 2010).

Chapter Two

1. John Elkington, *The Cannibals Have Forks: Triple Bottom Line for the 21st Century* (Gabriola Island, BC, Canada: New Society Publishers, 1998).

2. Michael Hammer and James Champy, *Re-Engineering the Corporation: A Manifesto for Business Revolution* (New York: HarperBusiness, 2003).
3. M. Kat Anderson, *Tending the Wild: Native American Knowledge and the Management of California's Natural Resources* (Berkeley: University of California Press, 2006).

Chapter Four

1. Joshua Cooper Ramo, *The Age of the Unthinkable: Why the New World Disorder Constantly Surprises Us and What We Can Do About It* (New York: Little, Brown, 2009).
2. Daniel Pink, *The Peril of Giving People What They Want* (blog entry), http://www.danpink.com/archives/2010/06/the-peril-of-giving-people-what-they-want (accessed July 18, 2010).
3. Dev Patnaik and Peter Mortensen, *Wired to Care: How Companies Prosper When They Create Widespread Empathy* (Upper Saddle River, N.J.: FT Press, 2009), p. 103.
4. Daniel Pink, *A Whole New Mind: Moving from the Information Age to the Conceptual Age* (New York: Riverhead Books, 2005), p. 153.
5. Howard Gardner, Mihaly Csíkszentmihályi, and William Damon, *Good Work: When Excellence and Ethics Meet* (New York: Basic Books, 2002).
6. Paul Bloom, *How Pleasure Works* (New York: W. W. Norton, 2010).
7. Marcus Buckingham and Donald O. Clifton, *Now, Discover Your Strengths* (New York: Free Press, 2001).
8. Dr. Seuss Quotes. ThinkExist, http://thinkexist.com/quotes/dr._seuss (accessed July 18, 2010).
9. Daniel Goleman, *Emotional Intelligence: Why It Can Matter More Than IQ* (New York: Bantam Book, 1995).
10. Helen Harrison and Newton Harrison, The Harrison Studio, http://theharrisonstudio.net (accessed September 28, 2010).
11. James Howard Kunstler, *The Geography of Nowhere: The Rise and Decline of America's Man-Made Landscape* (New York: Touchstone, 1993).
12. Living Education Group, www.livingeducationgroup.com (accessed July 18, 2010) and Developmental Economies Group International, www.degi.us.com (accessed July 18, 2010).
13. Nassim Nicholas Taleb, *The Black Swan: The Impact of the Highly Improbable* (New York: Random House, 2007).
14. Jonah Lehrer, The Frontal Cortex, http://scienceblogs.com/cortex/2010/05/patience.php#commentsArea (accessed July 18, 2010).

Chapter Five

1. Geoff Colvin, *Talent Is Overrated: What Really Separates World-Class Performers from Everybody Else* (New York: Penguin Group, 2008), p. 67.
2. Chip Heath and Dan Heath, *Made to Stick: Why Some Ideas Survive and Others Die* (New York: Random House, 2007), p. 89.
3. Frank Barrett, "Creativity and Improvisation Jazz and Organizations: Implications for Organizational Learning," *Organization Science*, September/October 1998, 9(5), 5.
4. Jeffrey Hollender with Bill Breen, *The Responsibility Revolution* (San Francisco: Jossey-Bass, 2010).
5. Jeffrey Hollender, "How I Did It: Giving Up the CEO Seat," *Harvard Business Review*, March 1, 2010, p. 2101.

Chapter Six

1. Gary Hamel with Bill Breen, *The Future of Management* (Boston: Harvard Business School Press, 2007).
2. Curtis Sittenfeld, "Powered by the People," *Fast Company*, June 30, 1999, p. 26.
3. Ori Brafman and Rod A. Beckstrom, *The Starfish and the Spider: The Unstoppable Power of Leaderless Organizations* (New York: Penguin Books, 2006).

Chapter Seven

1. Peter Senge, *The Fifth Discipline: The Art and Practice of the Learning Organization* (New York: Doubleday, 1990).
2. Joshua Cooper Ramo, *The Age of the Unthinkable: Why the New World Disorder Constantly Surprises Us and What We Can Do About It* (New York: Little, Brown, 2009), p. 164.
3. Richard Nisbett, *The Geography of Thought: How Asians and Westerners Think Differently and Why* (New York: Nicholas Free Press Publishing, 2003), p. 49.
4. Gerald Zaltman, *How Customers Think: Essential Insights into the Mind of the Market* (Boston: Harvard Business School Press, 2003).
5. Carol Sanford, "The Ethics and Practicality of Incentives," in *Learning Organizations: Developing Cultures for Tomorrow's Workplace*, eds. Sarita Chawla and John Renesh (Portland, Ore.: Productivity Press, 2006), pp. 305–321.

6. Daniel Pink, *Drive: The Surprising Truth About What Motivates Us* (New York: Riverhead Books, 2009).

Chapter Nine

1. Paul D. McLean, *The Triune Brain in Evolution: Role in Paleocerebral Functions* (New York: Springer, 1990).
2. Jonah Lehrer, *How We Decide* (New York: Houghton Mifflin Harcourt, 2009).
3. Charles Krone, materials from proprietary workshops, unpublished.
4. Gerald Zaltman, *How Customers Think: Essential Insights into the Mind of the Market* (Boston: Harvard Business School Press, 2003), p. 3.
5. Daniel Pink, *Drive: The Surprising Truth About What Motivates Us* (New York: Riverhead Books, 2009).

Chapter Ten

1. Daniel Pink, *Drive: The Surprising Truth About What Motivates Us* (New York: Riverhead Books, 2009).
2. Carol Sanford, "Science into Technique: A Systems Research and Development Process for Organizational Science" (Seattle: Springhill Publications, 1994), www.carolsanford.com/orders.htm (free download).
3. James Collins, *Good to Great: Why Some Companies Make the Leap . . . and Others Don't* (New York: HarperCollins, 2001).

Chapter Eleven

1. Paul Hawken, Amory Lovins, and L. Hunter Lovins, *Natural Capital* (New York: Bantam Books, 1998).
2. "Toyota Halts Sale of Lexus," *USA Today*, April 13, 2010, http://www.usatoday.com/money/autos/2010-04-13-consumerreports-lexus-gx460_N.htm (accessed July 18, 2010).
3. Laurence J. Peter, Raymond Hull, and Robert I. Sutton, *The Peter Principle: Why Things Always Go Wrong* (New York: Harper Business, 2009).
4. Nicholas Mang, "Regenerative Urban Planning: A Comparative Case Study of Successful Socio-Ecological Regeneration Initiatives and the Developmental Processes of Their Leadership Teams" (Doctoral dissertation, Saybrook Graduate School and Research Center, 2008), pp. 129–134.

5. John Knott Jr., "Noisette–Crafting the New American City," in *Lessons Learned: The Costs & Benefits of High Performance Buildings*, ed. Earth Day New York (New York: Earth Day New York, 2006), p. 3, www.noisettesc.com/pdf/news/29159161010643190.pdf (accessed July 18, 2010).

6. Beirut talks by Carol Sanford. (Carol Sanford speaking to business leaders from twenty Arab nations at a climate change conference sponsored by the Arab Federation for Environment and Development [AFED], November 19 and 20, 2009), www.youtube.com/user/carolsanford2.

Chapter Twelve

1. Google, "Our Philosophy: Ten Things We Know to Be True," www.google.com/corporate/tenthings.html (accessed October 6, 2010).

Chapter Thirteen

1. Gar Alperovitz, *America Beyond Capitalism: Reclaiming Our Wealth, Our Liberty, and Our Democracy* (Hoboken: John Wiley, 2005).

2. See also Newground Social Investment, www.newground.net.

3. B Lab, www.bcorporation.net (accessed July 18, 2010).

Epilogue

1. http:/en.wiktionary.org/wiki/affect (accessed July 18, 2010).

INDEX

A

Ableness, 281–282

Accountability: at Kingsford, 89–91, 99; locus of control and, 166–168

Accounting firms, 60

Accounting thinking, 99

Accrued equity, 239

Activists, 21, 45, 46, 270

Adams, S., 74

Administrative offices, 150

Adult responsibilities, xxxviii–xxxix

Advertising, 256

Advisory boards, 21

Advocacy, shareholder, 267–271

Affect, 282

Affectiveness, 282–283

Affordable products, 128

Africa, 52

The Age of the Unthinkable (Ramo), 54, 159

Agency, 280–281

Agendas, 136, 147

Agriculture industry, 238

Air pollution, 105

Airbags, 183

Airline industry, 176

Albertsons, 268–269

Alexandria Township Council, 129

Algebra, 165

Al-Herbish, S., 239

Allergies, 42

Alperovitz, G., 264–267

Altruism, 61, 167

Amazon.com, 97, 246

American Energy Innovation Council, 262, 263

Analog frequencies, 255

Anderson, K., 33

AND1, 272

Annoyed customers, 56

Annual reports, 263

Antioch University, 108

Apache tribe, 152–153

Apartheid, 122–123, 124, 126

Apple: responsibility indicators at, 243–259; stories at, 218

Arab Federation for Environment and Development, 238

Archetypes, 57, 87

Arithmetic, 165

Arthur, B., 159

Artisans, 113–114

Asia, 160–161

Assembly lines, 31, 35

Assumptions, 204, 209

Atwood, J., 148

Australian mines, 177–180

Authenticity: as essence, 111–112; example of, 5–7; importance of caring to, 58; strategic direction and, 140

Automobile recalls, 225

Avatars, 57

B

B Lab, 271–275

Babies 'R' Us, 121

Bandwidth, 255

Bank of America, xxvi

Banking industry, 43

Barbeque industry, 8–11, 86

Bard College, 269

Barrett, F., 102–103
Beckstrom, R. A., 152
Behavior management, 211
Being, 168, 169, 170
Benefits, 169
Berra, Y., 175
Berry, W., 25
Best practices: for co-creators, 58–59; dangers of, 24; development of, xl; opposition to, xxxv–xxxvi
Bias, 160, 161
The Black Swan (Taleb), 79
Blame, 159–160, 166
Bleaching agent, 65
Bloom, P., 59
Board of directors, 78, 79
The Body Shop, 52
Bohn, H. G., 3
Boston Consulting Group, xliv–xlv
Brafman, O., 152
Brain science, 187–199, 206
Brainstorming, 208
Brand identity, 234
Brand loyalty, 227, 269, 271
Brand, M., 230
Branded identities, 73
Breen, B., 115, 141
British Petroleum, xxvi
Buckingham, M., 59
Budget limits, 236
Budgeting systems, 148, 151
Burns, S., xxv
Bus systems, 235
Business acumen, 143
Business start-ups: after Kingsford layoffs, 106; co-creators in, 150; guidelines for starting, 150–152
Business strategies, 114–119
Business units, 261
Businesses: challenges of, xxxviii; characteristics of, xxxiiv; definition of, xxxvi, xxxvii; effects of, on society, 53; evolving corporate responsibility from, xxxix–xlii; as microcosms of

society, 52; purpose of, 25; uniqueness of, 140
Buyer classes, 116–118, 183
Buyers: versus customers, 30; salespeople's relationship with, 43–44; in winning business strategy, 116–118
Buying patterns, 55
Byerly, D., 283

C

C corporation, 271
Cable services, 255
Cannon, B., 78
Capability development: in business transformation, 142–144; common questions regarding, 142; at Consolidated Diesel Corporation, 151–152; as principle of Responsible Business, 23; versus training, 142–143; unlimited nature of, 229
Capital: co-creator investments of, 227–229; community investments of, 232–239; customer investments of, 224–227; definition of, xliii, 221, 223; Earth's investments of, 230–231; investor investments of, 240–241; power of, 221–222
Capitalism, 256–257
Carbon emissions, 20, 65, 68
Carbon neutral business, 65
Caring: cultures of, 56–58, 197, 282; mode of, 156, 275–276; for place, 234
Carrefour warehouse, 61
Cash flow, 143
Catalog companies, 15
Catering industry, 4, 111
CD player, 55
CDC. *See* Consolidated Diesel Corporation
Ceres conference, xxv–xxvi
Certified B Corporation, 272–275

Chain businesses, 70
Chambers Works Intermediate Chemicals, 45, 138
Champy, J., 31
Change blind people, 161
Change, in leadership, 201
Change processes: in businesses versus nonprofits, 16; at Colgate, South Africa, 12–15; components of, 145; at DuPont, 20; hazards to, 201–216; at Kingsford, 9–11; old systems and, 148; required time for, 201; resistance to, 146, 173–174, 215; skepticism about, 173; starting point for, 145
Character development, 75
Charles, Prince, 38
Checklists, 109–110
Chemical manufacturing, 45–48
Chesapeake Bay, 67
Child labor, 181
Childrearing, 187
China, 160–161
Chlorine, 65
Cleveland, Ohio, 264–267
Clifton, D. O., 59
Clorox, 7, 8, 69, 88, 193
Coalition building, 100
Co-creator indicators, of responsibility, 249–253
Co-creators: accountability of, 89; after change in structure, 149; best practices for, 58–59; capital investments of, 227–230; at Consolidated Diesel Corporation, 151; definition of, 58; description of, 30–32; at DuPont, 46–48; expression of essence by, 112; fundamental task of, 31; importance of, 31; intrinsic motivation of, 169–170; at Kingsford, 32, 88; lack of personal development of, 214–216; in Responsible Business framework, xlii, 39; return on investment for, 222, 223–224, 227–230; at Seventh Generation, 42–43, 119–121; in start-ups, 150; as stewards, 197; at U.S. Bank, 43; value-adding view of, 58–63
Colgate, Europe, 183–184, 207
Colgate, South Africa: business acumen at, 143; challenges of, 122–123; community building at, 14–15, 71; community focus of, 35–36; core teams at, 125; cross-functional teams at, 124, 125; decision making at, 139; description of, 11–15; health promotion at, 127–129; idea generation at, 124; impact of change at, 125–127; initiating change at, 123–125; management at, 125–126; management philosophy at, 141; mentors at, 126–127; Responsible Business framework at, 122–129; status at, 135–136; strategic direction of, 139; symbols at, 136; taboos at, 139; technological competence at, 144
Collins, J., 216–217
Collusion, 213
Colvin, G., 98
Commercial land, 238
Commitment, 99
Communication, caring, 156
"Communication on Progress," 21
Communities: branded identities of, 73; business analysis of, 69; businesses' ethical responsibility to, 73; businesses' view of, 69–70; capital investments of, 232–239; characteristics of, 70; culture of, 70; definition of, 34; education in, 72; effect of chain businesses on, 70; elevating governing principles of, 74–76; essence of, 72–74; human systems in, 71–72; identities of, 73, 233, 236; of Internet companies, 71; investors' relationships with,

181–182; Kingsford's effect on, 105–107; leadership of, 74; newsletters for, 95; promoting health of, 112–113; purpose of businesses in, 25; resources in, 35; in Responsible Business framework, xliii, 39; as stakeholders, 34–36; standardization and, 70–71; uniqueness of, 70, 72–74; value-adding view of, 69–76; ways for businesses to give back to, 76

Community building: at Colgate, South Africa, 14–15, 71; at Craft Warehouse, 44; responsibility indicators of, 258

Community indicators, of responsibility, 254–256, 258

Company picnics, 86

Compensatory programs, 204

Competition: business integrity and, 79; frames of mind and, 190; value-adding and, 55–56

Concept development, 251–252

Concept testing, 99

Conflict resolution, 13–14

Conscious capitalism, 256–257

Consciousness, 28

Conservation, of ecosystem, 65–66

Consistency, 240

Consol, 126

Consolidated Diesel Corporation (CDC), 150–152

Constitution, 162

Consultants, 8

Context, 161, 177, 232–233

Contractors, 120, 257

Contributions, from employees, 215

Core teams: at Colgate, South Africa, 125; at DuPont, 179; at Kingsford, 92, 94–95, 96

Corporate governance, 21

Corporate responsibility: challenges of, xxxviii–xxxix; description of, xxxvii; evolution of, xxxix–xlii; mandatory disclosure and, 21; problematic trends in, xxvi

Corporate responsibility reports, 63–64

Corporatewide responsibility programs, xxxix

Corporations: characteristics of, xxxvi–xxxvii; definition of, xxxvi, xxxvii; importance of, 261; makeup of, xxxix

Cost cutting, 176

Cotton farmers, 60

Covey, S., 147

Craft Warehouse, 43–44

Craftspeople, 180

Creativity: best practices and, 58–59; at DuPont, 47; familiarity and, 192–195; fostering of, 61–63; of improvisational players, 102; investment of, 227–230; at Kingsford, 88–89, 97–105; leadership and, 212–213; pattern-thinking and, 165; responsibility indicators of, 249, 250–251; at Seventh Generation, 42–43; stakeholder relationships and, 42–43; in urban development, 235; value-adding and, 59

Critical systemic thinking, 144

Critical thinking development, 98, 281

Cropping, 68

Cross-functional groups: at Colgate, South Africa, 124, 125; at Kingsford, 93–94, 100

Csíkszentmihályi, M., 59

Culture: blaming and, 159–160; at Colgate, South Africa, 12–15; of communities, 70, 73–74; at Consolidated Diesel Corporation, 152; at DuPont, 138; focus on investors and, 196; fragmented thinking in, 179; frames of mind and, 191; at Kingsford, 8–11, 90, 91–92, 193;

leadership and, 201, 203; locus of control and, 168; of open source communities, 83; pattern-thinking and, 166; at Procter & Gamble, 278; at Seventh Generation, 16, 18; and thinking, 160–161; transformation of, 134–138; view of investors in, 77
Curitiba, Brazil, 235
Customer champions, 182–183, 206
Customer indicators, of responsibility, 244–248
Customer loyalty, 56
Customer satisfaction rates, 206
Customer-focused business: achieving a, 182–185; at Apple, 246; benefits of, 177; at Colgate, Europe, 183–184; at DuPont, 182–183; example of, 5–7, 30, 179–180; at Google, 245–246; stakeholder relationships and, 42–43; at U.S. Bank, 184
Customers: anticipating the needs of, 247; archetypes of, 57; capital investments of, 224–227; description of, 29–30; education of, 121; feedback from, 182; function of, 30; internal versus external, 43; lack of insight by, 55; methods used to understand, 53–55; reasons for purchases by, 49; in Responsible Business framework, xlii, 39; return on investment for, 224–227; strategic direction and, 139–140; types of, 29; value of businesses to, 25; value-adding view of, 53–58
Customized products, 71
Cybernetic approach, 159

D

Damasio, A., 188
Data-based assessments, 54, 58
Debate, versus dialogue, 22

Decentralized organizational structures, 152–153, 217
Decision making: brain science and, 188–199; business acumen and, 143; at Colgate, South Africa, 139; efficiency driven, 175–176; emotions and, 188–189; importance of, 171; innovation and, 157; at Kingsford, 91, 100–101; managing principles and, 217; mental frames theory and, 189–192; responsibility indicators of, 248; in Responsible Business framework, 156–157; self-organizing capabilities and, 157–170; work redesign and, 149
Decision points, 100
Defensiveness, 191
Delayed gratification, 80
Deliberative practices, 98
Deliverables, 60
Demand, for products, 158
Democracy, 279, 281
Democracy Collaborative, 264
Democratization, workplace, 91
Dependability, 226
Design decisions, 248, 251–252
Detergent business: challenge of change in, 1; ecosystem specifics in, 66; prototype of responsibility in, xxvii–xxx; value-adding in, 55
Detroit, 35
Developmental approach, 202–203
Dialogue: among stakeholders, 43; common places for, 283; versus debate, 22; definition of, 22; development of, 281; at DuPont, 22; education through, 22–23; locked paradigms and, 193; personal development and, 198–199; at U.S. Bank, 43
Diatomaceous earth, 127
Discussion guides, 285
Dishwashing liquid, 53
Disruption, 147
Dissection, 163

Distributors: as co-creators, 62; feedback loops, 158; at Kingsford, 89

Diversity programs, xxxii

Dohrs, L., 268, 270

Dr. Seuss, 60

Drive (Pink), 168, 197

Drucker, P., 49

Duff, BJ, 3–7, 108

Duke Energy, xxvi

DuPont: core teams at, 179; cultural patterns at, 138; customer feedback to, 182, 183; customer focus at, 182–183; description of, 19–23; idea generation at, 138; leadership at, 203; petroleum products of, 33; stakeholder relationships at, 44–48; strip mining of, 269; technological competence at, 144; titanium dioxide mining of, 177–180; understanding of materials by, 65; use of dialogue at, 193–195

Dynamic relationships, 162

E

Earth: businesses' responsibility to, 34; capital investments of, 230–232; description of, 32, 63; in DuPont's initiatives, 45–48; fragmented view of, 63–64; humans as part of, 64; Kingsford's view of, 104–105; popular view of, 69; products that promote the health of, 18, 34; in Responsible Business framework, xlii–xliii, 39; Seventh Generation's responsibility for, 34, 42; as stakeholder, 32–34; value-adding view of, 63–69

Earth indicators, of responsibility, 253–254, 258

Ecology, 232

Economic crisis: business integrity and, 78; efficiency versus innovation and, 35; faulty use of

Responsible Business framework and, 175; stakeholder relationships and, 28

Economic development, 106, 107, 234, 238

Economy, understanding of, 159

Ecosystems: assessment of, 63–64; belonging to versus preserving, 65–66; businesses' responsibility for, 34; businesses' role in, 33, 34; description of, 63; effects of changes in, 66–67; fragmented view of, 63–64; importance of, 66; making improvements to, 66–68; purposeful evolution in, 164; responsibility indicators of, 253–254, 258; uniqueness of, 66

Education: to build capability, 142–143; at Colgate, South Africa, 12; in communities, 72; of customers, 121; fragmentation of, 262; of investors, 36; at Kingsford, 8, 9, 75, 87, 92–95, 106; ongoing nature of, 217; responsibility indicators of, 258–259; through debate, 22; through dialogue, 22–23; transparency for, 22–23. *See also* Personal development

Efficiencies: focus on, 31, 35; versus innovation, 35; mind-set of, 175–176

Einstein, A., xxxv, 133, 186, 221, 261

El-Ashry, M., 239

Elbert, S., xxvi

Emotional intelligence, 61

Emotions, 136; affectiveness and, 282–283; frames of mind and, 190–191; frontal lobe and, 188–189; management of, 198

Empathy, 54, 58

Employee accountability, 89–91

Employee engagement, 109–111

Employee evaluations, 102, 143, 167

Employees: contributions from, 215; exit strategies for, 106; managing behavior of, 211; motivation of, 110; as resources, 92; turnover of, 202

Enlightenment, 159

Enneagrams, 205

Enron, 155

Entrepreneur's Foundation of Colorado, 275

Entropy: causes of, 200–216; prevention of, 216–218

Environment, 232, 253

Environmental impact statements, 63

Environmental scans, 41, 140

Essence: articulation of, 111–112; clarity of, 115; of communities, 72–74; of contractors, 120; definition of, 59, 111; employee recognition and, 61; expression of, 112–114; of Herban Feast, 111–114; of improvisation, 102; meaningful work and, 60; of natural resources, 64–65; strategic direction and, 140; versus strengths, 59–60; systems thinking and, 162; value-adding and, 59–60; in winning business strategy, 115–116

Essential oils, 18, 42

Essentialism, 59

Estuaries, 66, 67

European Common Market, 12

European Union, 207

Exit strategies, 106

Expectations, 79

External considering, 166–168

Extrinsic motivation, 168, 169

F

Fabric durability, 55

Failure: learning from, 198; of product, 224, 225; sense of, 99

Familiarity, 192–195

Family dynamics, 162, 187

Family participation, 94, 95

Family responsibility, xxxviii

Favelas, 235, 236

Fear, 167, 191, 213

Federal Communications Commission, 255, 257

Feedback, customer, 182, 183

Feedback loops, 158–159

Feld, B., 275

Fertilizers, xxix

Field teams, 183

The Fifth Discipline (Senge), 158

Financial advisors, 181

Fishing industry, 67

Flow, 59

Focus groups, 86

Forests, 66, 68

Fragmentation, 179, 262

Fragrances, 18, 34, 42

Franklin, B., 243

Free Burma movement, 270

Free University of the Environment, 237

Freedom, 62, 85

Freon, 45, 46–47

Friendships, 187

The Frontal Cortex blog, 188

Frontal lobe, 188–189

Fukuoka, M., 38

Function, 168–170

The Future of Management (Hamel & Breen), 141

G

Garbage collection, 236

Gentrification, 238

Gilbert, J. C., 271–275

"Global Compact Governance Framework," 20

Global imperatives, 118–119

Global warming, 20, 66, 67

Globalization: business integrity and, 79; stakeholder relationships and, 38–39

Goldman, D., 61

Gold-mining operations, 126

Good to Great (Collins), 216–217
Google, 133; responsibility indicators at, 243, 244–259; storytelling at, 218
Gore, A., xxv
Gore, W. L., 33, 133, 153, 238, 244, 248, 252, 259
Gore-Tex, 33, 133, 248
Go-to-market time, 100, 101
Governing documents, 273
Governing principles, 74–76, 256
Gratz, R., 150
Grazing, 68
Greed, 212–214
Green space, 235
Green Works, 69
Greenpeace activists, 45, 46, 47
Green-washing, 69
Greeting Seeds, 155
Gurdjieff, G. I., 167

H

Habitual thinking, 92, 93, 166
Habituation, 190
Halloran Philanthropies, 272
Hamel, G., 141
Hammer, M., 31
Harley-Davidson, 58
Harrison, H., 67
Harrison, N., 67
Hawken, P., 274
Health: of communities, 74–76, 112–113; products to promote, 18, 34, 127–129; responsibility indicators of, 254, 255
Heath, C., 99
Heath, D., 99
Hendersen, R., 275
Henderson, R., 133
Herban Feast: customer focus of, 5–7, 30; employees' focus at, 5–7; essence of, 111–114; founding of, 3–5; growth of, 5; imaging at, 109; mission of, 112; purpose of, 5; regenerative work at, 113; Responsible Business framework

at, 108–114; rituals at, 137; staff engagement of, 109–111; strategic focus of, 108–109; sustainability of, 114; work redesign at, 112, 149
Herbert, B., 268, 270
Hierarchical structures, 90, 103
High-commitment work systems, 206
Hiring interviews, 146, 151
Hirshberg, G., xxvi
History projects, 44, 238
Hollender, J., 16–18, 114–122, 272
Holliday, C., 19–23, 44, 261–262
Home Depot, 274
Home ownership, 238
Honesty, 276
Hotels, 4
Houlahan, B., 271–275
Housecleaning, 118
How Pleasure Works (Bloom), 59
How We Decide (Lehrer), 188
Howard, T., 264–267
Hsieh, T., 97
Human resource programs, 204–208
Human responsibilities, xxxviii–xxxix, 64
Human systems: function of, 71–72; responsibility indicators of, 254
Human waste, 29
Hunt Wesson, 147
Hydrogen peroxide, 65, 144

I

IBM, 58, 83
Idea generation: at Colgate, South Africa, 124; cultural patterns regarding, 137, 138; at DuPont, 138; at Kingsford, 93–94; pattern-following and, 164; responsibility indicators of, 252; at Seventh Generation, 115–116
Imaging: definition of, 53–54, 162–163; example of, 163; at Herban

Feast, 109; at Kingsford, 104; at Procter & Gamble, 55; systems thinking and, 162–163

Imperatives, stakeholder: of co-creators, 58–63; of communities, 69–76; of customers, 53–58; definition of, 53; of Earth, 63–69; of investors, 76–81

Improvisational collaborators, 6–7, 102–104

Incentive systems: brain science and, 195; creativity and, 102; frames of mind and, 191; intention of, 195; locus of control and, 167

An Inconvenient Truth (film), xxv

Industrial revolution, 50, 59, 249

Infrastructure, 67

Innovation: co-creation of, 119–121; considering Earth and, 104–105; core teams and, 94; decision making and, 157; versus efficiency, 35; essence and, 115–116; intrinsic motivation and, 168; jazz improvisation and, 102–103; open-time practice and, 250; pattern-thinking and, 165–166; promises-beyond-ableness practice, 97–101; shielding of, 216

Insight, of customers, 55

Integrators. See Customers

Integrity, 78–79, 224, 225, 227

Intel, 246–247, 269

Intelligence, investment of, 227–230

Internal customers, 43

Internet: ads, 256; stakeholder relationships and, 39; and transparency, 23

Internet companies, 71

Intrinsic motivation, 168–170

Intuition, 190

Investment bankers, 28

Investment imperative, 223, 224

Investments: of co-creators, 224, 227–230; of communities, 232–239; of customers, 224–227; definition of, 223; of Earth, 230–232; economic crisis and, 28; of investors, 239–241

Investor indicators, of responsibility, 256–257

Investors: in business culture, 77; capital investments of, 239–241; community relationships of, 181–182; creating social and financial returns for, 79–80; description of, 36; development of, 36; expectations of, 79–80; focus on, 175, 180, 196; forces affecting, 79–80; importance of, 36; motivation behind, 77–78; in open source software, 84–85; in Responsible Business framework, xliii, 39, 175; return on investment for, 196, 222, 223f, 239–241; self-interest of, 36; in Seventh Generation, 121–122; trust of, 78; types of, 76; value-adding view of, 76–81

iPod, 55

Irresponsible capitalism, 257

ISO Quality Standards, 229

IT departments, 43, 184

J

Jain, P., 154–156

Jazz improvisation, 102–103

Job creation, 238

Job descriptions, 145

Job security, 136

Jobs, S., 247, 252

Johnson & Johnson: founding principles of, 217; integrity at, 78; trustable relationships of, 226, 227

Johnson, S., 120–121

Joint merchandising, 117

Jung, C. G., 57

K

Kabler, J., 88–89, 218
Kassoy, A., 271–275
Keller, P., xxvi
Kelly, W., 186
Kingsford: accountability at, 89–91, 99; business acumen at, 143; change processes at, 9–11; co-creators at, 32, 88; community principles and, 75–76; core teams at, 92, 94–95, 96; creativity at, 88–89, 97–105; culture at, 8–11, 90, 91–92, 193; decision making at, 91, 100–101; distributors at, 89; education of employees at, 8, 9, 87, 91–92, 92–95, 106; effects of, on local communities, 105–107; equity at, 103; hierarchy at, 90, 103; hiring of consultants at, 8; idea generation at, 93–94; improvisation at, 102–104; layoffs at, 7, 75–76, 105–107; leadership at, 203; meetings at, 147; mentoring at, 8, 96, 98; operations at, 8; past challenges of, 7–10; product development at, 10, 100–101; resource development at, 96–97; respect for teams at, 90; Responsible Business framework at, 85–107; simultaneous change at, 210; status at, 135; storytelling at, 218; technological competence, 144; use of dialogue at, 193–195; view of Earth by, 104–105; work redesign at, 97–105
Kissinger Associates, 54
Kiuchi, T., 49
Knott, J., 237
Knowledge, versus understanding, 163
Krone, C., xxvii, 19, 50, 189–190
Kuntzler, J. H., 71

L

Labels, product, xxix
Laing, R. D., 186
Languages, 207
Lawsuits, 269, 275–277
Layoffs: effects of, 107; at Kingsford, 7, 75–76, 105–107; responsibility indicators of, 252
Leadership: future role of, 263; greed in, 212–214; loyalty of, 276–277; philosophy of, 141; purposeful, 216–217; voids in, 201–203. See also Management
Leadership, community, 74
Leadership in Energy and Environmental Design (LEED) certification, 63
Leadership transitions: self-interest and, 212–213; at Seventh Generation, 121–122
Learning: co-creator investment in, 228–229; commitment as, 99; from failure, 198; lifelong process of, 200–201; love of, 93; mechanization of, 210–211; pattern-following in, 165; regeneration of, 200–201; through doing, 142–143. See also Personal development
Learning valleys, 72
Left Feat, 102
Left-brain function, 187
Legacy, 217
Legal structures, 271
Legal system, 162
Legislation, xxix
Lehman Brothers, xxvi, 176
Lehrer, J., 80, 188
Level five leaders, 216–217
Life, meaningful, 54, 55
Lillian, G., 100
Limbic brain, 187
Linux Expo, 83
Linux operating system, 84
Literacy rates, 87, 94, 123.

Living Education and Developmental Economies Group International, 72

Living systems, xxxvii; description of, 32; regenerative thinking and, 158–164; in value-adding view, 63

Locus of control: description of, 166–168; packaged programs and, 211

Lorimer, R., 9

Lovins, A., xlii, 274

Lovins, L. H., 274

Lynn, W., 7–11, 86, 90, 92, 105, 136, 218

M

Machine repairs, 148

Machines, as models, 159

Macho image, 87–88

Made to Stick (Heath & Heath), 99

Mammalian brain, 187

Management: accountability of, 89; at Colgate, South Africa, 125–126; at Consolidated Diesel Corporation, 150; leadership voids in, 201–203; philosophy of, 141–142, 205; reviews of, 204; top-down change from, 210–212, 214. *See also* Leadership

Management integrity, 78

Managing principles, 217

Managing systems, 145

Mandela, N., 13, 35, 122, 129

Maniscalco, C., 121

Manufacturing plant, 150–152

Manufacturing systems: at DuPont, 19–20, 47; Proctor & Gamble's redesign of, xxix, xxx; value-added versus value-adding, 51–52

Market chains, 31

Market conditions, 101

Market research, 140; versus buyer classes, 116–117; familiarity and, 192–193; value-adding and, 55, 56–58

Martens, R., 274

Mashile, I., 128

Mastery, task, 165

Mazur, E., 99

McDonald's, 269

McLean, P., 187

McNamara, P., 82–85

McNealy, M., 43, 184

Mechanical models, 159

Media, xxxiii, 267

Meditation, 270

Meetings, 136–137, 147, 263

Mental frame theory, 189–192

Mentoring: at Colgate, South Africa, 126–127; at Kingsford, 8, 96, 98; processes of, 146

Microsoft, 246–247, 250

Mid-brain, 187

Middle East, 238–239

Mining industry, 177–180

Mission: of Herban Feast, 112; of Red Hat, 85; of Seventh Generation, 16

Mistakes, 103

MIT Sloan School of Management, xliv–xlv

Mixed messages, 207

Molecules, 238

Money, 77

Monocultures, 70

Morale, 169, 203

Morgens, H., xxvii

Mortensen, P., 57–58

Mortgage holders, 28

Motivation, employee, 110, 147, 167

Motivational sessions, 136–137

Myths, of social responsibility, 275

N

Nant'un leadership, 152–153

Native American cultures, 33

Natural Capital (Hawken, Lovins, & Lovins), 274

Natural groceries, 117

Natural resources: businesses' responsibility for, 34; current use of, by businesses, 33; Earth's capital investments of, 230–232; essence of, 64–65; Kingsford's view of, 104–105; responsibility indicators of, 253–254, 258; roles of, 64–65

Neo-cortex, 187, 206

Nested systems, 161–162

Net carbon effect, 68

New products, 163

Newground Social Investment, 268–271

Newsletters, 95

Nisbett, R., 160–161

Noisette Company, 237–238

Nonprofits: versus businesses, 16; businesses' contributions to, 76; companies making donations to, 17

Now, Discover Your Strengths (Buckingham & Clifton), 59

Numi Organic Tea, 274

Nylon, 33

O

Objectives, development of, 208

Oil industry, 239

Okefenokee National Wildlife Refuge, 269

O'Malley, M., 273

1/1/1 model of philanthropy, 274, 275

Ongoing education, 217

On-time deliveries, 158

OPEC Foundation, 239

Open houses, 113

Open source software, 83–85

Openness, 226–227

Open-time practice, 250

Oral health, 127–129

Organic gardening, 111

Outdoor life, 73–74

Outputs, characteristics of, 29

Oversimplification, 24, 160–161

Ozone destruction, 45, 46

P

Packaged programs, 210–212

Palm oil, 121

Paonia, Colorado, 72

Paper industry, 65, 144

Paradigms, 192–195, 201

Parents, 140

Parkland, 235

Participatory democracy, 279, 281

Passion, 83–84

Patnaik, D., 57–58

Pattern generation, 165–166

Pattern-following, 164–166, 197

Pay structures, 145, 206

Peace Corps, 163

Pentad model, xlii, 2, 39–48

Performance indexes, 98; creativity and, 103; hazards of, 204–208; locus of control and, 167

Perishable products, 158

Personal care products, 17, 18

Personal development: benefits of, 198–199; exit strategies and, 106; to foster creativity, 62; importance of, 216; innovation and, 98, 101; at Kingsford, 10, 91–92, 106; lack of, 214–216; lifelong process of, 200–201; mandated, 215; at Proctor & Gamble, xxxi–xxxii; responsibility indicators of, 249; at Seventh Generation, 198–199; types of, 281. *See also* Education; Learning

Personal security, 136

Personality types, 205

Personnel systems, 145

Perspective, taking another, 156

Pesticides, 269

The Peter Principle, 229

Petroleum, 33

Philanthropy, 274, 275

Philosophy, management, 141, 205, 207, 252

Phosphates, xxviii

Picnics, 86–87

Pilot programs, 208–210
Pink, D., 58, 168, 197, 204
Planning officials, 181, 237
Planning systems, 145
Polarized thinking, 167
Policy development, 169–170
Politics: community leadership and, 74; in European Union, 207; in leadership, 214; relationships and, 181; in South Africa, 11–12, 122–123, 126; two-force model in, 267
Pollination, 164
Portland, Oregon, 73–74, 233
Poverty, 234
Pratchett, T., 186
Privacy, 95
Problem solving: at Apple, 246; blaming and, 159–160; at Google, 245–246; human resource programs for, 204–206; mechanical model and, 159; principles of, 185
Procedures, 146
Process-based worldview, 49
Processes: at Consolidated Diesel Corporation, 151; description of, 146; failed change and, 146–147; nature of, 147
Procter & Gamble: challenge of change in, 1; culture at, 278; guiding principles of, xl–xxxiii; lessons from, xxxiv, 9, 217; as prototype for responsibility, xxvii–xxx; system improvement at, 148; systems umbrellas at, 216; value-adding at, 50–51, 55
Product development: goal of, 54–58; at Kingsford, 10, 100–101; leadership and, 202, 212–213; responsibility indicators of, 244–248
Product testing: by avatars, 57; at Kingsford, 86–87
Production, 158

Profitability, of Responsible Business, xli–xlii
Profit-focused businesses, 176–177
Promises-beyond-ableness practice, 97–105
Promotions, 125–126, 145
Public transit, 235, 236
Publishing work, 95
Punishing teams, 61–62, 204
Purchasing departments, 164, 257
Purposeful evolution, 164
Purposeful frame of mind, 191–192, 197
Purposeful leaders, 216–217

Q

Quality of life, 235–236, 245
Quarterly meetings, 263
Quilting groups, 44

R

Rabbits, 41
Race riots, xxxii
Race sensitivity programs, xxxii
Rally Software, 274–275
Ramo, J., 54, 159
Raw materials, 230–231
Raynsford, B., 100–101
Reactive frame of mind, 190
Reactivity: environmental scans and, 41; frames of mind and, 190, 191; incentives and, 195
Reading groups, 285
Real estate, 238
Reality principle, 23
Recalled products, 225, 226
Recognition: essence and, 61; hazards of, 204; importance of, 61; motivation and, 168
Reconciliation, 267–271
Recyclable products, 33
Recycling programs, 236
Red Hat, 82–85
Reengineering, 211
Reflection, 96, 98, 103, 112
Refrigeration, 46–47

Regenerative systems thinking, 158–164

Regenerative work, 18, 113

Regenesis, 231–232, 234

Regulation: business integrity and, 78; community identity and, 73; DuPont's adherence to, 47; financial focus of business and, 177; legal infrastructure and, 272; to promote corporate responsibility, 21

Reinvesting, 240–241

Rejecting ideas, 248

Relational frame of mind, 190–191

Relational intelligence, 191–192

Relationships, dynamic, 162

Relationships, stakeholder: balance among, 41–44; in communities, 232; consciousness in, 28; at Craft Warehouse, 43–44; at DuPont, 44–48; dynamics of, 162; entering into, 28; fragmentation of, 40, 45–48, 49; framework for, 39–48; importance of, 180–181; interwoven nature of, 38–39, 48; recent economic crisis and, 28; at Seventh Generation, 42–43; third-party management of, 181; transparency in, 28; trust in, 226, 227; understanding buyer class and, 117; at U.S. Bank, 43

Reliability, 56

Reptilian brain, 187, 206

Research-based assessments, 54, 116–117

Resilience, 153

Resources: in communities, 35; at Consolidated Diesel Corporation, 152; definition of, 96; development of, 96–97; employees as, 92; function of, 96; at Kingsford, 96–97; need for, 27. *See also specific resources*

Responsibility: at Apple, 244–259; at the business level, xxxix; at

Google, 244–259; importance of, xxxvi, xxxvii; locus of control and, 166–168; perceived challenges of, 219; for personal development, 215; requirements for, 214–215; to stakeholders, 28; systemic indicators of, 244–257; three approaches to developing, xl–xlii

Responsibility Program, xl–xli

Responsibility Project, xl

The Responsibility Revolution (Hollender & Breen), 115

Responsible Business: benefits of, xli–xlii; characteristics of, xxxviii; definition of, xxxii; development of, xl–xli; example of, 196–197; goal of, 279; increasing popularity of, 133; indicators of, 244–257; outputs of, 29; principles of, 23; recognition of stakeholders by, 28; stakeholder development by, 29

Responsible Business framework: benefits of, 131; at Colgate, South Africa, 122–129; components of, xlii–xliii; decision making in, 156–157; description of, xlii–xliiii; development of, xlii; at Herban Feast, 108–114; at Kingsford, 85–107; model of, xlii, xliii, 2, 39–48; at Red Hat, 82–85; reversing chain of, 175; at Seventh Generation, 114–122

Responsible Business, transformation to. *See* Transformation of businesses

Responsible Industries, 263–264

Return on investment (ROI): for co-creators, 222, 223–224, 227–230; for communities, 232–239; for customers, 224–227; definition of, 219, 223; description of, 222; for Earth, 230–232; for investors, 196, 222,

223*f*, 239–241; levels of, 240; managements' goals and, 196
Revitalization, 238
Rewards, 169
Ridicule, 193
Right-brain aptitudes, 58, 187
Risser, L., xxviii
Rituals, 136–137, 138
Rivers, 66, 67
Rockefeller Foundation, 272
Roddick, A., 52
Rogers, J., xxvi
Roosevelt IV, Theodore, xxvi

S

Safety, 136, 177–178, 226
Sahtouris, E., 154, 221
Sales: buyers' relationship with, 43–44; at Colgate, South Africa, 128; at Kingsford, 10; at Seventh Generation, 120–121
Sales calls, 146
Salesforce.com, 246
Salvage companies, 113
San Francisco Bay, 67
Santa Fe Institute, 54
SAS, 133
Scale, 161, 162
Scapegoats, 159–160
School systems, 75
Scott, H. L., xxv
Sea level changes, 67–68
Second Use Materials, 113
Security and Exchange Commission, 268
Seitz, B., xxvii, xxxiii
Self-direction principle, 23
Self-improvement, 92–93
Self-interest: hazards of, 212–214; integrity and, 227; of investors, 36, 79–80; locus of control and, 167; misperception involving, 61
Selfishness, 167
Self-organization, 90; capabilities of, 157–170; in work redesign, 149
Self-preservation, 191

Self-reliance, 202, 205
Senge, P., 158
Service work, 60
Settlement patterns, 67–68, 238
Seventh Generation: B Corp certification and, 274; challenges of, 114; co-creators of, 62–63, 119–121; commitment to specific ecosystems of, 66; conservation practices of, 65; description of, 15–18; ecological responsibility of, 18, 34, 42; future of, 121–122; growth of, 114; idea generation at, 115–116; improved systems at, 148; innovation at, 119–121; investors in, 121–122; leadership transition at, 121–122; market research of, 192–193; personal development at, 198–199; Responsible Business framework at, 114–122; stakeholder relationships at, 42–43; strategic direction at, 139–140; taboos at, 137; winning business strategy at, 114–119
Shantytowns, 235, 236
Shareholders: advocacy for, 267–271; of DuPont, 20, 21–22; managements' goals and, 196
Shareware, 84
Shaw, G. B., 279
Shoemakers, 50
Six senses, 58
Six Sigma, 211, 215
Skepticism, 173
Skilling, J., 155
Skills, exercising, 281
Smiles, S., 200
Social capital, 232–239
Social fabric, 234–235
Social justice, 90, 119
Social programs, 233
Socialization, xxxviii–xxxix
Socrates, 167
Software service companies, 82–85
Soil, 34

Solipsistic point of view, 51
South African Dental Association, 128
South America, 52
Spontaneity, 102
Stability, 190
Stakeholders: agreements with, 37; balance among, 41–44; definition of, 25–26, 39; dialogue among, 43; entering into relationships with, 28; environmental scan of, 41; fragmented thinking of, 179; function of, 27–28; integrating initiatives of, 44–48; interwoven relationships of, 38–39; locus of control and, 167–168; most significant of, 39–40; in Proctor & Gamble, xxxi; in Responsible Business framework, xlii–xlv, 39–48; return on investment for, 222, 223f; types of, 29–36; understanding of, 26–27; value-added versus value-adding for, 51–52. *See also specific types*
Standardization, effects of, 70–71, 227, 229
Starbucks, 73, 252
The Starfish and the Spider (Brafman & Beckstrom), 152
Status, 135–136, 138
Stereotypes, 8, 117
Stewart, D., 45–46, 138
Stimulus-response mechanisms, 190
Stonybrook Farm, xxvi
Story of Place, 234, 238
Storytelling culture, 127, 217–218
Storytelling projects, 44
Strategic direction: of Herban Feast, 108–109; transformation of, 138–142
Strengths, versus essence, 59–60
Strikes: at DuPont, 45; in South Africa, 11, 15
Strip mining, 269

Structures: challenges of, 149; description of, 145; evolving new, 148–149; failed change and, 146–147
Subprime mortgage holders, 28
Success stories, 217–218
Suppliers, 257
Supply chains: B Corp certification, 274; creation of, 31; creativity and, 59; sustainable types of, 68; value-adding in, 68
Supply, inadequate, 158
Surprising customers, 247
Sustainability: Earth's capital investments and, 230–231; of Herban Feast, 114; importance of, xlv; in the Middle East, 238–239; recent trends in, xliv–xlv; in supply chains, 68
Swartz, J., xxvi
Sykes, B., xxxiv, 216
Symbols, 136, 138
Synergen, 154
Systemic effects principle, 23
Systemic wholes principle, 23
Systems: at Consolidated Diesel Corporation, 151; demand for change and, 148; description of, 145–146; failed change and, 146–147; meeting topics and, 147–148
Systems dynamics, 158–164
Systems thinkers, xxxi
Systems umbrellas, 216

T

Taboos, 137, 138, 139
Taleb, N. N., 79
Talent Is Overrated (Colvin), 98
Team leaders, 150
Team-building exercises, 192
Teams: at Consolidated Diesel Corporation, 150, 151; fostering creative expression in, 61–63; function of, 61; at Kingsford, 90, 92; past trends in, 61; in Proctor

& Gamble prototype, xxviii–xxxiii; punishing of, 61–62; responsibility indicators of, 249; in Responsible Business development, xli
Technological competence, 144
Tektronix, Inc., 154–155, 230
"The Ten Principles," 20
Tending the Wild (Anderson), 33
Theory of relativity, 186
Thinking: about thinking, 155–156; brain science and, 186–187; culture and, 160–161; deconstructing patterns of, 197; effectiveness of, 156–157; fragmented, 179; living systems framework and, 158–164; locus of control and, 166–168; machine-based metaphors for, 159; mental frames theory and, 189–192; pattern generation and, 164–166
Threats, 167, 191
360-degree feedback, 147, 204
Three-brain process, 188–189
Timber industry, 68
Timberland, xxvi
Titanium dioxide mining, 177–180
Tobacco products, 268–269
Toothpaste, 127–129
Top-down change, 210–212, 214
Torvalds, L., 83
Total Quality Management, 198, 211
Toxic products, 16, 17, 118
Toyota, 225
Toyota Community Action Award, 95
Traffic, 235
Training, versus capability development, 142–143
Transformation cycles, 59
Transformation of businesses: capability building in, 142–144; changing culture in, 134–138; guidelines for, 262–263; strategic direction in, 138–142; work redesign in, 144–149
Transparency: B Corp certification and, 273; benefits of, 276; business integrity and, 78; at DuPont, 21–22; for education, 22–23; Internet and, 23; risks of, 22; in stakeholder relationships, 28
Tribal conflicts, 13–14, 35
Tribal efforts, 196
True self, 59
Trust: customer investments of, 224, 225–226; exercises to build, 192; of investors, 78; in relationships, 226; shareholder advocacy and, 269–270; value-adding and, 56
Trustable relationship, 225–226
Tsezos, S., 12–15, 35, 122–129, 135–136, 139, 141
Turnover, 202
Two-force model, 267
Tylenol, 226

U
Ultimate game, 283–284
UN Global Compact, 20–21, 262, 263
Understanding, versus knowledge, 163
Unemployment rates, 35
Unions, 90, 179
United Nations Foundation, 239
University of Michigan, xxix
Urban acupuncture, 236
Urban development, 235–237
Urban renewal, 72
U.S. Bank, 43, 184
U.S. Treasury, 255
User manuals, 247

V
Value-added, 51, 63, 68
Value-adding: benefits of, 52; co-creator imperatives and, 58–63; community imperatives

and, 69–76; customer imperatives and, 53–58; definition of, 2, 49; Earth's imperatives and, 63–69; energizing caring and, 52–53; example of, 49–50; investor imperatives and, 76–81; levels of, 50; in the Middle East, 239; origin of, 50–51; responsibility indicators of, 245; stakeholder imperatives and, 53; versus value-added, 51–52, 63, 68

Values statements, 256

Venture capitalists, 84–85, 156

Vice presidents, 45–46

Violence, 11, 13, 123

Virtual personalities, 57

Vision, 201

W

WAGES, 118

Walmart, xxv, 41

Waste, 29

Water quality, xxvii–xxxiii, 105

Water use, 269

Weddings, 4, 5, 6, 110

Wessel, K., xxvii, xxxii, 88, 150, 217

Western culture, 160–161

White Dog Cafe, 274

White, L., xxxii–xxxiii

Whole Foods Market, 62–63, 117, 274

A Whole New Mind (Pink), 58

Will, 169, 170

Wilson, E. O., 82

Windows operating system, 247

Wired to Care (Patnaik & Mortensen), 57

Wireless services, 255

Woolard, E., 179

Work, levels of, 168

Work, meaningful: learning through doing, 142–143; strategic direction and, 140; value-adding and, 60

Work redesign: aspects of, 145–146; assessment of, 208; bringing customer focus into, 182–185; in business transformation, 145–149; at Herban Feast, 112, 149; at Kingsford, 97–105; locus of control and, 167–168; most challenging phase of, 149; simultaneous implementation of, 209–210; tasks in, 145

Work reports, 43

Work sessions, xxxi

World Economic Forum, 54

Z

Zaltman, G., 192–193

Zappos, 97